Improving
Test
Performance
of Students
With
Disabilities

Judy L. Elliott · Martha L. Thurlow

Improving Test Performance of Students With Disabilities

...On District and State Assessments

CORWIN PRESS, INC.
A Sage Publications Company
Thousand Oaks, California

For information:

Corwin Press, Inc.
A Sage Publications Company
2455 Teller Road
Thousand Oaks, California 91320
E-mail: order@corwin.sagepub.com

SAGE Publications Ltd.
6 Bonhill Street
London EC2A 4PU
United Kingdom

SAGE Publications India Pvt. Ltd.
M-32 Market
Greater Kailash I
New Delhi 110 048 India

Printed in the United States of America

Library of Congress Cataloging-in-Publication Data

Elliott, Judy L.
    Improving test performance of students with disabilities— on district and state assessments/Judy L. Elliott, Martha L. Thurlow.
          p.   cm.
    Includes bibliographical references and indexes.
    ISBN 0-7619-7558-6 (cloth: alk. paper) — ISBN 0-7619-7559-4 (pbk.: alk. paper)
    1. Educational tests and measurements—United States.
    2. Handicapped children—Education—Ability testing—United States. 3. Education and state—United States.
    I. Thurlow, Martha L.   II. Title.
    LB3051 .E48 2000
    371.9'043—dc21   00-038421

This book is printed on acid-free paper.

00   01   02   03   04   05   10   9   8   7   6   5   4   3   2   1

Corwin Editorial Assistant: Kylee Liegl
Production Editor: Astrid Virding
Production Assistant: Cindy Bear
Typesetter/Production: D&G Limited, LLC

Contents

Preface

A mere three years ago we were putting the finishing touches on our book, *Testing Students with Disabilities: Practical Strategies for Complying with District and State Assessments*. Just as the book was heading to print, the Individuals with Disabilities Education Act (IDEA) was being reauthorized. Several landmark amendments were added to the law in 1997, among them requirements that students have access to the general education curriculum (including the standards that are driving the curriculum) and that districts and states include students with disabilities in state and district-wide assessments with accommodations where appropriate. It also specified that an alternate assessment be used with those students unable to participate in the regular state and district assessments. Furthermore, states are required to report the number of students taking state and district assessments as well as the number taking the alternate assessment. They also are required to report on the performance of students with disabilities in both types of assessments.

Little did we know as we were completing that book that such tremendous changes would occur in so little time. As a result, we again put pen to paper (or, more accurately, fingers to computer) to begin to address the next step in all this: making sure that students with disabilities actually benefit from their inclusion in assessments and accountability systems. The way that they will benefit is by showing improvements in performance.

IDEA 1997 (and other laws) make it clear that we need to know how students with disabilities are performing (thus, the requirement that scores be disaggregated) and that their performances are expected to improve over time. Our discussions with many teachers, parents, and administrators, however, suggest to us that it is not obvious how to make sure that the performances of students with disabilities do increase.

We wrote this book to begin to address the need to work systematically to improve the test performances of students with disabilities. Of course, we do this with the belief that improving test performances translates into improved learning. In fact, our suggestions include ways for improving students' learning and performances on a variety of tasks, not just test-taking.

Audience

This book was written to be a resource to all district and school professionals, particularly those overseeing programs for students with disabilities or special needs (including students with limited English proficiency) and the individuals responsible for instructing these students, including IEP teams and teachers. This book is intended to help teachers-in-training as well as administrators and teachers working to understand and implement inclusive accountability and assessment systems for all students. As with our previous book, we hope that state-level personnel will read this book, even though it is directed primarily toward educators in schools. Because the learning of our children, all children, is a shared responsibility, we also address parents as we suggest how to improve the performance of students with disabilities.

Overview

We have organized this book to take you step-by-step through some approaches to improving the performance of students with disabilities. As we do this, we provide you with lots of materials you can use to make decisions, document what you have done, and track student progress. In each chapter, we provide you with a list of additional resources that might be helpful to you as well as a list of Internet sites with information on the topic of the chapter.

To further facilitate your use of the information and your presentation of the information to others, we have provided a resource section on professional development at the end of the book. This is designed to help in the delivery and dissemination of information about ways to improve the performance of students with disabilities on state and district assessments. It also provides a wonderful review that integrates information from several chapters.

The professional development section includes information on some of the most important points that need to be made about assessments, decision making, and instruction, as well as some specific activities in which people can engage. Reproducible handouts and overheads are provided in this section as well.

Finally, but still important, we have created a list of technical assistance and dissemination networks that can provide information relevant to the topics covered in this book. Some of them are national resources; others are regional.

We have tried to develop a book that will be very useable, with both information and strategies, and materials to support both. We hope that as you use this book, you will provide us with feedback on its usefulness in meeting your needs and in improving student performance.

Acknowledgments

This book takes us the next logical step from where we left off when we completed our previous book, *Testing Students with Disabilities: Practical Strategies for Complying with District and State Requirements.* It is a book that begged to be written, because as states and districts began to include students with disabilities, it became clear that they often were not well equipped for the experience. They needed both test-taking skills and the content-based instruction that is so often taken for granted.

We thank those individuals who took the time to review the text for us. They are Carl A. Cohn, Superintendent of the Long Beach Unified School District; Larry Gloeckler, State Director of Special Education of Albany, New York; Alexis Ruiz-Alessi, Director of Program Assistance for Language Minority Students of the Long Beach Unified School District.

Corwin Press would like to thank the following reviewers for their contributions: Dave Malouf of the Office of Special Eduation Programs, U.S. Department of Education, Washington, D.C.; Mark Goor, Assistant Dean of the Graduate School of Education at George Mason University, Fairfax, Virginia; and Mary Male of the Division of Special Education and Rehabilitative Services at San Jose State University, San Jose, California.

We would also like to extend our thanks to those professionals who through their public work provided us with quotes we have used throughout our book. We hope that their inspiring and profound words provide you a clear trailhead as you start your journey on the path toward improving the district and state test performances of students with disabilities.

Judy L. Elliott, jelliott@lbusd.k12.ca.us

Martha L. Thurlow, thurl001@tc.umn.edu

About the Authors

Judy Elliott, Ph.D., currently is Assistant Superintendent of Special Education in the Long Beach Unified School District, Long Beach, California. Formerly a research associate at the National Center on Educational Outcomes, she worked and continues to assist districts and state education departments in their efforts to update and realign curriculum frameworks, instruction, and assessments to include all students. Her research interests focus on effective instruction, IEP development and its alignment with standards and assessments, and IEP team decision making for accountability, accommodation, and assessments, as well as translating information on standards and assessments for various audiences including parents; teachers; school boards, both local and state; and other community groups. Dr. Elliott serves as a national consultant and staff development professional to school districts and organizations. She has trained thousands of staff, teachers, and administrators, both in the South Pacific and the United States, in areas of inclusive schooling including linking assessments to classroom intervention, strategies and tactics for effective instruction, curriculum modifications for students with mild to severe disabilities, intervention and teacher assistance teams, authentic and curriculum-based evaluations, instructional environment evaluations, prevention-intervention techniques, strategies for difficult-to-manage students, collaborative teaching, restructuring pupil personnel service delivery systems, program evaluations, and accountability and assessment practices. Some of Dr. Elliott's most recent copublished books are *Strategies and Tactics for Effective Instruction II*, *Timesavers for Educators* and *Testing Students with Disabilities: Practical Strategies for Complying with State and District Requirements*.

Martha Thurlow, Ph.D., is Director of the National Center on Educational Outcomes. In this position, she addresses the implications of contemporary U.S. policy and practices for students with disabilities, including national and statewide assessments, standards-setting efforts, and graduation requirements. Her work also involves addressing these issues for students with limited English proficiency. Dr. Thurlow has worked with diverse groups of stakeholders to identify important outcomes for youth through the post-school level and to address the implications of recent federal education laws including Goals 2000, the Improving America's Schools Act, and IDEA 97. She has conducted research involving special education for the past 28 years in a variety of areas, including assessments and decision making, learning disabilities, early childhood education, dropout prevention, effective classroom instruction, and the integration of students with disabilities in general education settings. Dr. Thurlow has published extensively on all of these topics and has among her publications several collaborative works with other organizations (such as the National Governors' Association, the Council of Chief State School Officers, the Federation for Children with Special Needs, and the Parents Engaged in Educational Reform). She also is a co-editor of *Exceptional Children*, the research journal of the Council for Exceptional Children.

Key Elements in Maximizing the Performance of Students with Disabilities

"From a little spark may burst a mighty flame."

—Dante

"An accountability system is needed for all students and at the broadest level should apply to all students regardless of their characteristics."

—Jim YsselDyke

Hot-Button Issues

- Whatever happened to "educate the best, forget about the rest?"
- Are we not kidding ourselves when we say that all students can learn?
- All of this is more work that it is worth, right?

We have all heard the saying, "Today is the first day of the rest of your life." That saying always seems to make sense on the surface, but it does not always make sense when we are faced with the day-to-day reality of educating students. We cannot just do what we want to do today, because we have to make sure that students are at a certain point by the end of the quarter—or by the end of the year, or by the end of their school careers.

You have probably heard the phrase, "All students can learn." Many schools, districts, and states have this phrase as part of their mission statements. More and more often, this phrase is now being followed by the phrase, "All means all." Also, federal law and state and district policies are clarifying that the "all" in "all means all" includes students who have disabilities, as well as students who have limited English proficiency. For some time, both of these groups were excluded from assessments and accountability systems—but no longer.

Recent changes in federal and state laws make it quite clear that education is for *all* students, particularly students who have disabilities. This point is illustrated through the requirement that students who have disabilities should be included in state and district-wide assessments and that their performance is reported. How these students are performing must be placed in public view for all to see. More than ever before, educators need to examine how to ensure that these students are learning the most that they can learn—and that they are demonstrating all that they know and can do.

This chapter is a preview of the chapters in this book—each of which is devoted to ways to improve the test performance of students who have disabilities. The tests that are the focus here are those that are used by states and districts to report on what students know and can do, and more and more often to determine significant consequences for schools (such as school awards, school accreditation, and other rewards and sanctions) and for students (such as promotion from one grade to another and graduation from high school). Because students who have disabilities generally have not been included in these kinds of assessments in the past, we have not necessarily examined how to make sure that when they sit down for a test or when they engage in a performance event—or when they put together a portfolio—that they will perform their best, and that their performance will be an accurate reflection of what they know and what they can do.

The goal of this book is to help you, as an educator, improve the test performance of each and every student who has a disability. We are confident that the suggestions in this book also can be of benefit to other students, but we suspect that many of the things that we suggest are already being used by other students—either because someone has already implemented them or because the students themselves have picked them up on their own.

Picking the Right Way to Participate

Federal law has clarified that students who have disabilities must participate in assessments and accountability systems in one or more of three ways: (1) a standard assessment, (2) an assessment with accommodations, or (3) an alternate assessment. Making good decisions about which is the best way for individual students to participate in assessments relates directly to making good decisions about student learning. Students must be placed into the curriculum that best reflects their learning goals—and the knowledge and skills that they should be gaining as a result of their schooling. Making good decisions does not mean picking the assessment that is most likely to produce the highest scores for the students; rather, it involves aligning the student's opportunity to learn with the student's instructional goals, and aligning the assessment with the desired opportunity to learn. The first step in making sure that students have the best opportunity to succeed and that performance reflects well on the school, district, and state is making sure that students are learning.

The concern about wanting student performance to reflect well on the school, district, and state is a reality of today's educational landscape. Accountability for the learning of all students is a new hallmark of educational reform rhetoric. As you think about improving the performance of students who have disabilities, you will have an advantage if you understand what educational accountability is and some of the legal and ethical issues that you might face, as well as a host of other facts that will help you best understand what you are dealing with in your own educational-accountability system. Chapter 2 provides you with all of this information and gives you several tools to help delineate those parts of the accountability system that are important to consider.

Aligning the Individualized Education Program (IEP) with Standards

A critical sequence must be followed if the test performance of students who have disabilities is to improve. The first and most basic step is to know what standards the student is supposed to be working toward and the extent to which the targeted assessment is aligned with these standards. This process involves doing some background work to really understand what is expected of students in the educational system.

Another critical step is ensuring that the student's instruction is directed toward those standards. This alignment must be addressed in the student's *Individualized Education Program* (IEP). No longer can IEPs be devoted to just what special education or related services will provide to the student. Instead, there must be a link to the general education curriculum and a clarification of how this process is to occur.

Understanding what is needed to align the IEP with standards is the focus of Chapter 3. Beyond this topic, the chapter clarifies how the IEP can be related to standards and instruction and how standards can be backmapped to the IEP. Then, all of this material is linked to what happens in the classroom, in the home, and in the community.

The decisions that must be made concerning the best way for a student to participate, after making sure of the appropriate goals for the student's instruction, are much more complicated than picking one of the three alternatives. A student might need to be included in one way for one test, but in another way for a second test. A student might need to have accommodations at one point in his or her school career, for example, but not at another point. Furthermore, if a student needs accommodations to participate, what these accommodations are or what combination of accommodations is best must be decided. Also, accommodations needed might change with subject area or from one time to another. Decisions also might be affected by other factors, such as whether the district or state test was developed to make comparisons among students (such as norm-referenced tests) or instead to compare students to certain criteria or standards (such as criterion-referenced tests and standards-based tests).

An important step in all of this decision making is not only equipping students with learning and study skills, but also helping them gain the knowledge that they need to make good decisions about their own learning and test preparation. This process involves helping them take the right kinds of classes as they get older and determining what kinds of accommodations they need to best learn in the classes that they take. This process also involves educating students who have disabilities about how to make good decisions for themselves as they get older, so that when they are in high school and as they proceed to post-secondary or work settings, they will know how to make sure that their own test performance is the best that it can be.

The topic of deciding the right way to participate—whether in a regular state or district assessment or in some alternate assessment—is addressed in Chapter 4. Related topics, such as picking the right accommodations and test-preparation skills, are addressed in later chapters.

Making Good Decisions About Accommodations

We have already alluded to the need to make good decisions about how students participate in assessments. This step is critical for improving the test performance of students who have disabilities. One way in which students can take tests is with accommodations. The right for students to have needed accommodations is guaranteed by law. Making good decisions about what accommodations are needed is an important part of ensuring that the students really demonstrate knowledge and skills.

Many kinds of accommodations exist, and many specific accommodations might be selected for an individual student. We know that there is a tendency to "over-accommodate" students who have disabilities (i.e., identifying more than they need or will use). This situation is not helpful. Accommodations are not best selected by knowing the category of the student's disability. Making decisions in the past has often been no more than guesswork.

Student performance can be improved by making good decisions about needed accommodations. How this task can be done is the focus of Chapter 5. Decision-making tools are provided, in addition to ways to help the student identify the accommodations that he or she will need in various instructional and assessment situations.

Helping the Student Prepare for Testing

Test preparation is an overlooked aspect of improving test performance. Many test-preparation skills are not even identified as critical, because they come naturally to students who do not have disabilities. These skills are test-taking strategies that are beneficial for all students; however, many of these strategies do not appear in typical test-preparation books. These strategies and other helpful hints are the focus of Chapter 6.

As with accommodations, the ultimate goal is to have the students eventually take over responsibility for test preparation. Thus, Chapter 6 also addresses how to help the student know what he or she must do in order to be prepared for a test and to perform well. These strategies will not be the same for every student. Therefore, educators must learn what specific strategies will be useful for individual students who have disabilities.

Generating Parent/Guardian Support —and the Support of Others, Too

"It takes a village to raise a child," said First Lady Hillary Rodham Clinton. Likewise, more than a single teacher is needed to improve the test performance of students—particularly, students who have disabilities. We all know that the support of parents is important in efforts to improve students' test performance. Of course, if parental support cannot be obtained, we can still do much more. We believe, however, that there are many ways to gain parental support that take a minimal amount of effort but are tremendously helpful.

When we talk about parent/guardian support, we really should be broader and talk about family support. This support includes siblings and also the extended family. Aunts, uncles, grandparents—whoever might be available—can contribute to efforts to improve the test performance of students who have disabilities. Also, generating support among a broader group of people is helpful as well, including other individuals in the school (e.g., the office secretary, school nurse, or counselor) and people in the community. Resources are available outside the school that can be engaged in efforts to improve the test performance of students who have disabilities.

Critical steps in gaining parental and family support for improving the test performance of students who have disabilities are provided in Chapter 7. In addition, the chapter gives the educator and family ideas about additional resources that are available to help in the effort to improve test performance.

Addressing the Really Tough Issues

You might wonder what this statement can possibly mean. We have already listed lots of tough issues. But, some other issues exist that have to be addressed as we think about and begin to devote our energies to improving test performance. Tests are not the only part of this world. We certainly cannot devote all of our efforts to increasing scores on tests.

Transition issues are ones that often fly in the face of increasing test scores. If we devote all of our energies to improving test performance, particularly for those students who are in middle and high school, will we not be neglecting the important transition needs of students who have disabilities? We are required to develop and carry out individualized transition plans for these students. How can we mesh this task with worrying about tests? These tough issues are addressed in Chapter 8.

Another tough issue is instruction. If we worry about including a particular student who has a disability in the general education assessment, what are we really worried about? Is it that the student has not been provided the needed instruction all along? How can we address the bigger issue of instruction so that we will not always have to be worrying about students who are not going to pass a test, or students whose scores are so low that they pull down the school's scores? Instructional issues are addressed in Chapter 9.

And, how are we going to know for sure that we are doing the best things for students when we insist that they take the general education assessment? Students exist who just do not seem to fit into either the general education assessment or the alternate assessment. What should we do for these "gray-area" students? Does it make any sense to devote our energies trying to increase their test scores? What should we be doing for these students? Chapter 10 is where you will find gray-area issues addressed.

Finally, if those issues are not tough enough, how about the challenges that are created by the student who has disabilities and who has a limited English proficiency? Increasingly, schools are facing the reality of a rapidly changing clientele. More and more often, this situation requires working with students who might speak a different language, who might or might not be literate in their first language, who might or might not have ever been exposed to a written language, and who might or might not ever have been in an educational setting before. Yes, we want to improve their performance on district and state assessments too, right? Refer to Chapter 11 for more about this tough issue.

Summary

Each of the chapters in this book provides a discussion and lots of resources for you to take into your school. To help you be sure that you are taking away the important points from the chapter, we provide you with a set of "Hot-Button Issues" at the start of each chapter and a "Test Your Knowledge" set of questions at the end.

After every few chapters, we present for you a personal survey to use to determine where you stand in relation to the information that has been presented thus far in the book. Finally, at the end of this book, we provide a section of professional development ideas and a set of overheads, activities, and handouts that you can use to carry this information to others.

Test Your Knowledge

Just to be sure that you have a general idea of what we hope to achieve in this book, complete the following fill-in-the-blank statements. Do not hesitate to reread parts of this chapter if the words that go in the blanks do not jump immediately into your head.

1. The phrases "all students can learn" and "all means all" include students who have _____ and students who have limited _____ proficiency.

2. Federal laws require students who have disabilities to be included in state and district-wide assessments and require their performance to be _____.

3. The chapters in this book are devoted to ways to _____ the test performance of students who have disabilities.

4. Students who have disabilities must participate in assessments and accountability in one or more of three ways: (1) a standard assessment, (2) an assessment with _____, or (3) an alternate assessment.

5. The first step in making sure that students have the best opportunity to succeed is making sure that students are _____.

6. IEPs must be aligned with _____.

7. Student performance can be improved by making good decisions about needed _____.

8. One goal is to have the students take over responsibility for test _____.

9. When we talk about parental support, we really should be broader and talk about _____ support.

10. Among the tough issues when considering improving test performance are transition, _____, gray-area students, and students who have disabilities and who have a limited English proficiency.

Answers

1. disabilities; English (p. 2)
2. reported (p. 2)
3. improve (p.2)
4. accommodations (p. 2)
5. learning (p. 3)
6. standards (p. 3)
7. accommodations (p. 4)
8. preparation (p. 5)
9. family (p. 5)
10. instruction (p. 6)

BOX 1.1

While we will not repeat this material in each chapter, you might want to apply a scoring rubric each time you test your knowledge. Something like the following scoring guide would work. You might need to adjust the number of points (most chapters have 10 questions), but the framework will work in all of the chapters.

How Did You Do? Use the Scoring Guide Below:

- 8–10 Way to go!
- 6–7 Getting there
- 5–6 Moving in the right direction
- 4–5 Reread the chapter again
- 2–3 Uh-oh
- 1–2 Not Yet!

Resources

McDonnell, L. M., McLaughlin, M. J., and Morison, P. (eds.) (1997). *Educating one & all: Students with disabilities and standards-based reform.* Washington, D.C.: National Academy Press.

Thurlow, M., Elliott, J., and Ysseldyke, J. (1998). *Testing students with disabilities: Practical strategies for complying with district and state requirements.* Thousand Oaks, CA: Corwin Press.

Internet Resources

Council for Exceptional Children: http://www.cec.sped.org/

National Center for Research on Evaluation, Standards, and Student Testing: http://cresst96.cse.ucla.edu/index.html

National Center on Educational Outcomes (NCEO): http://www.coled.umn.edu/nceo

National Center to Improve the Tools of Educators (NCITE): http://darkwing.uoregon.edu-ncite/

National Information Center for Children and Youth with Disabilities (NICHCY): http://www.aed.org/nichcy

2

Educational Accountability: What Is It?

"Pinch yourself and know how others feel."

—Japanese proverb

"Disability is not an inability to learn."

—Tom Hehir

Hot-Button Issues

- □ *What is the fuss over this accountability thing?*
- □ *I was hired to educate kids, not to deal with political agendas—whose idea was these rewards and sanctions anyway?*
- □ *Whatever happened to "excellence for a few, but not for you?"*
- □ *Why should we care about accountability reports or what is in them, or better yet, what counts?*

Responsibility and accountability are words with which we are all familiar. Some of us heard them more than we liked as we were growing up. Now, we throw them back at our students—saying that they are responsible for their behavior. And, as educators of students who have Individualized Education Programs (IEPs), we realize that we are accountable for completing the paperwork for these students, making sure that they have up-to-date IEPs and that we are complying with placement decisions that have been made for them. This situation defined responsibility and accountability as we knew it—until recently.

But now, these words are becoming a part of our work life beyond meeting IEP requirements. They are cropping up and appearing in ways that we might not want. They are being used to hold us responsible and accountable for some things over which we feel that we have little control. This world involves educational accountability, and in a large part, it is the reason for this book. If we are going to be held responsible for the learning of students who have a history of poor performance, then we need some strategies for ensuring that the performance of these students is the best that it can be. We do not want to be held accountable for performances that reflect simple things like not knowing how to take tests or being afraid of taking tests.

To help us all feel that it is fair to be held responsible for the performance of all students, including students who have disabilities, it is important to take that first step—to really understand what educational accountability is, how it is being implemented, and what issues surround educational accountability. Then, after really considering and understanding the assumptions about including students who have disabilities in these systems, we can get down to the business of improving the test performance of students who have disabilities.

This chapter is the prelude to developing improved test performance in students who have disabilities. In this chapter, we define what accountability is and describe what some common accountability systems look like. We examine how the systems are implemented in real schools and school systems, so that we have a better understanding of what they really look like. All of this information helps you, as an educator who is caught in some type of system, to understand the workings of your system. This material also helps you figure out the most important avenues for you to follow as you help individual students improve their test performance.

A Definition of Educational Accountability

Accountability goes hand-in-hand with most of the educational reforms implemented in the United States within the past two decades. The desire for accountability has been a driving force since the mid 1980s, when the National Commission on Excellence in Education (1983) first decried American education, warning that it was producing students who were ill-equipped for a competitive, global economy. The term *accountability* has been used freely within various educational reforms, yet its meaning has often not been made clear.

Accountability does have a historical foundation in educational literature. Probably the most frequent meaning of the term refers in some way to answerability to others. Still, what one is held answerable for can vary. Before this use of the term took over, there was a general belief that for schools to be accountable, they would need to reach a consensus on the educational outcomes of schooling. These outcomes could be immediate and tangible results of schooling, such as enhanced achievement scores (proximal outcomes), or they could be longer-term social benefits and costs to society (ultimate outcomes).

What Does This Information Have to Do With Me?

What does all of this information mean to you? Pick up any newspaper, weekly news magazine, or educational journal, and you are bound to see a media display of some state or school district's test results. Reporting results is viewed as a relatively low-stakes kind of accountability—it might have some impact, but not the amount that would be generated by other actions that might be taken, such as removing teachers whose students earn low test scores or providing schools with large cash rewards that are determined in part by how their students are performing. These kinds of actions are viewed as relatively high stakes—they have significant implications for things that people hold dear, such as their jobs, earnings, and prestige.

What Educational Accountability Systems Look Like

Educational systems are typically depicted as consisting of *resources*, such as per-pupil funding or student characteristics; *processes*, such as instructional procedures or related services; and *outcomes*, such as student performance, attendance, or behavior (refer to Box 2.1 for one of the more common portrayals of this relationship). Generally, educators agree that before anyone can be held accountable for any of these three aspects of the system, defining clear goals, having a reliable assessment of achievement toward those goals, and developing a set of consequences attached to the success or failure of achieving those goals is essential.

Together, these elements form an accountability system. According to Linda Darling-Hammond and other policy researchers, these systems are designed to accomplish three goals: (1) to heighten the probability that good practices will occur for students; (2) to reduce the likelihood that harmful practices will occur; and (3) to encourage internal self-assessment to identify, diagnose, and change courses of action that are harmful or ineffective.

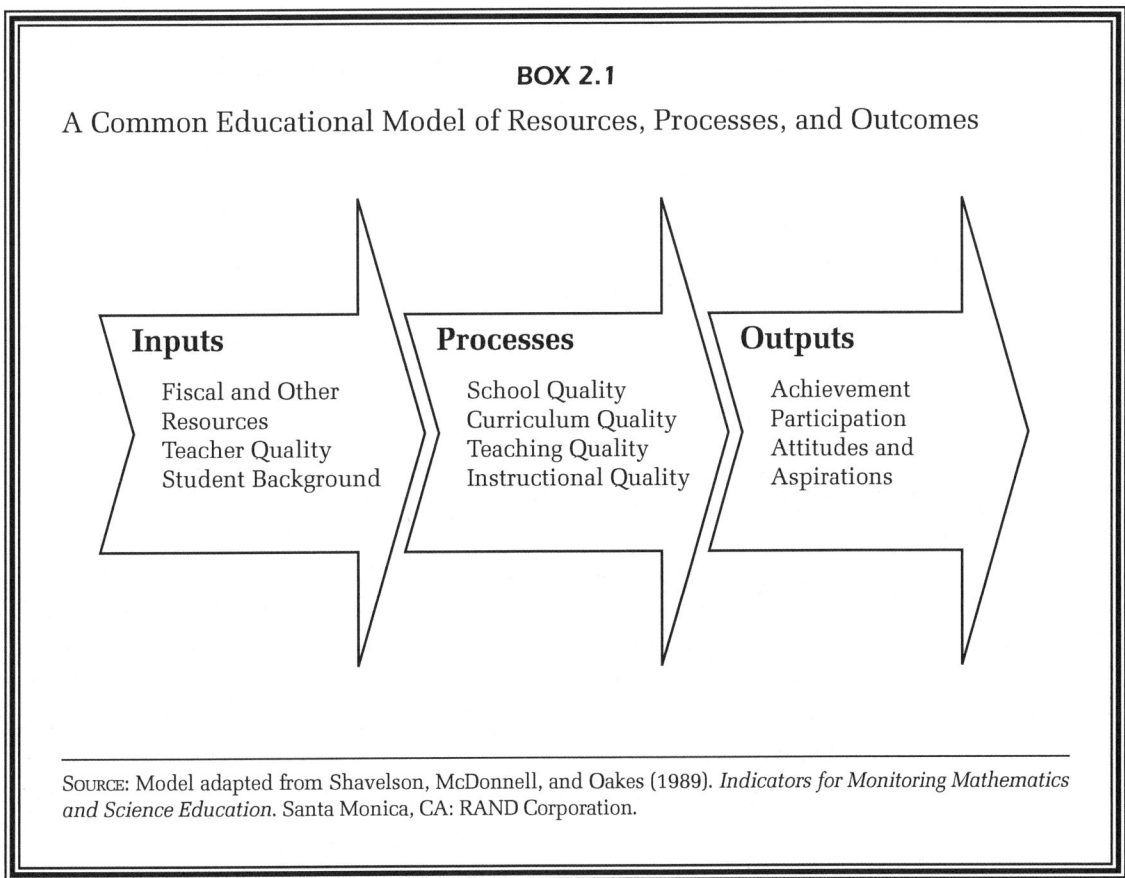

BOX 2.1

A Common Educational Model of Resources, Processes, and Outcomes

Inputs

Fiscal and Other
Resources
Teacher Quality
Student Background

Processes

School Quality
Curriculum Quality
Teaching Quality
Instructional Quality

Outputs

Achievement
Participation
Attitudes and
Aspirations

SOURCE: Model adapted from Shavelson, McDonnell, and Oakes (1989). *Indicators for Monitoring Mathematics and Science Education.* Santa Monica, CA: RAND Corporation.

Accountability Systems in Practice

Educational accountability systems look different in different states—and in different locations within states. The first step in improving students' test performance (and, in turn, improving how they affect various educational-accountability systems) is to really understand the accountability system within which you are working.

The clearest distinction to keep in mind is that basically, two kinds of accountability exist: system accountability and student accountability. In system accountability, the educational system—district offices, schools, principals, or teachers—are the focus of accountability. In student accountability, the student is the focus of accountability. Student accountability mechanisms include various promotion and graduation exams.

Accountability systems vary along a number of dimensions, and you should consider each of these:

- Who or what is the **target** of accountability?
- What are the **consequences** of accountability?

- What **information** is used to determine accountability?
- What **specific instruments** are used to collect student-performance data?
- Against what **standard** is the information held?

Each of these points combine to form unique accountability systems that vary from one place to the next.

The **target** of accountability is perhaps the most obvious way in which systems vary. Usually, the target is either the system or the student, but sometimes accountability can be directed at both at the same time. Also, when talking about the system as the target of accountability, you can target any one or more of several aspects of the system. In other words, it can be the principal, the school as a whole, the district, or the teachers.

The **consequences** attached to the accountability system can also vary tremendously. Sometimes the consequences are significant (they are called high stakes). For example, a school might lose its accreditation if student performance is low. Other times, the consequences are relatively low. Low-stakes consequences include having scores reported in a document that few people ever see.

Are they high stakes or not? These terms are relative. What might seem to be low stakes or medium stakes (such as simply reporting data) can actually function in a high-stakes manner (for example, when scores are reported in the newspaper with schools listed according to scores, and real estate agents begin to promote certain neighborhood locations because of high scores). The most common consequences for systems include the following:

- School performance reporting
- School warnings, probation, or watch
- School accreditation
- School takeover
- School monetary rewards or exemptions from regulations
- School awards or recognition
- High school skill warrantees, where schools guarantee to re-educate students if employers or post-secondary institutions determine that the students do not have the needed, basic skills for success

This list does not include teacher salaries or principal jobs. Yet, there are states in which those are the consequences of the accountability system. There are even states in which school accreditation status is determined in large part by test scores, and in which school accreditation determines whether or not money is contributed to teachers' retirements funds.

The **information** that is used for accountability purposes typically is more than just student test scores. The most common types of information used in state accountability systems are as follows:

- Student test scores
- Dropout rate
- Attendance rate

Individual states and districts, however, might use other information as well. For example, one state uses information from student follow-up surveys, six months after they leave school. Another state uses suspension rates in schools. Box 2.2 shows several commonly used student-level indicators and the extent to which each is used in some of the states that have high-stakes accountability systems.

Over time, there has been increasing reliance upon statewide assessments of student performance, as well as other selected outcome indicators (such as attendance and dropout rates) to provide data for accountability. While we might be held accountable for providing education in certain ways (e.g., using appropriate textbooks or good teaching techniques), what is facing us now is the need to show that students are reaching certain standards of learning. This situation typically comes down to the need to demonstrate that students can earn certain scores on achievement tests. Usually, these tests are standardized, multiple choice, or short answer tests of language arts, mathematics, writing, and maybe science or social studies. In other words, we are being held accountable for the scores that students obtain on tests. And, when students have disabilities, we already have some evidence that they do not perform well on these standardized tests.

Beyond the types of information that are used to determine accountability scores, you should know the **specific instruments** that are used to collect the information. This knowledge is most important for determining what makes up students' scores that are entered into accountability systems. A summary of the types of instruments used to collect student performance data used in state accountability systems is shown in the table in Box 2.3. This table shows the number of assorted measures that are used in selected states and how many of them count in the accountability system. You should be aware that accountability systems do change. In other words, the instruments used to produce information in systems also change.

You or someone in your school should be aware of specifically what instruments are used to determine school-accountability scores. To help you, use the worksheet in Box 2.4.

The final piece of information that you need about your accountability system is the **performance standards** that are used to determine adequate performance. Is a specific score identified as a satisfactory score for a student to achieve? Are the scores of individual students added to get an average score for the school, which is then used as the indicator of whether the

BOX 2.2

Some Student-Level Indicators Used in States that Have High-Stakes Accountability Systems for Schools or Districts

State	Attendance	Dropout Rate	Expulsion Rate	Graduation Rate	Retention Rate	Suspension Rate	Test Scores	Transition	Truancy
AK	X	X		X	X		X		
AL	X	X		X			X	X	
AR	X	X			X		X	X	
AZ	X		X			X	X		
CT	X	X					X	X	
DE	X						X		X
FL	X	X			X	X	X		
GA	X	X		X			X	X	
HI						X			
IL	X	X		X			X		X
IN	X	X	X	X		X	X	X	
KS	X	X	X	X		X	X		

BOX 2.2

Some Student-Level Indicators Used in States that Have High-Stakes Accountability Systems for Schools or Districts
(Continued)

State	Attendance	Dropout Rate	Expulsion Rate	Graduation Rate	Retention Rate	Suspension Rate	Test Scores	Transition	Truancy
KY	X	X			X		X	X	
LA	X	X	X	X		X	X		
MA	X	X	X			X	X		X
MD	X	X					X		
MI				X		X			
NC	X						X		
NH	X	X	X	X		X	X		X
NJ	X	X		X			X	X	
NY				X			X	X	
NV	X	X	X			X	X	X	
OH	X	X	X	X	X	X	X		
SC	X					X			

BOX 2.2

Some Student-Level Indicators Used in States that Have High-Stakes Accountability Systems for Schools or Districts
(Continued)

State	Attendance	Dropout Rate	Expulsion Rate	Graduation Rate	Retention Rate	Suspension Rate	Test Scores	Transition	Truancy
TN	X	X					X		
TX	X	X		X			X		
VA	X	X					X		
VT	X	X			X		X		
WA	X	X	X	X	X	X	X		
WI	X	X	X	X	X	X	X	X	X
WV							X	X	

Source: Information adapted from the Education Commission of the States (1999). *Accountability in the 50 States*. Denver, CO: Author.

BOX 2.3

Table of Student Performance Instruments Used by States

State	Number of Measures	Account-ability Measures	Measures that Contribute Information on Student Performance to Accountability Index
Alaska	2	2	Alaska Writing Assessment; Norm-Referenced Test
Alabama	5	4	Alabama Direct Assessment of Writing; Exit Exam; End-of-Course Exam; Stanford Achievement
Arkansas	2	2	Criterion-Referenced Test; Stanford Achievement Test
Arizona	1	1	Stanford 9
California	2	0	
Colorado	1	0	
Connecticut	2	2	CT Academic Performance Test; CT Mastery Test
Delaware	1	0	
Florida	2	2	FL Writing Assessment Program; FL High School Competency Test
Georgia	4	3	GA High School Graduation Tests; Norm-Referenced Testing; Writing Assessments
Hawaii	3	1	Stanford Achievement Test 8
Iowa	0	0	
Idaho	3	3	Direct Mathematics Assessment; Direct Writing Assessment; ITBS/TAP
Illinois	1	1	IL Goal Assessment Program
Indiana	1	1	Statewide Assessment
Kansas	1	1	KS Assessment Program

BOX 2.3

Table of Student Performance Instruments Used by States (Continued)

State	Number of Measures	Account-ability Measures	Measures that Contribute Information on Student Performance to Accountability Index
Kentucky	4	3	KIRIS On Demand; Open Response Questions; Portfolio Assessment
Louisiana	4	3	Gr 3, 5, 7 Criterion-Referenced Test; LA Graduation Exit Examination; Norm-Referenced Test
Massachusetts	3	0	
Maryland	2	2	MD Functional Testing Program; MD School Performance Assessment Program
Maine	1	0	
Michigan	3	3	Gr 4 and 7 Reading and Mathematics; Gr 5 and 8 Science; MI High School Proficiency Test
Minnesota	1	0	
Missouri	2	2	MO Mastery and Achievement Test; Missouri Assessment Program
Mississippi	3	2	Norm-Referenced Testing; Subject Area Testing Program
Montana	1	1	Student Assessment Requirement
North Carolina	3	1	NC Testing Program
North Dakota	1	1	Norm-Referenced Testing
Nebraska	0	0	
New Hampshire	1	1	NH Education Improvement and Assessment Program

BOX 2.3

Table of Student Performance Instruments Used by States (Continued)

State	Number of Measures	Account-ability Measures	Measures that Contribute Information on Student Performance to Accountability Index
New Jersey	2	2	Gr 11 High School Proficiency Test; Gr 8 Early Warning Test
New Mexico	4	3	NM Achievement Assessment; NM High School Competency Exam; NM Portfolio Writing Assessment
Nevada	3	3	High School Proficiency Examination Program; Norm-Referenced Test; Writing Proficiency Examination—Gr 8
New York	7	5	Occupational Education Proficiency Examinations; Preliminary Competency Tests; Pupil Evaluation Program Tests; Regents Competency Tests; Regents Examination Programs
Ohio	4	4	Gr 4, 6, 9, 12 Proficiency Testing
Oklahoma	2	2	ITBS, OK Core Curriculum Tests (CRTs)
Oregon	1	1	Reading, Writing, and Mathematics Assessment
Pennsylvania	2	1	Reading and Mathematics Assessment
Rhode Island	4	4	Health Performance Assessment; Mathematics Performance Assessment; MAT 7; Writing Performance Assessment
South Carolina	2	2	Basic Skills Assessment Program; Norm-Referenced Testing
South Dakota	1	0	
Tennessee	4	1	TCAP Achievement Test -NRT
Texas	1	1	TX Assessment of Academic Skills (TAAS) End-of-Course Exams

BOX 2.3

Table of Student Performance Instruments Used by States (Continued)

State	Number of Measures	Account-ability Measures	Measures that Contribute Information on Student Performance to Accountability Index
Utah	3	1	Norm-Referenced Testing
Virginia	2	2	Literacy Passport Test; VA Student Assessment Program
Vermont	2	2	New Standards ELA; Portfolio Assessment
Washington	1	1	Norm-Referenced Test
Wisconsin	2	2	Gr 3 WRCT; WSAS Knowledge and Concepts
West Virginia	2	1	Norm-Referenced Testing
Wyoming	1	0	

SOURCE: Part 3.2.3 (pp. 244–249) in Roeber, E., Bond, L., and Connealy, S. (1998) *Annual survey of state student assessment programs, Vol II: Fall 1997.* Washington, D.C.: Council of Chief State School Officers.

school is performing adequately? Such indicators are called school indexes, or other similar names. Or, on the other hand, is a student's score on a single test placed within a proficiency level? Then, are the numbers of students who are achieving satisfactory proficiency levels counted to determine whether the school is performing adequately? For example, if 350 students obtained inadequate proficiencies, 600 students obtained satisfactory proficiencies, and 225 students obtained high proficiencies, then is it only those students in the last group (the high-proficiency group) who count in determining a school index? Or, is it those students who are earning either satisfactory or high proficiency who count?

The examples that have been given here are just a couple of the approaches that are now being used. Actual systems are, of course, much more complicated because most states and districts use information from more than just a single measure of student performance. Sometimes, the exact makeup of an index that is used for district or school accountability is not common knowledge.

BOX 2.4

School Accountability Worksheet

To determine what factors contribute to school accountability in your school or district, find answers to the following questions. Complete this with your colleagues.

- Define the "stakes" associated with your accountability system(s) and specify exactly what they are:

	District Level	**State Level**
For students		
For staff		
For administrators		

- Which indicators are currently included in your accountability system(s)?

Student performance

Attendance

Dropout rate

Other

- What methods are used to gather data on each of the indicators that are used in your accountability system?

Student performance

Attendance

Dropout rate

Other

You might wonder again why you need to figure out all of this information. While it is not mandatory that you do so, understanding the exact workings of the accountability system will help you understand the most efficient approaches to improving student performance—both when the object of the accountability system is the student (as in grade promotion and graduation tests) and when the object of the accountability system is the school (or the principal, or the staff, or individual teachers).

Examples of Real Accountability Systems

The examples provided thus far have been hypothetical. Here, we provide some real examples. These examples will give you ideas about the kinds of things that you need to look for as you are mapping out the accountability system within which you are working.

In Kansas, an array of information is considered when calculating a school-accountability index. The information includes student performance, attendance, demographics, discipline, dropout rates, expulsion rates, graduation rates, and suspension rates, as well as information about staff development, the learning climate, parental or community involvement, and expenditures and use of resources. These factors together are used to determine whether a school receives accreditation from the state. If the school is accredited, then everything is fine. Everything continues as before. If the school is not accredited, however, then contributions are no longer made to the retirement accounts of staff in that school.

In New Jersey, in order for schools to be considered satisfactory, they must show that they have reached a desired level of performance on their school performance indicators. While 80 percent of students passing the state test, for example, is the level that schools must attain for students who are not receiving special services, questions are being raised about what criteria should be used for students who have disabilities (who are not included in the general accountability system). Determining consequences for schools once students are included is an important part of the accountability system.

Now, take some time to jot down some notes about your accountability system. You will find that you will come back to this list as you are contemplating how to improve students' performance in district or state assessments. If you do not have any ideas about where to begin, start asking questions and requesting information about policies. Talk to your district administrators and curriculum and instruction directors or state personnel.

Legal and Ethical Issues

Perhaps now is the best time to discuss some important legal and ethical issues that face educators as they explore accountability systems. Two considerations exist here: (1) those that comprise illegal activities, and (2) those that comprise unethical activities. We, of course, consider both to be inappropriate in the push for improved student scores. No one should encourage you to use either of these approaches as you work with students.

Illegal activities   In the recent past, there have been numerous examples of illegal activities within district or state assessment programs. One of the more prevalent illegal behaviors that we know about is erasures—in other words, erasing students' wrong answers and replacing them with correct answers. The reason why we know about these erasures is because the test developers and scorers have programs for detecting erasures and for analyzing whether unexpectedly large numbers of erasures have occurred and have resulted in changes that turned incorrect answers into correct answers.

Another example of illegal activity is that of changing student identification numbers. In many accountability systems, only the scores of students who have been in the school for at least one year count. So, by changing identification numbers, a student who was really in the school for a year would appear not to have been there, and that student's scores would not be figured into the accountability index. This kind of illegal activity is more difficult to detect. But, this activity is detected, as shown in Box 2.5.

We provide these examples because you might run into this technique as a strategy proposed by someone as the way to improve accountability scores. You should not even consider this type of approach. This tactic does not improve individual student performance.

Unethical activities   Unethical activities are more subtle but are just as inappropriate as illegal activities. Examples of these activities include providing students additional information through an accommodation (information that is not available to students who are taking tests without accommodations). For example, a person reading a test to a student might emphasize passages that contain the correct answers to questions that will be encountered later. Another example would be the scribe who, because he or she knows that the student really knows something, adds information to that student's answers that the student did not directly indicate when providing the answer.

Just as unethical is deciding that a student needs an accommodation that is not approved, thereby knocking that score out of the accountability system. Many similar kinds of actions and decisions border on the unethical. One such example would be encouraging the student to stay home the day of the test. Another would be suggesting to the student that a good test-taking strategy is to mark the same bubble if answers are not known—a strategy that is highly likely to result in the test being identified as invalid.

The perception that accommodations provide students with advantages is one reason why we need to be especially certain that any accommodations that are provided do not give any clues to answers that are not available to other students. For example, if someone decides that a student needs a person to record answers on a reading test in a timely manner, or to bubble in answers on a scanned bubble sheet, then it is critical that the scribe does not give clues to the student by asking the student to repeat only incorrect answers (or to ask questions like, "Are you sure that is what you mean?" or "Are you thinking carefully about what you read?"). Guidelines for readers exist that have been developed by Education Testing Services (ETS). The Council for Exceptional Children also has developed materials with details about specific accommodations and how they should and should not be used. Other guidelines probably exist in your

BOX 2.5

Example of Illegal Accountability Activity

A recent case in Texas, where a school administrator lost his job after a problem with student identification numbers was discovered, was described in a couple of articles in **Education Week**. In an article on March 17, 1999, Johnston wrote the following:

> In the state capital, Austin, a several-month criminal investigation into a different type of records-tampering is drawing to a close before a grand jury. The case began last fall, when Commissioner Moses asked the Austin city schools to look into changes to student records by district officials.
>
> An investigation commissioned by the 76,000-student Austin schools found that because of changes to student-identification numbers, some students' low scores on last spring's TAAS exams were not factored into school accountability ratings. As a result, two district administrators were reprimanded, and four school principals received letters of warning last fall.
>
> "It is important that the Austin community realizes that we have returned integrity to our accountability system," said Andy Welch, the district's spokesman. The investigation also resulted in the ratings of Travis Heights and Blackshear elementary schools being dropped one level to "low-performing" from "acceptable." Bryker Woods Elementary School's rating fell two levels to "acceptable" from "exemplary."
>
> "The changes [were] undertaken . . . with the specific purpose of impacting school ratings," according to the report prepared for the Austin schools by Moak, Casey & Associates, a school consulting firm in Austin. Austin's not out of the woods. Mr. Oden, the county attorney, is presenting evidence to a grand jury of possible criminal misconduct by school system employees. He has expanded the initial scope of his investigation to include dropout statistics, personnel information, payroll records, and other data.
>
> He hopes his investigation sends a strong message elsewhere. "Where there is evidence of intentionally falsifying records to produce a false result," he said, "that is the same kind of intent that makes behavior criminal in other areas."

In a follow-up article on April 14, 1999, Johnston and Galley wrote the following:

> The probe of the Austin Independent School District began last fall after the Texas Education Agency asked school officials to explain why several students' Social Security numbers were used in place of the state-assigned student numbers on 1998 test data. An independent probe commissioned by the Austin schools found that student identification numbers for several low-scoring students at three schools were intentionally altered. The substitutions of student information effectively invalidated the student scores, which in turn raised the state ratings of those schools.

BOX 2.5

Example of Illegal Accountability Activity (Continued)

Following that investigation, Ms. Psencik, whose office was in charge of student test data, was reprimanded by the district. In February, she announced her intention to retire at the end of the school year. Ricky Arredondo, a systems analyst who worked under Ms. Psencik, was also reprimanded.

While the district had contended that no laws were broken, County Attorney Oden disagreed and took his case to a Travis County grand jury. He claimed that district officials broke the law by tampering with government records. Mr. Oden later expanded his investigation into Austin's dropout records and other school documents. That probe is continuing.

Last month, Mr. Arredondo pleaded no contest to charges that he changed government documents. Sentencing for Mr. Arredondo, who resigned from the district, is slated for June.

This case and the threat of problems with student identification numbers is one of the reasons why states and districts try to monitor the numbers of students who are taking and not taking tests and try to relate the numbers of students who are taking tests to the school population. This situation is another driving force for ensuring that all students are included in assessments and accountability systems.

---

district or state, and additional guidelines are sure to be developed as state and district tests continue to be used for accountability purposes.

Accounting for the Alternate Assessment

Although we have devoted an entire chapter to the new alternate assessment (refer to Chapter 4), we want to take a minute to point out that accounting for the performance of all students really means also accounting for the learning of those students who are taking the alternate assessment. As a result of the Individuals with Disabilities Education Act (IDEA) 1997, states and districts have had to take a serious look at standards and curricula for all students. We know, however, that there are students who even with accommodation will not be able to take the regular assessments for a variety of reasons. Our point is that regardless of what test a student takes, the score must count. Students who are taking an alternate assessment might be assessed on something totally different from the regular assessment. For example, the regular assessment might be a multiple-choice and/or short-answer test, while the alternate assessment is a portfolio measuring a different curriculum. So, how can scores obtained from different assessments count? Surely we cannot aggregate or combine them. That is right—we cannot. But read on.

Only one state so far, Kentucky, has found a way to count scores on the alternate assessment *and* scores from the regular assessment system—partly because one of the parts of the regular assessment system uses a portfolio approach, and Kentucky's alternate assessment is an alternate portfolio approach. Both the regular and alternate portfolios are scored by using the same rubric. In other words, a 4 on the alternate assessment counts the same and is weighted the same as a 4 on the regular portfolio assessment. In this manner, the scores from both assessments can be aggregated or combined. The trick to this system is that the assessments are similar and are scored by using the same rubric. The Kentucky school system embraces the "all kids count" concept, and this perspective is reflected in how the two assessments count equally. We must also point out that in addition to the regular portfolio, the general-education students take multiple-choice assessments.

High Stakes on the Rise

The high-stakes nature of accountability that states are placing on local school districts is creating pressures in classrooms like never before. Not only are there high stakes for students (with nearly half of the states requiring students to pass an exam to earn a high school diploma), but there are also high stakes for schools and districts. Consider the situation in California. An Accountability Performance Index (API) now exists that is being used across the state. The APIs have been determined by the previous year's test performance on the Stanford Achievement Test-9 (SAT-9). Sanctions will be applied for schools that do not reach the API index that is set for them by the state. The sanction can be in the form of school or district takeovers by the state or loss of accreditation and the like.

Basically, there are two areas in the API: cognitive and non-cognitive. Within each area are several indicators that are used to calculate the school and school district API. In the cognitive area is the SAT-9, California Standards Test, soon-to-be high school graduation test (in 2004), and a primary language test. Sixty percent of the API counts for this area. In the non-cognitive area, 40 percent of the proposed API is teacher attendance, student attendance, the number of credentialed teachers, and the graduation or dropout rate.

The caveat to this new legislation is that unless reliable data can be collected for all of these components, the data cannot be included in the API. To date, only the scores on the SAT-9 are recognized as producing useable data. All of the other indicators will not be used in the API until a statewide student information system is developed and implemented. So, in the meantime, the pressure is on to raise test scores.

Looking for loopholes In most states that are using norm-referenced tests or even some standard-based criterion-referenced tests, there is a set of assessment accommodations that has been identified. Students who require other accommodations that are not on the approved list usually take the assessment, but their scores are not counted in the school building and on district reports. Hence, there is incentive to have students with disabilities take the test with non-standard accommodations, because then their scores do not count. In some districts, such as the Long Beach (California) Unified School District, accountability reports include all students, including students who took non-standard assessments. Scores are disaggregated and aggregated to ensure that all students have been accounted for. What is new is that school buildings are now beginning to get testing reports on students who have disabilities who took the same district and state tests. Not until recently have people been concerned about the assessment performance of students who have disabilities. True, there are people who are looking for ways to exclude students who have disabilities from accountability reports, but why? Could it be because of the following points?

1. Little or no instruction is taking place in special-education classes?

2. Instruction in these classes bares little or no resemblance to that of the standards that are set for what all students should know and be able to do?

3. An attitude exists that special education is a baby-sitting service for kids?

4. In general, learning expectations are low for students who have special needs?

Tough questions need to asked and answered:

1. Who is responsible for evaluating and supervising special education teachers at the site?

2. Are special educators not part of a building's teaching staff?

3. Who is the instructional leader on site?

4. Who supervises and evaluates instruction at the school site?

Too often, we hear administrators say, "I don't know how to evaluate special education teachers." Guess what? Good teaching is good teaching. The "special" in special education does not mean a different set of teaching standards; rather, it connotes the type of student needs that must be considered when teaching.

For too long, special education classrooms and teachers have been considered a separate program. As a result, we have perpetuated a dual system of service delivery or instruction to students. Unfortunately, this dual system has not carried accountability. Now, schools and districts across the nation are faced with increasing the performance of all students, including students who have disabilities. Prevalent and current conditions of special education classrooms and instruction are beginning to surface—lack of books, curriculum, technology, professional development, etc.—yet teachers are expected to improve performance for all students. Is it any wonder why people at a building site are looking for ways to exclude students from accountability reports? Things must change from the top down and from the bottom up.

Assumptions about Including Students Who Have Disabilities

The bottom line is that all kids count and must be accounted for. Although current practices sometimes suggest otherwise, including all students and including special-needs students in accountability systems is the right thing to do. Often, folks cannot get close enough to this goal due to their perceptions and expectations of special populations.

A number of key assumptions underlie the inclusion of students who have disabilities in educational-accountability systems. We will list these assumptions here, and you should make sure that they are assumptions with which you agree. If you find that you do not agree with any of the assumptions listed here, you should take a few moments to review the justification for each of the assumptions. Many good sources exist for reviewing the underlying basis for the assumptions (refer to Box 2.6).

Assumption 1: All students can learn.   This seemingly simple statement lies at the core of including all students in educational accountability systems. This philosophy encompasses a recognition that all learning is important, be it deciphering a complex mathematical formula, recognizing the letter *a*, or using involuntary muscles to roll over. This idea also encompasses an understanding of the dramatic effects that expectations can have on the learning of individuals and the need to be aware of a ten-

---

BOX 2.6

Resources on the Underlying Basis of Assumption on the Inclusion of Students Who Have Disabilities in Assessments

High Stakes: Testing for Tracking, Promotion, and Graduation (by Heubert & Hauser, 1999).
Testing, Teaching, and Learning: A Guide for States and School Districts (by Elmore & Rothman, 1999).
Educating One & All: Students with Disabilities and Standards-Based Reform (by McDonnell, McLaughlin, & Morison, 1997).
Testing Students with Disabilities: Practical Strategies for Complying with District and State Requirements (by Thurlow, Elliott, & Ysseldyke, 1998).

dency to hold inappropriate expectations for individual children, particularly those who are performing below the level of other children who are the same as them in one way or another.

Assumption 2: Schools are responsible for the learning of all children. Long ago in the history of American education, the decision was made that schools were public institutions and were open to all citizens of the United States of America. In fact, a strong premise underlying the development of American public education was that schools were the mechanism to bring equality to all, regardless of background. Over time, policymakers have recognized that individuals who have disabilities are people first, and that they have the same rights as other citizens. Students who have disabilities have the same right to an appropriate public education as all other students. While it has taken some strong public laws to ensure that these rights are recognized and upheld (refer to Box 2.7), these rights remain an integral part of the assumptions underlying an inclusive accountability system.

Assumption 3: Whenever children are counted, all children must count. Educational-accountability indexes invariably assign numbers or scores to children, add them up in one way or another, and use them to determine some type of consequence. To have an inclusive educational accountability system, students who have disabilities must count in the same way as other children. Not all students have to take the same test to be counted, but they must count in the evaluation system of the educational system. Without a doubt, special approaches have to be taken in order to ensure that scores are comparable in agreed upon ways, and this approach must be decided on up-front with stakeholders talking to each other. But the bottom line is that all students must count—no ifs, ands, or buts.

Summary

If we start from the assumptions of an inclusive accountability system, then there is no tendency toward either illegal or unethical behavior. Instead, the focus can be unequivocally on how to improve the test performance of all students, including those who have disabilities. That is the goal of this book—to help you know how best to ensure that students who have disabilities perform their best on tests and other assessments that are used in district and state accountability systems.

Test Your Knowledge

Either rely on what you remember about what you have just read, or reread parts of this chapter as you complete the following fill-in-the-blank statements. The answers should jump into your head immediately. If not,

---

BOX 2.7

Federal Laws that Ensure the Rights of Individuals Who Have Disabilities

Americans with Disabilities Act (ADA)

(1990). This act requires that youth who have disabilities should be provided with the same benefits and services that are available to youth who do not have disabilities. The ADA is known as a major employment act, with implications for both physical plant accommodations and other accommodations for individuals who have disabilities. The ADA also requires accommodations to be provided to youngsters who have disabilities.

Improving America's Schools Act (IASA)

(1994, reauthorization pending). Formerly known as the **Elementary and Secondary Education Act** (ESEA), this law funds Title I programs (also known as Chapter I in the past). Title I is a major funding source for schools that have disadvantaged students. The 1994 IASA and its reauthorization created the requirements that students who have disabilities are to be included in the programs and in the evaluation systems for the programs, which were to be based on standards and assessed through state and district assessments.

Individuals with Disabilities Education Act (IDEA)

(1997). This far reaching reauthorization emphasizes standards-based reform, access to the general-education curriculum, and inclusion in state and district assessments. As a result of IDEA 1997, states must establish goals and performance indicators for the performance of children who have disabilities that are consistent with those indicators and goals that are set for other children by the state. Students who have disabilities must be included in state and district assessments or in an alternate assessment developed for them, and their performance must be reported publicly in the same way and with the same frequency as students who do not have disabilities.

Section 504 of the Rehabilitation Act of 1973

(1973). This law prohibits discrimination in federally funded programs on the basis of disability. Section 504 provides support to ensure that youth who have disabilities have an equal opportunity to gain the same benefits, obtain the same results, and reach the same level of achievement as their peers who do not have disabilities. This section of the Rehabilitation Act is the basis for 504 accommodation plans.

---

review what you have read, or jot down some notes. Do not hesitate to reread parts of this chapter if the words that go in the blanks do not come to you at once.

1. A key piece in most educational reforms in the past decade or so is some kind of _____.

2. The terms *high stakes* and *low stakes* refer to the relative _____ of the consequences in an accountability system.

3. The three parts of an educational system for which educators might be held accountable include its resources, its processes, and its _____.

4. Understanding the accountability system in which you are working is one of the first steps in improving students'_____ _____.

5. _____ are one of the main reasons why accountability systems have any impact at all.

6. The most common types of information that are used in accountability systems are student test scores, dropout rates, and _____ rates.

7. One truth about accountability systems is that they _____ over time.

8. Both illegal testing activities and _____ activities are inappropriate.

9. A core assumption that supports including students who have disabilities in accountability systems is that all students can _____.

10. A key belief of inclusive accountability is that whenever children are counted, all children must _____.

Answers

1. accountability (p. 11)
2. impact (p. 12)
3. outcomes (p. 12)
4. test performance (p. 13)
5. consequences (p. 14)
6. attendance (p. 15)
7. change (p. 15)
8. unethical (p. 25)
9. learn (p. 30)
10. count (p. 31)

Resources

Bond, L., Roeber, E., and Connealy, S. (1998). *State student assessment programs database: School year 1996–97.* Washington, D.C.: Council of Chief State School Officers.

Darling-Hammond, L. (1992). *Standards of Practice for Learner-Centered Schools.* New York: Columbia University, National Center for Restructuring, Education, Schools, and Teaching (NCREST).

Education Testing Services. (1989). *ETS guide for the use of readers in non-standard test administrations.* Princeton, NJ: ETS.

Elmore, R. F. and Rothman, R. (1999) (eds.) *Testing, Teaching, and Learning: A Guide for States and School Districts.* Washington, D.C.: National Academy of Sciences.

Huebert, J. P. and Hauser, R. M. (1998) (eds.) *High Stakes: Testing for Tracking, Promotion, and Graduation.* Washington, D.C.: National Academy Press.

Johnston, R. C. (1999, March 17). "Texas presses districts in alleged test-tampering cases." *Education Week.*

Johnston, R. C. and Galley, M. (1999, April 14). "Austin district charged with test tampering." *Education Week.*

Levin, H. (1974). "A conceptual framework for accountability in education." *School Review, 82,* 363–391.

Macpherson, R. (1996). "Educative accountability policy research: methodology and epistemology." *Educational Administration Quarterly, 32,* 80–106.

McDonnell, L. M., McLaughlin, M. J., and Morison, P. (1997). *Educating One & All: Students with Disabilities and Standards-Based Reform.* Washington, D.C.: National Academy Press.

National Commission on Excellence in Education. (1983). *A Nation at Risk: The Imperative for Educational Reform.* Washington, D.C.: Author.

Thurlow, M. L., Elliott, J. L., and Ysseldyke, J. E. (1998). *Testing Students with Disabilities: Practical Strategies for Complying with District and State Requirements.* Thousand Oaks, CA: Corwin Press.

Internet Resources

Council of Chief State School Officers: http://www.ccsso.org/

Education Commission of the States: http://www.ecs.org/

National Association of State Boards of Education: http://www.nasbe.org/

National Association of State Directors of Special Education (NASDSE): http://www.nasdse.org/

National Center on Educational Outcomes (NCEO): http://www.coled.umn.edu/nceo

Standards-Based Instruction: The Backbone of Educational Accountability

"Excellence for a few, but not for you"

—unknown

"If you treat students as they are, they become worse. If you treat them as they could be, they become better."

—Gerald Tirozzi

Hot-Button Issues

- What standards? Who developed them? What were they thinking?
- Not all students, including students who have disabilities, will meet the standards. Then what?
- Why do all students need to work toward the same standards, anyway?
- Linking the IEP to standards is just more busy work.
- What has happened to the "I" in IEP?

So what is all the noise about standards, anyway? And why do parents, teachers, and administrators need to know about them?

The backbone of educational accountability is the evaluation of how students, including students who have disabilities and those who have a limited English proficiency, are learning and progressing in today's schools. How can we really account for student learning if we do not have a common measure by which to judge learning? Standards identify the goals of learning.

Basically, two kinds of standards have been established in states and districts. Content standards are those that define what students should know and be able to do. Performance standards, on the other hand, describe to what extent or degree of mastery that students must demonstrate achievement of content standards. In other words, how good is good enough? Each state has the responsibility of answering that question relative to the content standards that it has developed.

States have developed performance descriptors or performance rubrics to serve as the measure of what students need to demonstrate in order to show various levels of proficiency. Here are two examples of performance rubrics: (1) Partially Proficient, Proficient and (2) Beginning, Emerging, Developing, Proficient, Strong, Exemplary, Advanced. Each performance descriptor defines what and how students must demonstrate a skill in order to obtain a score within a specific level (refer to Box 3.1).

Changing of the Tide

In the midst of this process is the strong undercurrent (or should we say, riptide) of how schools will be held accountable for the integrity and implementation of standards. In order to make any sense of the standards-based movement, there must be an accountability plan. Also, without

---

BOX 3.1

Examples of Content and Performance Standards

Reading

Content Standard 5: Students will read to locate, select, and make use of relevant information from a variety of media, reference, and technological sources.

Performance Descriptors for Grades K–4

Partially Proficient: Students inconsistently find and make use of information by using organization features of a variety of printed texts and electronic media. Students take notes and outline and identify main ideas in resource material, but there might be inaccuracies, limited understanding, omission of important facts and details, or direct copying.

Proficient: Students are able to find and make use of information by using organizational features of a variety of printed texts and electronic media for a specific topic or purpose. Students accurately take notes, outline and identify main ideas in resource materials, and give credit by listing sources.

Advanced: Students can easily and without assistance find information by using organization features of a variety of printed texts and electronic media. Students sort, record, and synthesize information from a wide variety of sources and give credit by listing sources.

BOX 3.1

Examples of Content and Performance Standards (Continued)

Mathematics

Content Standard 6: Students link concepts and procedures as they develop and use computational techniques, including estimation, mental arithmetic, the paper-and-pencil method, calculators, and computers in problem-solving situations and communicate the reasoning that is used in solving these problems.

Performance Descriptors for Grades 9–12

Partially Proficient: With some procedural errors, students uses ratios, proportions, and percents in problem-solving situations. Students use a limited range of methods for computing with real numbers, selecting from among mental arithmetic, estimation, the paper-and-pencil method, calculator and computer methods and they make an attempt to determine whether the results are reasonable. Students describe some limitations of estimation, and incompletely assess the amount of error resulting from estimation.

Proficient: In problem-solving situations, students use ratios, proportions, and percents. Students select and use appropriate methods for computing with real numbers. Students select from among mental arithmetic, estimation, the paper-and-pencil method, calculator and computer methods and determine whether the results are reasonable. Students describe the limitations of estimation and assess the amount of error resulting from estimation within acceptable limits.

Advanced: In problem-solving situations, students use ratios, proportions, and percents. Students select and use appropriate methods for computing with real numbers. Students select from mental arithmetic, estimation, the paper-and-pencil method, calculator and computer methods and provide insightful arguments that the results are reasonable. Students thoroughly describe the limitations of estimation and assess the amount of error resulting from estimation within acceptable limits.

SOURCE: Reprinted with permission from Hansche, L. (1998). *Meeting the Requirements of Title I: Handbook for the Development of Performance Standards*. Washington, D.C.: United States Department of Education.

---

meaningful and aligned assessments, the current standards movement can be dissolved into nothing more than another education bandwagon that has tried to function without all of the cogs in the wheel.

Standards-based education continues to top the list of reforms that are sweeping the nation. This form of education is at the top of both national and state educational agendas. By the year 1998, 49 states had established content standards, and almost half of the states had approved performance standards or descriptors. We say "approved" because each state, in order to receive its federal money from the office of Elementary and Secondary Education, had to submit proposed performance standards to a review team that examined the *process* by which states set their performance standards.

Where is Lake Wobegon, Anyway?

Like it or not, all schools must be accountable for their students' performances. No matter how large or small or on what side of town the schools are located, we must continually ask ourselves, "Are students learning what they should? How do we know that schools are making progress in educating all students? What are we doing for schools that are not making progress?" Because no one has ever been able to locate the community of Lake Wobegon, where "all the children are above average," the need to take a close look at standards and assessments that include all students continues to be central to reform today.

Some basic principles exist that we need to be sure are in place before the standards-based reform in today's schools really has purpose or impact. Examine the following principles, and see which ones you have in place in your school, district, or state:

- The accountability system is accountable to itself.
- Accountability is built on standards that reflect all students in our schools.
- The opportunity to learn is a primary element in the accountability system.
- All constituents of the accountability system have a clear understanding of the components of the accountability system, including rewards and sanctions.

Setting standards and announcing an accountability plan is one thing. Actually providing the support and resources that are needed to provide students the opportunities to learn and meet those high expectations is another. Although resources will look different wherever you go, some basic resources include sustained professional development, technology, teaching materials, and qualified teachers.

Current Status of Standards in States and School Districts

Establishing content standards   Across the nation, 49 states have established content standards. Many districts have also established their own standards. Standard-setting is the process by which states have identified what they want all students to know and to be able to do as a result of their years of K–12 schooling. Typically, standards-setting has been done by a group of stakeholders, including parents, general education and special education teachers, administrators, students, and community groups and/or local business representatives. But this method is not how it was done everywhere. You should know how content standards were established in your state and in your district. Stakeholder groups typically use a consensus process to decide what they want students to know and to be able to do. As you can imagine, this task is not small. Each stakeholder brings to the task his or her own views. One might come with 13 years of classroom experience, another might come with one year of experience, and another might have 30 years' experience. Add to this mix parents, administrators, and maybe community representatives. Opinions vary widely, as do perspectives and philosophies of what constitutes a well-rounded education.

An analysis of 47 states' content standards conducted by the National Center on Educational Outcomes in 1997 showed that standards were quite varied and included several non-academic standards (such as vocationally oriented and life skill-oriented standards). Of course, we know that most district and state assessments emphasize academics only. Although states indicated that standards were established for *all* students, 11 states did not mention students with disabilities at all, and only four states simply indicated that students who have disabilities were included in "all students." Nine states seem to have more thoroughly considered students with disabilities as part of "all" by suggesting that accommodations would be needed to give them access to achieving the standards. Still, few states indicated that special educators were part of the standard setting process.

Establishing performance standards   Similar consensus processes are being used to establish performance standards. The fact that only 22 states had performance standards (as of spring 1999), however, suggests that there are other issues to face. Deciding what to require students to know and to be able to do is one thing, but deciding how good is good enough is quite another.

Relevance for all students   When examining your state and district standards, you will find that it does not take long to notice that not all students will be able to attain the content and/or performance standards. Most students who have disabilities, however, will be able to work toward the standards that have been set for all students. As we have noted elsewhere, it has been estimated that 85 percent of students who have disabilities are able to participate in the typical district or state assessment. Some can do so without accommodations, while others need accommodations. These same students must be learning the standards and skills, with instructional accommodations when needed, and they should be taking the standards-based assessments that are designed to measure progress toward meeting these standards.

So, what about students for whom existing standards are not relevant? You could easily argue that many of your existing standards are more relevant for some students than others, depending on their life goals. For example, what about students who have more significant cognitive disabilities? Are your state or district standards appropriate for them? If your answer is yes, then hooray! But in most cases, your answer will be no. Then what? Generally, people have made the decision to expand, extend, or bridge established standards so that they will be relevant for these other students. In other words, districts and states have taken existing standards and have made them more functionally relevant for students who have more significant cognitive disabilities. Other places are working to rewrite or create another set of standards for these students.

The impact on school districts   The tricky part of standards is implementing them at the school district, building, and classroom levels. In light of the diversity that exists in schools today, this task is a challenge. The 1997 changes in IDEA have been one force behind creating standards for all students, including students who have disabilities. Because the general nature of standards is academic and few special educators were at the table during their development, states have been faced with the task of re-examining the standards, keeping all students in mind and including students who have more significant cognitive disabilities.

As required by IDEA 1997, students who have disabilities not only must have access to general education, but they also must be working toward the same standards as other students. That is, students' IEPs must reflect and align with the standards toward which all other students are working. In order to accomplish this goal, there must be relevant standards toward which students can work. States and districts have begun to take many approaches to reach compliance with this aspect of IDEA.

Some states and districts have selected several broad standards that are embedded in the general standards and have identified them as the ones toward which students who have more significant cognitive disabilities will work. In this case, the content standards remain the same; however, the performance indicators are different. Others have decided to create a separate set of broad standards that are tailored to the daily skills and domains upon which these students are working (refer to Chapter 4 for more discussion).

Still, there are those who have taken the existing standards and expanded, bridged, or extended them to encompass a broader spectrum of skill levels. In Box 3.2, we provide you with three state examples that demonstrate expanding or extending standards for students who are taking

BOX 3.2

Examples of Expanded Standards

New York—Social Studies

Standard 1: Students will use a variety of intellectual skills to demonstrate their understanding of major ideas, eras, themes, developments, and turning points in the history of the United States and New York.

Alternate Level: Students will study family, neighborhood, community, New York State and United States history, culture, values, beliefs, and traditions and the important contribution of individuals and groups.

Performance Indicators: Identify individuals who have helped to strengthen democracy in the United States.

Missouri (one of four general state goals)

Goal 4: Students in Missouri public schools will acquire the knowledge and skills to recognize and solve problems.

Functional Context: Students will respond to their environment.

Performance Indicators: Demonstrates an understanding of cause and effect; uses trial and error to solve simple problems and make decisions

Kansas—Reading

Standard 1: Learner will demonstrate skill in reading a variety of materials for a variety of purposes.

For the purposes of the alternate assessment, reading is defined as receptive communication. Receptive communication is the processing of a message mediated through one or more of the senses.

Benchmark 1: The learner understands basic vocabulary.

Indicators (selected excerpt):

1. Retell reading material in accurate sequence.
2. Identify simple detail and/or facts in the written passage to support understanding.
3. Read to get information.
4. Understands basic message of text
5. Responds to photographs

BOX 3.2

Examples of Expanded Standards (Continued)

Delaware—English Language Arts

Standard ELA 3: Student will access, organize, and evaluate information gained by listening, reading, and viewing.

Functional Standard: Student will develop and maintain the ability to attend to, respond to, and utilize information from others.

Key Concepts: The student will:

1. Attend/orient to others
2. Follow request/directions
3. Access, organize, evaluate, and use information though some mode in order to make choices

---

the alternate assessment. In these examples, it is clear that effort was made to bridge the general standards to those students for whom the regular assessment is not appropriate. The presentation of each state's information is quite different (e.g., different terminology and format); however, we think it paints the picture.

In almost all cases, efforts to develop broader standards have been the result of an effort to include students who have more significant cognitive disabilities in assessment and accountability reports that are required by the federal government. Also, in turn, these standards are what states are using as the basis for the development of their alternate assessments (refer to Chapter 4 for more discussion).

Trademarks of a Standards-Based Classroom

Standards-based instruction, standards-based classrooms, or standards-based anything nicely rolls off your tongue. But what does it really look like in the classroom? What are the trademarks of a successful standards-based classroom? Try the following concepts on for size:

Students know the standards and level of proficiency required. Effective educators announce up-front the standards, goals, and proficiency requirements—at the start of each semester, lesson, and unit of instruction—and they reinforce these requirements throughout instruction. They see instruction and assessment as inextricably linked. Nothing is kept secret. In fact, students are part of some of the instructional planning. After all, it is proficiency—not seat time—that matters in standards-based classrooms.

Students are provided multiple opportunities to learn. Students are given opportunities to revise, review, and debate work over the course of days or during a unit of instruction. This method is not how it has been typically done in the past. Often, students are given one chance to get it right. We all know of teachers who give assignments and never return them or give students a grade without corrective feedback or the opportunity to revise. Whatever happened to mastery learning? Only in turn when these things occur—when students are allowed to reach mastery—do students really learn from their work.

Student assignments reflect an integration of facts, concepts, and strategies. Assignments reflect the depth and breadth of skills that are being taught. They do not simply skim the surface. Students are given the opportunity, over the period of several days or during an even more extended period of time, to integrate their knowledge of a topic with other academic areas. In a standards-based classroom, teachers are aware of the standards in other content areas and integrate and reinforce them wherever and whenever possible.

Each assignment is an assessment in itself. The purposes of classroom activities are to build skills in ways that can be assessed by using different techniques. Proficiency is required of more than the one skill that is being taught. This standard reflects cumulative knowledge and proficiency. Teachers in standards-based classrooms understand the instruction-assessment cycle. Instruction feeds assessment, and vice-versa.

Aligning IEPs with Standards

Among the many changes in special education law is the restructuring of the IEP to include (1) what assessment that students who have disabilities will participate in, and (2) what accommodations are needed. Before the changes in law, the IEPs of most students who have disabilities have reflected only individualized goals and objectives, without linking to anything even remotely related to the general education curriculum. There are a variety of reasons why this situation might have been true:

- Lack of general expectations for students who have disabilities to achieve the general education curriculum

- Lack of professional development for administrators and general and special educators
- Lack of collaboration between special educators and general educators in general education reforms
- Lack of visionary leadership
- TTWADI (pronounced ta-waa-di), or, "That's the way we've always done it."

The bottom line is that we know more today than ever before about what works in learning, instruction, and assessment. The tragedy is that we do not always show what we know.

Linking the IEP to Standards

Today, more and more states are beginning to move in the direction of recommending a format for all IEPs. Past practice has been to list all required components of the IEP and to provide an example or model IEP. In many districts, IEPs have been redeveloped to guide teachers through an errorless method of linking a goal and an objective to a state or district content standard. For example, the teacher identifies the goal and objective for the student, then indicates what content standard it addresses.

If you are in a state that has established a set of broad standards (let's say eight) for students who have significant cognitive disabilities, then you would perhaps have at least eight IEP goals and objectives reflecting instruction in these required areas. Some argue that this method takes the "I," or individualization, out of the IEP. This statement is false. In addition to these areas, a student's IEP must reflect his or her current levels of need in the areas that might not be covered by standards. In this manner, a student's IEP reflects the standards being worked toward by other students, as well as individual areas that are in need of further development. Box 3.3 is an example of a standards-based IEP. The goals and objectives reflect the district standards for all students. Each objective is linked to a standard or area in the general curriculum.

Backmapping standards to instruction   Once we have the IEP linked to the standards, then what? How do we *teach* the standards? What do the standards look like in the instructional process? How do we know that we have taught to the standard? All of these questions are critical in the process of aligning standards, instruction, and assessment. Although we will discuss instructional approaches in Chapter 9, it is useful to look at the process of backmapping.

The term *backmapping* is a relatively new one. This term has evolved from the need to link standards to instruction in order to align the instruc-

---

BOX 3.3

IEP Format Linking District Standards and Student Annual Goals

Example 1

Student: Yu Kanduit   DOB: 10/24/93

Content Area: Language Arts   **District Standard Area:** Participating in Discussion

District Standard: Students will engage productively in discussions to clarify thoughts; to explore issues, feelings, and experiences; to extend understanding; and to interact effectively with others.

Annual Goal: Yu Kanduit will use the Picture Exchange Communication System (PECS) to indicate wants and needs with 70 percent accuracy.

Objective 1: Yu will use PECS to indicate the need for water and/or the restroom with 70 percent accuracy by December 2000.

Objective 2: Yu will use PECS to request an activity of his choice with 100 percent accuracy by February 2001.

Objective 2: Yu will count the number of girls and the number of boys in the class and draw a bar graph with 100% accuracy.

Objective 3: Yu will draw a bar graph that depicts his physical education class, including the total number of students, boys, and girls with 90 percent accuracy by January 2001.

---

tion with assessment. Backmapping makes sense in that once you have identified the desired result of learning (standards and benchmarks), you can then begin the instructional process by asking assessment questions. Educators need to think like assessors:

- How will I know my students have an in-depth understanding of what I have taught?

- What will the evidence be?

- What assessment tasks will enable me to determine the extent to which students have learned the content?

- How can I use these assessment tasks to anchor my unit of instruction, lessons, and assignments?

BOX 3.3

IEP Format Linking District Standards and Student Annual Goals (Continued)

Example 2

Student: Ima Gonatry   DOB: 8/29 /85

Content Area: Mathematics   **District Standard Area:** Discrete Mathematics

District Standard: Students will solve problems in the areas of counting, identifying the problem to be solved, and finding the best solutions.

Annual Goal 1: Ima Gonatry will create her personal daily schedule by using 24-hour and standard time.

Objective 1: Ima will write out her morning routine/schedule with 100 percent accuracy by September 20, 2000.

Objective 2: Ima will write out to the minute, using standard time, her morning schedule with 80 percent accuracy by October 31, 2000.

Annual Goal 2: Using counting techniques, Ima will chart and graph the results to various mathematic problems with 80 percent accuracy.

Objective 1: Ima will count the total number students in the class and draw a bar graph of the results with 80 percent accuracy.

Objective 2: Ima will count the number of girls and the number of boys in the class and draw a bar graph with 100 percent accuracy.

Objective 3: Ima will draw a bar graph that depicts her physical education class, including the total number of students, boys, and girls with 90 percent accuracy by January 2001.

The key is to explore the answers to each of these questions prior to the start of instruction or during your planning stage. Looking for the extent to which students can explain, interpret, apply, and give perspectives is a good place to start.

Here is how backmapping works. Start with a standard—any standard. Examine the standard in terms of its elements of instruction. For example, let us examine the following science standard:

Students will identify different kinds of energy and describe how energy can be transmitted, reflected, and absorbed.

This standard has several elements or skills embedded in it, including but not limited to the following:

- Concepts—identify, same, different, reflection, and absorption
- Vocabulary words—energy, transmission
- Ability to comprehend and apply knowledge to produce examples
- Student abilities—cognitive, processing information, producing examples, following a strategy or procedure, reading for understanding

In other words, we have many skills packed into one standard. How do we know that students have the necessary prerequisite skills to work on the standard? Well, we do not know unless we pre-assess the specifically identified skills that are needed to learn and demonstrate mastery of the standard. Once the components or skills are listed, we can begin to create a blueprint for instruction. You must locate where in the curriculum the identified facts, concepts, or strategies are taught. If they do not appear anywhere, you have just discovered an existing gap in the alignment of standards, instruction, and assessment (in Chapter 6, we discuss aligning tests with instruction). Be sure to incorporate the needed (but missing) skills into the curriculum. Begin to identify units of instruction and corresponding curricular materials. Then, develop the instructional strategies and materials that can be used to teach these units. Be sure to keep in mind the cognitive demands of tasks (refer to Box 3.4).

If you are preparing students for a published test, perhaps a norm-referenced test, you should look at the test matrix. Here, you will find the types of skills that are measured as well as the number of items that will test each skill. More information about the test-specification matrix appears in Chapter 6. Frameworks for backmapping the curriculum (refer to Box 3.5) are best done with teams of teachers. This process can be accomplished at state, district, or site levels. Although time intensive initially, the time invested in this process is worth its weight in the results—comprehensive instruction and aligned assessment.

Remember Benjamin Bloom (may he rest in peace) and his Bloom's Taxonomy (refer to Box 3.6)? Well, you should dig out this book and dust it off. (Good things die hard or never at all.) We mention the learning taxonomy because, besides being an oldie but goodie, this book is important for looking at the breadth and depth of knowledge that you are requiring of students and then to match your instruction to this level.

In addition, Bloom's Taxonomy helps with developing assessments that reflect exactly what was taught. This procedure has been around for a long, long time, but too often we have misplaced it (maybe in Lake Wobegon).

BOX 3.4

Steps in Backmapping Standards to Instruction

1. Select a standard.

2. Identify or break down the standard according to the elements or skills that are embedded in it.

3. Locate these skills in the scope and sequence of the curriculum. Are they present or not?

4. Create an instructional blueprint of all skills that are needed to achieve the standard. Be sure to indicate those that are prerequisite skills and those that are component skills.

5. Break identified skills into units of instruction.

6. Identify instructional strategies and materials to teach the embedded skills.

7. Assess whether students have the prerequisite skills that are needed to engage in learning the standard.

8. Identify methods to assess student knowledge and understanding of the taught skills.

9. When assessment is conducted by using a norm-referenced test, review the table of specifications. This table outlines the types of skills measured, the method of assessment, and the number of items assessed. This table helps you plan for instructional areas of concentration and importance.

BOX 3.5

A Framework for Backmapping

Standards (Domains)	Instructional Blueprint	Units of Instruction/ Materials	Instructional Strategies	Assessment

---

BOX 3.6

Bloom's Taxonomy

KNOWLEDGE: Rote recall of specific information, such as facts, terminology, procedures

Example: What is the name of the assessment required by the state?

COMPREHENSION: Understanding of material; able to translate, paraphrase, interpret, or extrapolate information

Example: What concept and strategies does the reading subtest measure?

APPLICATION: Able to transfer information to new situations or settings

Example: Using the provided student test protocol, tell where the student performed the best.

ANALYSIS: Able to find the parts to a whole, finding the interconnectedness or relationship among parts

Example: Tell how effective instruction impacts improving student performance.

SYNTHESIS: Structuring, organizing, or assembling parts into a logical whole (or vice-versa)

Example: Propose a plan for improving student performance on assessments for your school.

EVALUATION: Able to make judgments about the value, usefulness, and/or utility of materials or ideas, according to certain criteria

Example: Based on your plan, how will you know whether it accomplished the goal of improving student performance on assessments?

Summary

In this chapter, we have discussed the trademarks of standards-based instruction. We have illustrated what expanded or bridged standards look like and why many states have developed them. We examined the importance of incorporating standards into the IEP and showed a simple process for mapping them into instruction. Critical to the discussion of improving student performance was the need to align instruction with assessment. We reviewed Bloom's Taxonomy and the need to align the cognitive demands of how you teach with how you test. Finally, we raised issues and concerns about accountability for all students. Included here was the imperative participation and supervision of special educators in school-site activities and agendas. For too long, special education teachers have been islands unto themselves and have been considered hands-off by many building administrators. If we truly are accounting for all students, and if all students are to count in the building and in the district accountability reports, then it makes sense that folks should be sure that all staff and students are on board the assessment and accountability train.

Test Your Knowledge

In keeping with standards-based instruction, see how well you have learned the facts, concepts, and strategies presented in this chapter.

1. Standards provide a common _____ of student learning.

2. Performance standards tell us how _____ is _____ enough.

3. For the most part, state and district standards have been developed without the participation of _____ _____.

4. In accordance with IDEA 1997, students who have disabilities not only must have access to general education, but also must be working toward the same _____ as other students.

5. In some places, in order to include students who have significant cognitive disabilities in standards-based instruction and accountability, people have _____ established standards.

6. More and more states and districts have developed IEP forms that link goals and objectives to the _____ standard.

7. TTWWADI is the age-old saying _____ _____ _____ _____ _____ _____ _____. This statement can be viewed as one of the reasons for the lack of progress in the fields of general and special education.

8. IDEA 1997 has forged a link between standards and students' _____.

9. The process of backmapping is a way to _____ standards to instruction.

10. Backmapping better assures that instruction and assessment are _____

Answers

1. measure (p. 35)
2. good, good (p. 36)
3. special educators (p. 39-40)
4. standards (p. 40)
5. extended or bridged or expanded (p. 40)
6. content (p. 50)
7. That's the way we've always done it (p. 44)
8. IEPs (p. 44)
9. link or connect (p. 44)
10. aligned (p. 44)

Resources

Bloom, B. (1956). *Taxonomy of Educational Objectives: The Classification of Educational Goals: Handbook 1. Cognitive Domain.* New York: McKay.

Elliott, J. L. and Thurlow, M. L. (1997). *Opening the Door to Educational Reform: Understanding Standards.* Boston, MA: Federation for Children with Special Needs, Parents Engaged in Educational Reform (PEER) Project.

Reeves, D. B. (1998). *Making Standards Work: How to Implement Standards-Based Assessments in the Classroom, School and District.* Denver, CO: Center for Performance Assessment.

Linn, R. L. (1999). *Standards-Based Accountability: Ten Suggestions.* Los Angeles, CA: National Center for Research on Evaluation, Standards, and Student Testing.

Education Week (1997, January 22). "Quality counts: A report card on the condition of public education in the 50 states." *A Supplement to Education Week,* Vol. 16.

Hansche, L. N. (1998). *Meeting the Requirements of Title I: Handbook for the Development of Performance Standards.* Washington, D.C.: United States Department of Education.

Internet Resources

American Federation of Teachers: http://www.aft.org
Council of Chief State School Officers: http://www.ccsso.org
Education Commission of the States: http://www.ecs.org

Federation for Children with Special Needs: http://www.fcsn.org

National Center on Educational Outcomes: http://www.coled.umn.edu/nceo

National Center for Research on Evaluation, Standards, and Student Testing: http://www.cse.ucla.edu

National Education Association: http://www.nea.org

Chapters 1–3
Self Check:
Where Do I Stand?

Inventory yourself the following statements as a personal survey of where you stand in relation to the information presented thus far. Base your answers to these questions on the topics that are presented in this book and on what you think that you already know and are doing.

- I have a good sense of what I have been emphasizing to increase the test performance of students and what I still really need to learn about to be more effective. I understand why there are accountability systems, and I know that most systems involve more than just looking at student performance. (Chapter 1)

- I know how to check what the specific indicators of accountability are in my state and district and the sources of information for these indicators. (Chapter 2)

- I know what to do if I were to encounter illegal or unethical testing procedures. I have checked district policies so that I will never be surprised by policies in this area. (Chapter 2)

- I know the core assumptions that underlie the decision to include students who have disabilities in accountability systems. (Chapter 2)

- I know my district and state accountability policies. For example, I know what is counted and included when reports are released to the public. When test scores are released, I know that all students' test results, including those results of students who have disabilities, are reported. (Chapter 3)

- I have a sense of our district/state content standards; that is, whether they are broad or narrow and whether they include non-academic areas. I also know how the content standards and the performance standards were developed. (Chapter 3)

- I understand the concept of backmapping. I am able to take a standard and backmap or link it to the scope and sequence of the curriculum and instructional sequence. I see the final result of backmapping as an IEP goal and objective that reflects learning standards established for all students. (Chapter 3)

Improving the Performance of Students in the Alternate Assessment

"All of us do not have equal talent, but all of us should have an equal opportunity to develop our talent."

—John F. Kennedy

"When schools are required to account for all students and report on the results of their performance, schools are more likely to focus on improving the results for 'all,' including students with disabilities."

—Jim Ysseldyke

Hot-Button Issues

- Why should we not use the Individualized Education Program (IEP) as the alternate assessment for special education students?

- If the alternate assessment does not count in the big picture of district/state accountability, why do the kids have to take the assessment?

- Like any district or state assessment, the alternate assessment will just be another test.

- It would be nice if someone could come up with a test that made sense to kids and instructional improvement.

- How can we test these kids when they are not even learning the same curriculum?

We realize that there might be many unhappy campers. The 1997 IDEA has created much ado about something—something incredibly important—namely, accountability for the learning and progress of all students who have disabilities. To date, virtually the only indication of how students who have disabilities are doing in school is in the Annual Report to Congress. If you are unfamiliar with this report, imagine a big, fat telephone book that lots of people use as a door stop. In it, you will find information about the number of students who are classified within the 13 federal categories of disabilities, dropout rates, the number of students who exit programs, and the like. What you will not find is information about the achievement of students who have disabilities. Nowhere in the report is there documentation of how students who have disabilities are learning and progressing in schools today. Get the picture? Until IDEA 1997, we had no information about the performance of these students.

In this chapter, we talk about the ins and outs of the alternate assessment. We explore the alternate assessment in terms of why it was developed, who takes it, and how it can be used to improve student learning and performance. After all, if we are going to give students an assessment for accountability purposes, why would we not use the results to drive instructional improvement?

In Which Assessment Should Students Participate?

Effective July 1, 1998, IDEA 1997 requires all students who have disabilities to participate in state and district assessments, with accommodations where necessary. Those students who are unable to take the district or state tests are required to take an alternate assessment, effective July 1, 2000. Sounds pretty straight-forward, right? Sure, if you have students who neatly fit into either assessment option.

Right now, states and districts have different criteria for deciding whether a student will take the regular assessment or the alternate assessment. Some states and districts indicate that if a student is pursuing a standard high school diploma, then the student cannot take the alternate assessment—while others indicate that the alternate assessment is a valid way to obtain a high school diploma. Some states say that the alternate assessment is only for students who have significant cognitive disabilities, while others say that this assessment is for anyone who is not on the grade level. Making good decisions—decisions that are good for kids—on the basis of existing criteria is difficult.

What should we do? To some extent, you must pay attention to what your head tells you. Is the student working on the same knowledge and skills as other students who are in general education classrooms?

The tricky part in making these decisions revolves around those students who, as we will discuss in Chapter 10, are caught in the middle or gray areas of assessment systems. As we see it, there are at least three types of students who make these decisions more difficult than they appear: students who (1) are participating in the regular assessment but require accommodations that are not permitted on the test, (2) are learning the general curriculum but have characteristics that necessitate different ways to show what they know and can do (different from the standard pencil-paper tests), or (3) are struggling in the general curriculum but do not qualify for special education. Do you know one or two students who fall into one or more of these areas?

In our opinion, none of these students would be appropriate participants for an alternate assessment. An alternate assessment should be for students who are working on life skills and knowledge that is different from the rest of the students who take the regular district and state assessments. These students might be working on the same content standards as other students, but they are meeting different performance standards (refer to Box 4.1).

Without a doubt, by now you have been directly or indirectly involved in discussions about the alternate assessment for your state or district. One of the first hurdles facing you is deciphering who is eligible to take the alternate assessment. Discussion always comes full circle back to the gray-area kids. Right on the heels of that discussion is the discussion that focuses on the standards to be used in developing the alternate assessment. In other words, what standards are students who are taking the alternate assessment working on?

We know that there are some people who are not at all excited about the idea of an alternate assessment for students who have significant

---

BOX 4.1

Example of Standards for All Students with Different Performance Benchmarks

Standard for All Students	**Alternative Performance Benchmark**
Students describe the basic processes of photosynthesis.	Student will point to various kinds of leaves.
Students will demonstrate an understanding of perimeter.	Student will walk around the outside of the school grounds.
Students will demonstrate their understanding of the governmental system of the United States and the United States Constitution.	Student will say the Pledge of Allegiance to the United States flag.
Student will vote in a school/class election.	Student will participate in a July 4 celebration.

cognitive disabilities. As one teacher put it, "Why would the superintendent of my district care if one of my students is working on an objective to keep drool off his chin?" Our response is, "What part of 'all' don't you understand?" Of course, kids who are working on these types of skills are important. Kids are kids. They come in all shapes, sizes, and abilities and have the right to develop their skills and talents just like any other student.

In our work with a local school district and board of education somewhere in the United States, to help them understand the importance of the concept "all kids count," one school board member adamantly opposed any of "those special-education students" participating or counting in the district reports. Another member (off the record, of course) mentioned that "the district is spending too much money on students who are never going to contribute to society anyway." The tragedy of this story ends as follows: About one month after this meeting, a school board member's son was in physical education class and was hit in the head with a softball. After this board member's son was diagnosed with traumatic brain injury, the school board soon changed its approach to educating "those special-education students."

So why would we not want to know how all students in our schools are progressing? We owe it to ourselves and to the public at large to make sure that every student becomes everything that he or she is capable of. The alternate assessment was developed as a means to account for the learning of students who, from the beginning of time, have been left out of schools, programs, activities, and accountability systems.

Alternate Assessments—What They Look Like

Between 1997 and 2000, states across the country worked feverishly to develop, field test, and pilot their versions of what an alternate assessment would be. In some states, frameworks or criteria for developing an alternate assessment were crafted and handed down to school districts, which in turn created the assessment. No matter where your state or district landed in the process, you should know what continuing issues and challenges remain regarding the development, administration, and use of the alternate assessment results for improving student learning and performance.

The original focus of the alternate assessment was an assessment for students for whom the regular assessment system was inappropriate, due to the content of the test. Alternate-assessment kids should be, in our opinion, those students who on a day-to-day basis work on learning skills ranging from working in a competitive but supervised work environment to feeding themselves and making their personal needs known. Clearly, the Stanford Achievement Test-9, the Metropolitan Achievement Test, or the Iowa Test of Basic Skills or any other norm-referenced test is not a good measure of these skills. None of the skills that should be assessed by an alternate assessment are easily measured by pencil-paper tests. They are skills that need to be measured by performance assessments.

Kentucky was the first state to develop an alternate assessment. Kentucky developed the Alternate Portfolio Assessment, which includes eight entries that are measured through the use of a variety of methods (refer to Box 4.2). Standards that were used for Kentucky's portfolio were taken directly from the learner expectancies that were developed for all students in the state. In general, the standards for the alternate portfolio assessment are broad and focus on a wide range of skills (refer to Box 4.3).

BOX 4.2

Kentucky's Alternate Portfolio Contents

A complete table of contents
A letter to the reviewer
A letter from a family member or caregiver

An additional 7–10 entries must reflect (in order) the following areas:

A student activity schedule or routine
A resume of job experiences
A sample of the student's present mode(s) of communication

BOX 4.3

Examples of Kentucky's Academic Expectancies for the Alternate Portfolio Assessment

Nature of scientific activity: Students use appropriate and relevant scientific skills to solve specific problems in real-life situations.
Democratic choices: Students recognize issues of justice, equality, responsibility, choice, and freedom and apply these democratic principles to real-life situations.
Writing: Students communicate ideas and information to a variety of audiences for a variety of purposes through writing.
Physical wellness: Students demonstrate skills and responsibility in understanding physical wellness.

Maryland was the second state to develop an alternate assessment and is now in the final stages of pilot-testing its program. Called the Independence Mastery Assessment Program (IMAP), this Maryland program has an entirely different set of eight standards for its assessment. These standards encompass broad content and learner domains and focus on the skills that they expect students to know and to be able to do as the result of schooling (refer to Box 4.4). The domains are broken down as follows:

Content Domains (subjects): personal management, community, career/ vocational, recreation/leisure
Learner Domains (skills): communication, decision making, behavior, academic

Maryland's IMAP has two basic components: the portfolio (which includes performance tasks) and a parent survey. The portfolio has two parts (refer to Box 4.5). Part I contains the student's daily portfolio of work samples and completed projects. Part II, called "Pick and Take," is comprised of elements that describe the student's strengths and needs. Part II also reflects the IMAP performance tasks. Maryland has developed specific performance tasks that the student must complete. The teacher picks one of these tasks, and a second task is randomly assigned by the Maryland State Department of Education. Examples of such tasks for personal man-

---

BOX 4.4

Excerpts from Maryland's Eight IMAP Content Domains

Academic: Students will demonstrate the ability to apply correct and appropriate academic skills and knowledge at all times. Isolated academic skills (e.g., that are taught in inclusion-content classes) that are tested for their value (identified in the IEP) must be co-developed by both of the students' teachers (general and special education).

Community: The student will demonstrate his or her ability to access community resources and navigate safely in the environment.

Behavior: Students will demonstrate their ability to behave in chronologically age-appropriate ways in various situations. Students' outcomes should be measured across and complement content outcomes. Support systems should be in place for behavior outcomes.

BOX 4.5

Maryland's Student IMAP Portfolio

Part I: Student Global Portfolio

Student Information Data
Documentation of Opportunities to Learn
Support Documentation
Student Performance
(Within each of these entries are multiple examples and products of the student's best daily work.)

Part II: "Pick and Take"

Portfolio Label (contains identifying information, such as student, teacher, and school name, age of students, and the performance task completed)
Student Description
List of Accommodations and Support Services
List of Key Modifications, Adaptations, Supports, Scaffolding, and/or Strategies
Task Questions and Directions
Task Products

---

agement include the student demonstrating skills in grooming, washing his or her hands, following class rules, or selecting the appropriate clothes for the weather. In the learner domain of career/vocations, students must demonstrate skills in making a beverage (instant tea or Kool-Aid), using a computer, planting a seed, and/or exploring a job.

Other states have taken the Kentucky approach in the development of their standards. That is, they are using the standards for all students as the foundation for building the alternate assessment. The state of New York is following suit. Although the standards are reported to be the same for all students, some argue that New York's standards have been extended downward to make them more accessible and realistic for students who have significant cognitive disabilities (refer to Box 4.6).

Kansas provides an example of how the Kansas Curricular Standards for all students in reading, writing, and mathematics have been extended to explicitly define what is expected of students who are taking the alternate assessment (refer to Box 4.7). Kansas has incorporated extended standards, benchmarks, and indicators for students. The extended standards have been written to address a wide variety of response and communication modalities/methods that are required by students who take the alternate assessment. These standards are individually determined by the IEP team.

The intent of all of these states has been to develop an assessment that reflects the standards and curriculum that students who have sig-

---

BOX 4.6

Examples and Excerpts of New York Standards

Area: English/Language Arts

Standard 1—Language for Information and Understanding

Students will read, write, listen, and speak for information and understanding.

Alternate Level—Listening and Reading

Listening and reading in order to acquire information and to understand involves collecting data, facts, and ideas; discovering relationships, concepts, and generalizations; and using knowledge from oral, written, and electronic sources.

Students will:
Attend to the speaker (visually and/or auditory) or to the task
Follow directions that involve one or two steps
Use functional reading sight vocabulary

Area: Mathematics, Science and Technology

Standard 4—Science

Students will understand and apply scientific concepts, principles, and theories pertaining to the physical setting and living environment and recognize the historical development of ideas in science.

Alternate Level—Physical Setting

The Earth and celestial phenomena can be described by principles of relative motion and perspective.

Students will:
Recognize patterns of daily, monthly, and seasonal changes in their environment
Use a chart to keep track of daily weather by using picture symbols to denote sunny, rainy, and cloudy days

---

nificant cognitive disabilities are learning. These efforts have emphasized keeping these students involved in the educational process. The next step for states and districts that are implementing alternate assessments is to figure out how to make sure that these students count in the same way as other students.

Not all states are considering portfolios for the alternate assessment. Minnesota is proposing the use of two surveys of student skills: one called

---

BOX 4.7

Examples of Kansas Standards for Alternate Assessment

Area: General Curriculum Standard 1—Reading

Extended Standard—Receptive Communication

Benchmark: 1—The learner demonstrates observable responses to a variety of relevant stimuli.

Indicator: 2—The learner responds to objects.

School	Vocational Career	Community	Recreation and Leisure	Home
Uses switch to activate computer	Begins work when materials are placed at work station	Gets cart or basket to carry shopping items	Assists with putting on personal floatation device in preparation for swimming	Activates switch to make a toy move across the floor
Changes take effect when the school bus approaches the school building	Responds to signs within the school	Gathers belongings for outings	Recognizes video-game machines	Recognizes his or her own towel and washcloth
Retrieves and places toys in the toy box	Places name tag on shirt	Carries money in wallet or purse for small purchases	Returns play equipment to proper place	Assists in covering self with sheet and/or blanket at bed time
Rests on own rug, mat, or blanket during rest time	Places lunch in community refrigerator	Rings doorbell before entering friend's home	Activates switch to play video or audio tape	Sits in chair at dinning room or kitchen table during meal time

---

the Developmental Assessment, and the other called the Functional Assessment. The Developmental Assessment focuses on hierarchical skills that are needed for skills in mathematics and reading. The Functional

---

BOX 4.7

Examples of Kansas Standards for Alternate Assessment (Continued)

School	Vocational Career	Community	Recreation and Leisure	Home
Carries lunch tray	Uses switch to activate machine at work station	Puts money in vending machine to retrieve desired item	Pushes bowling ball down ramp	Uses remote control to select appropriate TV program

---

California has identified several domains that it feels should be reflected in the instruction of students for whom the alternate assessment is appropriate. The domains are communication, self-care, functional academics, pre-vocational/vocational, mobility/motor skills, behavior, and other. California, however, has not identified any standards to which these students should be taught. The alternate assessment is a practice of mapping a student's IEP goals and objectives to the domain that seems to fit. For example, a student who has autism might have an IEP objective of "Student will use PECs to request needed materials, such as a pencil, marker, etc., to complete an assigned task with 70 percent accuracy." This objective could be mapped to the domain of communication. The tricky part of California's alternate assessment is that the lack of standards in the identified domain areas means that students and teachers are not being held accountable to standards that reflect what students should know and be able to do. In this example, all we know is what the objective says—and we know nothing about its relation to any standard. Likewise, an objective of "Student will attend to an assigned task for five minutes, four out of five trials" could fit under any of the following domains: functional academics, pre-vocational/vocational, or behavior. The lack of standards in the domains makes it anyone's guess as to where this objective really fits.

Some states are simply recording the percent of students who meet IEP goals and objectives. For example, states/districts are collecting the percentage of students who met 100 percent of their IEP goals, those who met 70–90 percent of their IEPs, and so on. The objection that we have to this practice is that there is no way to monitor the validity or integrity of the IEP goals. How do we know, then, that they are connected to standards and that they are written to appropriate levels of expectation?

Variations on a Theme

You might reside in a district or state that has expanded student eligibility for the alternate assessment to students other than those who have significant disabilities. Some districts and states argue that gray-area kids should be eligible for the alternate assessment. For example, one argument is that if the regular test is given in grade eight and the student is reading on a grade-three level, then the alternate assessment should be the viable assessment choice for this student. (Of course, we do not agree with this approach—more details about this subject appear in Chapters 5 and 10.)

Accountability in the Making:
Making Alternate Assessments Count

No matter where your district or state falls on the continuum of options for developing an alternate assessment, the most important goal must be improving student outcomes. We have all heard the old saying, "Never assess for assessment's sake"—or was it, "If you are going to assess, be sure to use the results." This statement applies to students who will participate in the alternate assessment.

Two parts exist to making the alternate assessment count. The first part is to make sure that you and the student know the goals of instruction—i.e., what standards you want to help the student reach. This step involves the instruction that precedes the assessment. Instruction toward meeting standards is just as important for students in the alternate assessment as it is for all other students.

The second part in making the alternate assessment count is, perhaps, a bigger leap: What do we do with the results of the alternate assessments? Once the scoring is completed, we need to decide what to do with the results and determine how they can be used to impact instruction and improve student learning.

Let us explore an example of how to use the results of an alternate assessment for improving the learning and performance of students. For this example, we are in a state/district that has developed the alternate assessment by using a portfolio approach. Entries for the portfolio include the following:

1. A letter to the reader
2. **Student information**, including a brief description of the student's abilities, a photograph of the student, parent-teacher conference logs, and grading/report cards that reflect IEP goals and objectives
3. **Opportunities to learn**, including a copy of the student's schedule and a summary of the student's daily activities and routines

4. **Program components**, including accommodations and/or assistive technology, a behavior-management system, current IEP goals and objectives, and a description of the student's prompt hierarchy used in the instructional program

5. **Student work products**, including no fewer than five current samples of the student's best work and other testimonials (e.g., videos, interviews, job evaluations, etc.) spread across domain areas

The foundation of the alternate assessment revolves around several learning domains that have been identified. The domains are as follows: physical health, responsibility and independence, citizenship, academic and functional literacy, and personal and social adjustment.

Within each domain are standards that students must know and be able to do. In this case, some of the standards are exactly the same as standards for other students (broad in scope and non-academic), while others are extensions of the general standards (refer to Box 4.8). As is the case in most states and districts, established standards are academic or content

---

BOX 4.8

Excerpts of Domains and Standards for Kindergarten through Grade Two

Physical Health	Responsibility and Independence	Citizenship	Academic and Functional Literacy
Health Education: Make good food selections and participate in exercise and recreation as part of growth and development **Consumer Sciences:** Demonstrate appropriate eating skills	**Social Studies— Principles of Civics & Government:** Learn to share, engage in fair play, and respect the rights of others. **Language Arts— Listening:** Listen and respond thoughtfully to a variety of messages	**Social Studies— Cultural Anthropology:** Recognize that all people are important and can make positive contributions to communities **Social Studies— Political Systems:** Recognize their membership in groups	**Earth Science:** Tell how weather affects our daily lives; tell why the sun is important to us **Algebra:** Use manipulatives, models, illustrations, graphs, and technology **Language Arts— Presenting Ideas:** Speak audibly and clearly

SOURCE: Taken from Long Beach Unified School District Standards Documents.

oriented and often narrow in scope. This state/district requires at least one goal and objective to fall in each of the domain areas. The majority of objectives will fall into the domains that reflect current levels of instruction for each student.

This list provides an example of taking the standards that are required for all students in kindergarten through grade two and mapping them to appropriate domains. This task is relatively easy. All of the academic and functional literacy standards come directly from the standards for all students, as are those that are listed under responsibility and independence and citizenry. Physical health contains newly created standards, because this domain represents a non-academic area and has not yet been developed.

Assessment of these domains can be completed through a variety of methods. In our example, the state/district has identified four major methods of assessment: (1) observation, (2) interview, checklist, and rating scales, (3) record review, and (4) testing. At least two of the four methods must be used in assessing each domain area. That is, the standards within each area that students are working on must be evaluated by two methods of assessment.

The scoring for the alternate assessment is done via the use of a four-point rubric. The scoring range is as follows:

4 means **Distinguished**—The student has shown mastery of the standards selected within the domain areas.

3 means **Proficient**—The student has demonstrated understanding of the standards.

2 means **Progressing**—The student is making substantial progress toward the standards.

1 means **Not Yet**—The student has made little or no progress toward standards.

Marla, age 13, is a student who has significant cognitive disabilities. Here is a list of some of the goals and objectives from Marla's IEP:

1. Identify her phone number upon request, four out of five trials with 100 percent accuracy

2. Orally repeat her phone number when orally dictated by an adult, with four out of seven digits correct

3. Complete a vocational task requested with minimal physical prompts, five out of 10 trials

4. Trace her first name independently with 100 percent accuracy

5. Trace the letters k, t, and l independently with 100 percent accuracy

6. Label 20 pictures of safety signs with 90 percent accuracy

7. Identify 15 pictures of safety signs with 80 percent accuracy

8. Kick an 8.5-inch stationary ball forward 10 feet without physical prompts, three out of five times

For the purpose of her alternate assessment, the majority of Marla's areas of needed skill development fall into the domains of academic and functional literacy (4, 5); responsibility and independence (1, 2, 3); personal and social adjustment (6, 7); and physical health (8). Although citizenship has been identified as a required learning domain, none of Marla's IEP objectives reflect this factor. Therefore, we have discovered an area that needs to be addressed for Marla.

Each domain must have an objective toward which the student is working. Because all of the alternate assessment learning domains are important and have standards that are critical for what students should know and be able to do, Marla's IEP will need to be amended in order to include an objective for citizenship.

Without providing you with a complete version of the learning domains and specific standards within each domain (similar to Box 4.8), we have placed Marla's objectives into the listed domains. A general lack of clarity exists due to the absence of specified standards in each domain. This information is what states (such as California, for example) will have as a result of simply identifying learning domains with nothing prescribed in them. Here are the results of Marla's domain assessments:

Domain: Physical Health
Score: 3
Method of Assessment:
  observation, interview

Domain: Responsibility/Independence
Score: 2
Method of Assessment:
  curriculum-based assessments,
  observation/role play

Domain: Academic and
  Functional Literacy
Score: 1
Method of Assessment:
  curriculum-based
  assessments observation

Domain: Personal/Social Adjustment

Score: 2
Method of Assessment:
  curriculum-based assessments
  observation in class outing

Domain: Citizenship
Score: 2
Method of Assessment:
  interview with cafeteria monitor, checklist (As noted previously, this objective was missing. We added one for the sake of interpretation.)

Marla received a "Not Yet" in the area of Academic and Functional Literacy. In taking a closer look at the tasks and work samples included in her portfolio, it is clear that more concentrated instruction is needed in the area of tracing her name and various letters (as reflected in her IEP goals and objectives). Therefore, we must take a look at where the breakdown in skill and learning has occurred. In the case of this student, Marla demonstrates great difficulty in attending to and completing tasks. Three of the five work samples in her portfolio are incomplete, even with documented prompts for assistance.

Based on this result, we will examine the contingency or management system that is used with Marla. Is this system effective and efficient? Apparently not, given her scores on the work samples. How can we better tailor the incentive and/or hierarchical prompt system for Marla to remain on task to eventual completion? Perhaps we need to work with others in order to re-examine what works in other environments. Perhaps we need to break down the instructional task that we are requiring into smaller pieces. Is this situation a "can't-do," "won't do," or "don't know when to" skill for Marla? In other words, is she truly unable to complete the tasks due to difficulty? Is this situation a result of mere boredom and lack of motivation? Or, perhaps she is unable to discriminate when to do certain skills within the larger task.

Based on this discovery, it might make sense to add an instructional objective for task completion, which would fall under the learning domain of responsibility and independence. In the learning domain of personal and social adjustment, Marla received a score of "Progressing." A closer look reveals that Marla lacks the beginning skills of identifying safety signs to enable her to successfully move around the community. Therefore, we need to review our teaching strategies in this area. Perhaps we need to provide errorless learning opportunities for Marla in order to give her more structured, correct practice on pointing to, identifying, demonstrating, and producing safety signs.

Marla is a profile of a typical student who takes the alternate assessment. We hope that we have demonstrated how straight-forward it is to take Marla's IEP goals and objectives, link them to domains and standards, use an alternate assessment, and use the results and parlay them into instruction that can improve Marla's learning. In order to keep track of how Marla is progressing in each area, we recommend that you chart her progress throughout the year. (Refer to Chapter 9 for information about how to create aimlines that reflect learning.)

Focusing on Improvement: Report It

No matter what kind of alternate assessment your district or state has developed, it is imperative that the main focus is accountability and improving the performance of students who have disabilities. In the case of any assessment—but especially the alternate assessment—students' scores need to be included and reported in the overall evaluation of the education system. A difficult task in the development of the alternate assessment is reporting results. Some states have agreed to report just what is asked of them by the regulations—the number of students who are taking the alternate assessment and their disaggregated performance. Others struggle to find a way to reasonably integrate scores of the alternate assessment into the existing assessment, thereby including scores in the overall accountability system for all students.

In our example, we used a portfolio approach to assess Marla's progress in the curriculum that reflected her IEP goals and objectives. So, what do we do with her scores? Try this idea on for size. Consider reporting the number of students who took the alternate assessment and the scores that they earned on their assessments. For example, your district has 50 students who are eligible to take the alternate assessment. Let us say that eight students receive an overall portfolio score of 4 (Distinguished); 15 students earn a score of 3 (Proficient); 20 students receive scores of 2 (Progressing), and the remaining seven students earn a 1 (Not Yet). The results could be reported by the number and total percentage of students who achieved a score (refer to Box 4.9).

Reporting can be this easy. Even if your state/district does not perform this sort of reporting, you can do it yourself in your own classroom and school building. This way, you can generate a report of the performance of your students who participated in the alternate assessment. Then, the next year—when the alternate assessment is given—you will be able to watch

---

BOX 4.9

Sample Scoring Summary

Any District, U.S.A.

Number of students eligible for the alternate assessment: 50
Number of students who took the alternate assessment: 50
Number of students scoring in each category:

Distinguished	Proficient	Progressing	Not Yet
8	15	20	7

Percent of total students taking the alternate assessment scoring in each level:

Distinguished	Proficient	Novice	Not Yet
16%	30%	40%	14%

for movement in student scores. That is, you can determine how many students moved from "Not Yet" to "Progressing" or "Progressing" to "Distinguished," and so on. This type of information is usually collected for students who take the regular assessment. Why not do the same for students who are taking the alternate assessment? They count, too.

Summary

In this chapter, we have presented the challenge of making the alternate assessment count. The goal of any assessment is to use the results in order to improve learning and instruction. This concept applies to the students who will take the alternate assessment. We have shown you how states have created alternate assessments and how they have demonstrated how these assessments can truly be used to improve instruction. You might be in a state that has prescribed a narrow version of an alternate assessment (e.g., a teacher survey, checklist, student observation, etc.). If that is the case, we appeal to you to extend the assessment to make sense for kids.

The federal mandate per IDEA for having a state alternate assessment has come and gone (July 1, 2000). The assessment does not have to be written in stone, however. Perhaps you live in a state that put something together to meet the deadline. Or, perhaps you participated in the thoughtful development of an alternate assessment for your state and/or district. Now that you have lived with the alternate assessment for a testing cycle or two, re-evaluate the assessment. Is the assessment getting at the information to which it was intended? Does it provide information that teachers can use to drive instructional improvement and learning for students? Does the assessment need to be adjusted in order to be more meaningful for the population of students it was intended to assess? Like other state and district assessments, this assessment can be a work in progress until we obtain the intended outcomes that we set out to achieve from the beginning. Take the time to review, revisit, and revise your state or district's version of the alternate assessment to be sure that it counts toward improving outcomes for kids.

Test Your Knowledge

Take a peek at this little assessment and show what you know.

1. To date, the only record of information about students who have disabilities in today's schools is the _____ _____ _____ _____.

2. The alternate assessment mandated by IDEA 1997 was required to be in place by _____.

3. The alternate assessment was developed for students for whom the regular assessment is not meaningful, even with accommodations. These are typically students who have significant _____ _____.

4. Students who are working on life-skills curricula are candidates for the _____ _____.

5. A popular format for the alternate assessment is the _____ approach.

6. Some states have used the same standards for the alternate assessments, while others have _____ standards.

7. No matter what type of alternate assessment your state or district develops, the most important goal must be _____ student outcomes.

8. The results of the alternate assessment should be used to impact _____ and improve sudent learning.

9. No matter what your alternate assessment looks like, student performance should be linked to _____.

10. There are _____ basic methods of assessment.

Answers

1. Annual Report to Congress (p. 55)

2. July 1, 2000 (p. 55)

3. cognitive disabilities (p. 55)

4. alternate assessment (p. 56)

5. portfolio (p. 58)

6. extended (p. 60)

7. improving (p. 64)

8. instruction (p. 64)

9. standards (p. 64)

10. four (p. 66)

Resources

Burgess, P. and Kennedy, S. (1998). *What Gets Tested, Gets Taught. Who Gets Tested, Gets Taught.* Lexington: University of Kentucky, Mid-South Regional Resource Center.

Guy, B., Shin, H., Lee, S., and Thurlow, M. (1999). *State Graduation Requirements for Students with and Without Disabilities.* (NCEO Technical Report 24). Minneapolis: University of Minnesota, National Center on Educational Outcomes.

Long Beach Unified School District. *Academic Standards: A Guide for Parents, Teachers, Administrators, and the Community.* Long Beach, CA: Office of Curriculum and Instructional Resources.

LaCount, N. and McLaughlin, M. (1996). "Alternate Assessments" (Video). Available from NASDSE, Products, ID Audio ANA-603.

New York State Education Department. *The Learning Standards and Alternate Performance Indicators for Students with Severe Disabilities.* Albany: The State University of New York, Office of Vocational and Educational Services for Individuals with Disabilities.

Olsen, K. and Ysseldyke, J. (1997). "Alternate Assessment" (videotape recording). Alexandria, VA: National Association of State Directors of Special Education.

Thurlow, M., Elliott, J., and Ysseldyke, J. (1998). *Testing Students with Disabilities: Practical Strategies for Complying with District and State Requirements.* Thousand Oaks, CA: Corwin Press.

Thurlow, M., Olsen, K., Elliott, J., Ysseldyke, J,. Erickson, R., and Ahearn, E. (1996). *Alternate Assessments for Students with Disabilities: For Students Unable to Participate in General Large-Scale Assessments* (NCEO Policy Directions 5). Minneapolis: University of Minnesota, National Center on Educational Outcomes.

Ysseldyke, J. and Olsen, K. (1997). *Putting Alternate Assessment into Practice: Possible Sources of Data.* Minneapolis: University of Minnesota, National Center on Educational Outcomes.

Ysseldyke, J., Olsen, K., and Thurlow, M. (1997). *Issues and Considerations in Alternate Assessments.* Minneapolis: University of Minnesota, National Center on Educational Outcomes.

Warlick, K. and Olsen, K. (1998). *Who Takes the Alternate Assessment? State Criteria.* Lexington: University of Kentucky, Mid-South Regional Resource Center.

Ysseldyke, J., Thurlow, M., Erickson, R., Gabrys, R., Haigh, J., Trimble, S., and Gong, B. (1996). *A Comparison of State Assessment Systems in Kentucky and Maryland, with a Focus in the Participation of Students with Disabilities.* (Maryland/Kentucky Report 1). Minneapolis, MN: University of Minnesota, NCEO.

Internet Resources

National Association of State Directors of Special Education (NASDSE): http://www.nasdse.org

National Center on Educational Outcomes: http://www.coled.umn.edu/nceo (see the Alternate Assessment Cyber Survey)

Accommodations—How to Make Sound Decisions for Instruction and Assessment

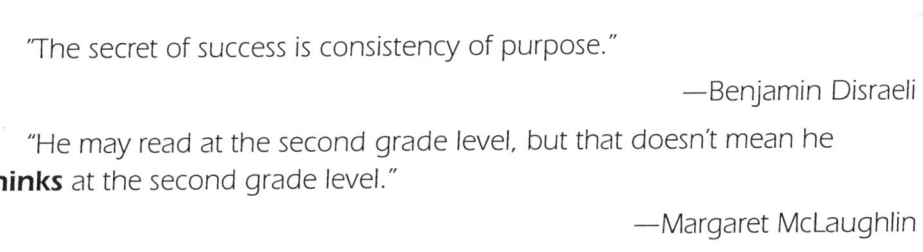

"The secret of success is consistency of purpose."

—Benjamin Disraeli

"He may read at the second grade level, but that doesn't mean he **thinks** at the second grade level."

—Margaret McLaughlin

Hot-Button Issues

- □ There is too much to do during instruction already. How can we be expected to provide accommodations, too?

- □ Instructional accommodations are designed to help students learn, so why should they be carried into assessments?

- □ Because we do not have a good accommodations research base, shouldn't we just allow as many accommodations as possible during instruction and assessment?

- □ My major adjustment for this student is to simplify and lower the level of instruction. Shouldn't out-of-level testing be the accommodation that this student gets for state and district tests?

Accommodations are changes in the way that materials are presented or in the way that students respond, as well as changes in setting, timing, and scheduling. The reason for providing accommodations is that they enable the student to bypass (or partially bypass) the effects of a disability, so that the student can learn or demonstrate knowledge and skills. Examples of some accommodations that fall within each of these categories are shown in Box 5.1. The goal of this chapter (and of other chapters to follow) is to assist you with becoming a sound decision-maker about accommodations.

The kinds of accommodations that are easiest to understand and justify are those that are typically provided to students who have sensory or physical disabilities. For example, the need to have instructional materials magnified so that students who have significant visual impairments can see them is obvious. Similarly, it is easy to respect the need for students who have hearing impairments to be provided amplification equipment, such as hearing aids, so that they can benefit from instruction. These kinds of accommodations are akin to those that are provided to individuals with

---

BOX 5.1

Examples of Different Types of Accommodations

Setting	Presentation
Study carrel	Repeat directions
Special lighting	Larger bubbles on multiple-choice questions
Separate room	Sign language presentation
Individualized or small group	Magnification device

Timing	Response
Extended time	Mark answers in test booklet
Frequent breaks	Use reference materials (e.g., dictionary)
Unlimited time	Word process writing sample

Scheduling	Other
Specific time of day	Special test preparation techniques
Subtests in different order	Out-of-level test

SOURCE: This table is a reproduction of Box 3.2, "Examples of Six Types of Assessment Accommodations," with permission from M. L. Thurlow, J. L. Elliott, and J. E. Ysseldyke (1998), *Testing Students with Disabilities: Complying with District and State Standards*. Thousand Oaks, CA: Corwin Press.

wheelchairs—without an elevator (or a chair lift), these individuals do not have access to instruction that is provided on the second floor of a building. In the same way, individuals who have difficulty seeing or hearing do not have access to instruction that is provided visually or orally, unless they can use accommodations.

These same arguments apply (but are more difficult to understand) for individuals who have less-obvious disabilities, such as learning disabilities, emotional disabilities, and mild mental retardation. Teachers (and others) are commonly heard to say, "Accommodations are nothing but a crutch. Johnny is just lazy. He could do it if he wanted to do it." When disabilities are less obvious, they are more difficult to recognize—and it is more difficult to realize that the students' access to learning is impeded in much the same way as for students who have visual or hearing impairments.

In Box 5.2, we have an illustration of a student, Kyle, who has a learning disability and who struggles to access the curriculum in the same way that other students do. Also illustrated in the example is how accommodations can increase the student's access to the curriculum and how the resulting classroom performance better reflects the student's knowledge and skills than the non-accommodated learning.

This chapter addresses questions of how to make sound decisions about which accommodations a student might need during instruction or assessment. To start, we make a distinction between opinions about accommodations and research-based knowledge. Then, we identify some considerations to ponder before making accommodation decisions for both classroom instruction and assessments. Following this section, we delve into making decisions about accommodations that are needed for instruction and for classroom tests. Finally, we suggest ways to roll instructional and classroom test accommodations into district or state assessments. In conclusion, we address several related issues, such as how to be sure that accommodation information is connected to the IEP and strategies for assisting students when current accommodations policies are not consistent with student needs.

Making decisions about accommodations might sound simple, given what we have said thus far. But these decisions are far from simple. Many people have struggled with how to make good accommodations decisions. This ability is a skill, like most others, that is improved through information and practice. The benefits of making good accommodation decisions are great. Students have access, as they should, to the content that is conveyed by instruction—and are then able to demonstrate their true knowledge and skills. Skill-building takes practice. Certainly, if we expect that students must practice in order to learn things well, then we (as teachers or administrators) also can be expected to learn by engaging in sufficient practice.

BOX 5.2

Kyle's Access to the General-Education Curriculum with and without Accommodations

Kyle was first diagnosed as having a learning disability in third grade. His reading skills were poor, but his math computation skills were excellent. He had trouble listening to the teacher and to classroom discussions and never seemed to be able to complete assignments when he was in the classroom. Sometimes when he bothered other students and kept them from doing their work, Kyle was sent into the hallway, where he was carefully watched by a hall monitor. Here, he could do his work without distraction. Despite his quick completion of tasks, particularly if they were math problems, he was made to stay in the hallway as punishment. As a result, he missed worksheet reviews and discussions between the teacher and his classmates as they reviewed how problems were solved or how word problems were comprehended.

When the IEP team met for Kyle's annual review, it became obvious that something was not working right. Despite his excellent math skills, Kyle was not enjoying the same access to the curriculum as his classmates. The IEP team identified several accommodations to restore and upgrade his access to the general curriculum.

First, being sent to the hallway to work undistracted was no longer used to help focus on his math problems (nor as punishment). Instead, Kyle was assigned to a carrel in which he could work undistracted if he needed it. Kyle was taught to figure out when he needed an accommodation to help him work undistracted. Also, to help Kyle pay attention during teacher instruction, he was given a desk at the front of the room, slightly ahead of other students so that he could not bother them. He also was given instruction in self-regulation skills, so that he monitored whether he was on task, and was rewarded for bringing himself back on task (or for remaining on task without redirection).

With these instructional accommodations, Kyle rarely missed teacher instruction or review and discussion periods. Also, he resumed his excellent math performance. As he regained his skills and began again to surpass his classmates, Kyle was allowed to help other students (as long as he remained on task). Because he had access to the general education curriculum, his skills and behavior demonstrated that it was good not only for him but also for his classmates. Also, as a result of the careful consideration of what accommodations would work and which ones he would need to be taught, Kyle gained skills in knowing when he needed accommodations and asking for those that he needed when he needed them.

Opinions Versus Research-Based Knowledge on Accommodations

In the early 1980s, research was conducted by two large test development companies: ACT and ETS (see the Resources section for lists of some of their publications). For several reasons, the relevance of this research to state and district tests is limited. For example, the ACT and ETS research included only limited samples of students (those who were headed for college), and most of the research lumped together disabilities that probably needed to be studied separately, such as physical disabilities and learning disabilities. Commonly cited findings from this research about reasonable time extensions (up to 1 1/2 times the standard testing time, for example) really do not apply to state and district assessments. We need new research involving state and district tests before we can develop guiding principles like those from the college entrance-testing work.

In the mid-1990s, policymakers realized the need for additional research focused directly on state and district assessments. The United States Department of Education provided funds for this research, with the hope that this research would answer many of the questions that surrounded the use of accommodations during district and state assessments. While this research is still occurring, to a great extent the research has revealed that the effects of accommodations are complicated—varying as a function of the test, the characteristics of the student, and attitudes about what accommodations should accomplish.

In Box 5.3, we summarize some of the major findings about accommodations from recent research. Glancing over this list helps us see the complexities of the research, but it also reinforces the importance of decisions about whether an individual student *needs* any accommodations and specifically *which accommodations* are needed. Several of the studies point to a tendency toward "over-accommodation" of students who have disabilities. In other words, a tendency exists for people who are making decisions about the accommodations that a student would use during an assessment to pick nearly every accommodation possible—with the mistaken belief that accommodations might increase the student's score, and the more the better. This tendency was revealed in research conducted by the National Center for Education Statistics and was suggested by others' research, as well. Research has now confirmed that the unneeded accommodations might actually interfere with a student's performance.

Considerations in Making Decisions About Accommodations

Regardless of whether we agree with the assumptions of some of the research that has been conducted, the research does point to the need to

make careful and informed decisions about accommodations and to identify the considerations that inform our decision making. With these concepts as a foundation, we can achieve the purpose of this chapter—to help
you and your colleagues make sound, supported decisions about accommodations. These decisions will not only hold up to scrutiny by administrators and parents, but they will also be the best decisions for the
students. We will list and then briefly discuss each consideration:

Consideration: Whether an accommodation is needed and what
accommodation is needed should *not* be determined by the student's category of disability.

The clues provided by the disability category are as follows:

BOX 5.3

Summary of Selected Research on Accommodations

Fuchs, L. S., Fuchs, D., Eaton, S. B., Hamlett, C., and Karns, K. "School Psychology Review"(in press). Supplementing teacher judgments about test accommodations with
objective data sources.

In this article, the authors report on research that looked at the effects of accommodations on
(1) an assessment that was similar to those in statewide assessments and (2) curriculum-based
measures, which are short measures of students' knowledge and skills. The effects of the
accommodations were examined for students who have learning disabilities and students
who do not have learning disabilities. Several effects of accommodations were evident on the
curriculum-based measures, even when they were not evident for the traditional assessment.
For example, on math curriculum-based measures, effects were greater for LD than for other
students for accommodations involving extended time, reading, and writing the student's
responses. The extended time effect was not evident on the traditional assessment.

Tindal, G., Heath, B., Hollenbeck, K., Almond, P., and Harniss, M. "Exceptional
Children," 64 (4), 439–450(1998). Accommodating students with disabilities on large-scale
tests: An empirical study of student response and test administration demands.

In this article, the authors report on a study of a cluster of presentation accommodations via
videotape, which included the reading of problems and answer options, color cueing of
answer options, one problem per page, and problem pacing. In addition to looking at the
number of test items correct, the authors looked at performance on a variety of other measures, including math computation, math vocabulary, an open-ended problem, and a reading
measure. Data from about 2,000 students indicated that the videotaped cluster of accommodations improved the performance of some (but not all) students who have disabilities. The
findings pointed to the limitations of group designs.

BOX 5.3

Summary of Selected Research on Accommodations (Continued)

Trimble, S. (1998). *Performance trends and use of accommodations on a statewide assessment.* (NCEO Assessment Series, Maryland/Kentucky Report 3). Minneapolis, MN: University of Minnesota, National Center on Educational Outcomes.

Trimble analyzed the performance of approximately 4,000 students who have disabilities—some using a variety of accommodations during the state test, and others using none. In addition, the performance of students without disabilities was examined relative to the performance of students who have disabilities. Findings indicated that the use of accommodations was relatively high (nearly 85 percent of students who have disabilities in grade four), yet the performance of these students generally was lower than that of students who have disabilities and who did not use accommodations and students without disabilities. The performance of students using accommodations was higher than that of the total group of students in only four of the 104 accommodation comparisons. These four cases involved accommodations of paraphrasing and dictation.

SOURCE: A comprehensive summary of research on a variety of test changes was produced by the Mid-South Regional Resource Center (http://www.ihdi.uky.edu/msrrc). The studies in this box, as well as more than 100 other studies, are summarized in that document (refer to Tindal and Fuchs, 1999, in the Resources section).

- If the student has a sensory disability, it is *almost* certain that some kind of accommodation will be needed.

- In all categories, the more severe the disability, the more likely the student is to need an accommodation.

Disability categories provide only some clues about the need for accommodations or the specific accommodations needed. The disability category never should be used as the sole basis for deciding that a student does or does not need an accommodation or what accommodation is needed. Decisions about specific accommodations needed by a student always must start with a consideration of the student as an individual; i.e., what the student's learning and behavior characteristics and skills are.

Consideration: Whether an accommodation is needed and what specific accommodation is needed should *not* be determined by the availability of accommodations.

Starting from available accommodations and then determining whether students need them is a backward approach to deciding on the need for accommodations. Clear reasons exist for decision making to proceed in the other direction—to start from student characteristics and needs—and on the basis of this information to determine whether accommodations are needed in instruction, in classroom tests, and then in district and state assessments.

Making decisions about accommodations by starting with the student's needs is more difficult with some tests than with others. Criterion-Referenced Tests (CRTs), in which student performance is compared to a criterion that is to be reached, seem to be more accommodation friendly than norm-referenced tests (in which student performance is compared to the performance of other students). When between-student comparisons are made, the mindset of test developers (and many test administrators) is that all students must take the test exactly the same way. We are not saying that this mindset is correct, but this mindset should be recognized and countered if a student truly cannot accurately show his or her knowledge and skills without a needed accommodation. Until test developers have included all students in their standardization samples, with needed accommodations, the use of "non-approved" accommodations when taking CRTs will continue to be an issue. This issue must continue to be pushed forward for students who have disabilities, however.

Basing accommodations decisions on the availability of specific accommodations could be interpreted as a violation of federal law, because this process might result in an individual not being provided a necessary accommodation. Thus, availability should never be a consideration when identifying which specific accommodations a student might need. The time to consider availability of accommodation is when you are figuring out the *logistics* of providing accommodations to students. Sometimes, this task can be quite a challenge. Nevertheless, this process should not be a consideration during decision making about specific accommodations that individual students need.

Consideration: Whether an accommodation is needed and the specific accommodations that are needed by a student might change over time as a function of the student's age or skills.

This concept is sometimes difficult to understand. In fact, you might have been taught that once an individual has a disability, that disability is there to stay. This belief might also be bolstered by some research that has concluded that once students are placed in special-education services, they almost never escape from them. But, other evidence exists that suggests that this situation is not always the case, and this evidence supports the idea that a student's particular needs can change over time.

Improvements in students' skills and a greater maturity both probably play a role in the possible change in whether a student needs accommodations and in the specific accommodations that are needed. Think about what happens to people who need glasses. As they get older, their vision disability does change to where the need for far vision assistance usually decreases, while their need for near vision assistance usually increases.

Just as the decision about whether a student needs any accommodations might change over time, so can the decision about specific accommodations that are needed. To understand this point, let's go back to the example of what happens to people who need glasses. While a person's vision disability can change over time to where there is a need for magnification rather than far vision assistance, during the same period of time a need for amplification equipment for hearing might be needed, although this equipment was not previously needed. Maturation and skill development can affect the specific accommodations needs of youngsters, just as they obviously affect the assistance needs of those who are older.

Consideration: Whether an accommodation is needed, and the specific accommodations that are needed, should *not* be determined by how well a student is performing.

A tendency exists to think that low student performance is a sure fire way to determine whether an accommodation is needed. This statement is not necessarily true. Similarly, the fact that a student is performing well in class and on tests is not a sure fire indication that the student does not need an accommodation. Students can perform poorly simply because they have never been exposed to the general education curriculum or to a particular content area. They are not going to perform better just by receiving accommodations. For example, providing extended time to a student who has not been exposed to the curriculum that is being tested is not likely to improve test performance. Similarly, students who perform well in the classroom and during tests might be doing so despite their disabilities. Their performance, although high, might be much lower than it would be if they were provided the needed accommodations.

Still, one of the most obvious signs of the need for accommodations is probably poor performance. The poor performance, however, must be linked to some obvious limitation in behavior or skill that interferes with demonstrating other skills.

Selecting Accommodations for Instruction and Classroom Tests

The considerations that we just highlighted serve as reminders that decisions about accommodations—especially those concerning specific accommodations that are needed—must be individualized. They should *not* be made for groups of students; rather, they should be made for specific students based on their learning and behavior characteristics and skills.

Box 5.4 shows a list of several common instructional accommodations. Many of these are transferred into classroom tests, as well. We do not mean, however, that they can be *directly* transferred into district and state

---

BOX 5.4

Common Instructional Accommodations, A through Z

Altered assignments	Natural supports
Audio-taped directions	Note-taking aids
Bold print	On-task reminders
Bulletin board strategy reminders	Outline text
Color coding	Paper holders (magnets, tape, etc.)
Crib notes	Peer support
Darker lines	Quality monitoring
Directions clarified or simplified	Questions in margins
Enlarged materials	Reader
Extended time	Raised print
Fewer tasks per assignment	Shorter assignments
Finger spacing, counting strategies	Seat location change
Graph paper for calculations	Touch talker (communication device)
Green color as cue to continue	Tutoring (cross-age, peer)
Harder items first	Underline key points
Headphones	Use reminders
Individual work area	Visual prompts
Isolated items	Vocabulary cues on paper/board
Key words highlighted	Wider margins
Knock-on-desk cues	Word processor
Large pictures	Word list on board
Limit number of tasks	X-out text to reduce reading
Manipulatives	Yellow paper
Memory aids	Zero-wrong strategies

---

tests. Some instructional accommodations should not be transferred into the testing situation. For example, during reading instruction, an appropriate accommodation might be to read along with the student, perhaps having the student follow along as someone reads to him or her. When the student is taking a reading test that is designed to assess decoding skills, then the read-along accommodation is not appropriate. Making decisions about what accommodations confuse the construct that is being measured requires a good understanding of the test. More about this subject will appear in Chapter 6.

Although the easiest approach to deciding what accommodations a student will use during instruction and during classroom tests is to start from a checklist of all possible accommodations, that approach generally fosters over-accommodation. Likely, this action will result in identifying accommodations that are only minimally related to the student's needs.

You can take several steps to identify the accommodations that individual students need for classroom instruction and classroom tests. These steps include the following:

- Ask the student about what helps him or her learn better. What gets in the way of him or her showing what he or she really knows and can do?

- Ask parents about the things that they do to help their child complete household tasks or homework. Often, parents and other family members have wonderful insights about needed accommodations, although they will not use the term "accommodations."

- Consider the strengths and weaknesses of students in areas linked to the curriculum. Identify those skills or behaviors that seem to consistently get in the way of learning.

- Teach the student how to use accommodations that might be provided. You should perform this task in order to determine whether an accommodation really is needed by the student. Making this determination is impossible if the student does not know how to use an accommodation.

- Observe the effects of provided accommodations to determine whether the accommodation is being used and the extent to which the accommodation seems to be useful to the student

- Collect data on the effects of accommodations that are used by the student. With the current lack of concrete research data on the effects of accommodations in general, there must be a more objective way to judge the effects of accommodations for individual students, not just through observations of whether they seem to make a difference. Simple curriculum-based measures might be the easiest and the most accurate way to get this kind of information.

These steps and others are incorporated into a worksheet for your use (refer to Box 5.5). We discuss each of these steps in a little more detail here, because they are so critical for making sound accommodations decisions.

Ask the Student   Students are usually knowledgeable about what helps them perform better on tests. While they might be better able to explain their needs as they age, even young students have ideas about what does and does not help them. Getting at the information might have to be done in slightly different ways, but it is possible to obtain.

BOX 5.5

Classroom Accommodations Worksheet

Follow these steps to identify accommodations that are needed for classroom instruction and for classroom tests for a specific student. Be sure to consider the specific characteristics, strengths, and weaknesses of the student for whom this worksheet is being completed. For each step, be sure to separately consider instruction and tests, and use the questions to spark ideas about useful accommodations. You will find it helpful to complete this worksheet with other individuals who know the student.

	Reflections on Each Question	Possible Instructional Accommodations	Possible Classroom Test Accommodations
1. What helps the student learn better or perform better? What gets in the way of the student showing what he or she really knows and can do?			
2. What has the student's parents or guardian told you about things that they do to help the student complete household tasks or school homework?			
3. What are the student's strengths and weaknesses? What skills or behaviors often get in the way of learning or performance?			
4. What accommodations has the student been taught to use? Are there other accommodations on which the student needs training?			
5. For which accommodations have effects been observed? What accommodations is the student willing to use?			

BOX 5.5

Classroom Accommodations Worksheet (Continued)

	Reflections on Each Question	Possible Instructional Accommo-dations	Possible Classroom Test Accommo-dations
6. Have any quantitative data (e.g., from one-minute tests) been collected on the effects of accommodations?			
7. Is there any other relevant information that might affect the provision of accommodations, either during classroom instruction or during tests?			

Among the questions that you will want to ask students are the following (refer to the worksheet in Box 5.6). Remember to adjust the questions for students of different ages.

- The format of the test is [indicate the format]. Do you think that this format will be okay for you, or is there some way that the format could be changed to help you perform your best on the test?

- The timing of this test is [insert information about how the test is timed]. Is there anything about the timing procedures that could be changed to help you perform your best on the test?

- The test is scheduled to occur [indicate when in the day or week that the test is scheduled]. Is there any way that this scheduling could be changed to help you perform your best on the test?

- The test is typically presented in the following manner [indicate the manner of test administration]. Is there any way that the presentation format could be changed to help you perform your best on the test?

BOX 5.6

Student Accommodations Questionnaire

Students often are the best source of information about accommodations that they need and that they are willing to use (the two are not always the same). Students' skills at answering questions about their accommodations needs are naturally better as they mature. Still, being able to identify needed accommodations is an important skill for students who have disabilities (and is a skill that can be developed). By asking students questions about accommodations (using a different term) even at young ages, you will help students hone their skills in identifying needed accommodations (as well as clue you in to important information).

The following questions can be used to ask students about accommodations. Be sure first that you understand the assessment that students will be taking so that you can convey this information to the student. Adjust your vocabulary and question complexity for the age of the student.

- Do you think that the test [describe for the student] will be okay for you, or is there some way that it could be changed to help you perform your best?
- Is there anything about the content of the test or what it asks you to do [describe for the student] that could be changed to help you perform your best?
- Is there anything about the test's timing procedures [describe for the student] that could be changed to help you perform your best?
- Is there anything about when the test is given [describe for the student] that could be changed to help you perform your best?
- Is there anything about the way the test is presented [describe for the student] that could be changed to help you perform your best?
- Is there anything about how you have to answer the test [describe for the student] that could be changed to help you perform your best?
- Is there anything about the test that could be changed to help you perform your best on the test?

- The test typically enables you to respond to the test by [indicate the test-response methods]. Is there any way that this response format could be changed to help you perform your best on the test?
- Are there any other changes in the assessment that could help you perform your best on the test?

These questions can be adjusted for younger children by giving examples of some possible accommodations that fit within each of the types of accommodations. For older students, the questions can be merged into one general question about whether there are any changes in testing that would not change what is measured, but which would help the student perform better.

Ask Parents and Other Family Members   Parents spend a lot of time with their children—time during which they pick up cues as to what helps their children learn and what interferes with their learning. While parents might not necessarily use the word "accommodations," they can respond to questions that describe the essence of accommodations. For example, they usually know whether providing directions one time is enough for their child to understand what is to be done. They usually know whether there are ways to tune in the attention of the child in order to obtain the best performance possible. They often know what times during the day the student will perform best and when the student's down time occurs.

Consider Strengths and Weaknesses   Accommodations that a student needs are determined by individual student characteristics. Perhaps one of the easiest ways to determine what these needs are is to examine the student's strengths and weaknesses. The weaknesses help focus on what characteristics might interfere with showing knowledge and skills. These are the factors that accommodations are needed for in order to "bypass" the disability. Examining the student's strengths is also advantageous, because you can see the characteristics upon which accommodations can capitalize.

For example, if a student is easily distracted, that student's adequate math skills might be hidden because of the student's inability to complete items under standard test conditions. Yet, this same student might have good skills in organizing materials, keeping track of what is next in sequences, and so on. While we typically think of accommodations such as extended time and breaks for students who are easily distracted, for the student in our example, there are some additional logical approaches to "bypassing" the effect of distraction. One way is to build upon the strength of organization and sequencing to develop a template that covers everything but the problem on which the student is working. Because the student has skills in sequencing and organization, the student will be able to move the template down the page as each problem is completed—and, at the same time, curb the effects of distraction.

Box 5.7 provides a form that can be used to keep track of students' strengths and weaknesses in a way that informs not just the development of instructional plans, but also the identification of reasonable and useful accommodations. Use a separate page to insert a completed form into each student's IEP, or use one form for all students in a classroom or building who need accommodations.

BOX 5.7

Form to Track Students' Strengths and Weaknesses

Student	Strengths	Weaknesses	Implications for Accommodations

Teach the Use of Accommodations   Much discussion has occurred about the need for accommodations that are used during assessment to be accommodations that the student has received during instruction. Some places, in fact, have made it a requirement that documentation of an accommodation that is being used in instruction for at least three months must occur before the accommodation can be used in an assessment. The message is that students must be used to using accommodations before they use them in assessments.

An implicit assumption is that if accommodations have been used during instruction, then the student knows how to use them. This statement could not be farther from the truth. Simply providing accommodations to students during instruction does not assure that the students really know how to use them.

Students need to be directly taught how to use accommodations and the best ways to use them. This lesson is obvious for certain accommodations. For example, students must be taught how to read Braille before it is a reasonable accommodation for them to use during assessment. While the need for instruction on the use of an accommodation is relatively clear here, the need is less obvious for other accommodations, such as using a template or using a tape recorder to read directions to the student. If a student has not been directly instructed on how best to use these accommodations, these accommodations might be misused, and their effects might not be what was originally intended.

Observe the Effects of Accommodations   While making sure that the student has been instructed in how best to use accommodations, this instruction does not ensure that any of the accommodations will be effective. To be able to document that accommodations are having intended effects, you should collect data about their effects.

One way to collect data is to observe the effects. Anecdotal comments about what was observed are the least satisfactory for this purpose. The more that the observations can be systematized and recorded, the better the data. In other words, you need to show the impact of the accommodation.

Collect Data about the Effects of Accommodations   Observational data are one kind of evidence that can be useful in documenting the effects of accommodations. Even better are data that are more objective, such as collecting direct measures of performance. Simple measures that are repeated over time can serve this function. These simple measures are one to three minute mini-tests in which the student either reads words or passages, computes the answers to calculation problems, or writes for one minute in response to a sentence prompt. Counting the number of words read, the number of problems solved, or the number of words written comprises the data that can be used to judge the effectiveness of accommodations. Comparing performance on these simple measures with and

BOX 5.8

Tracking the Effects of Accommodations

Charting the performance of a student on the same type of task (e.g., reading a list of words) when using one or more accommodations (and without the accommodations) provides an excellent way to track the effects of accommodations. This task can be done easily by having the student spend one to five minutes on the task. On some days, the student has no accommodations—and on other days, the student uses an accommodation. By charting the performance on a graph and noting when accommodations are used and when they are not used, you can easily obtain a good picture of whether the accommodation has an effect on the student's performance.

The following is the type of chart that can easily be drawn on graph paper and used to track the effects of one or more accommodations.

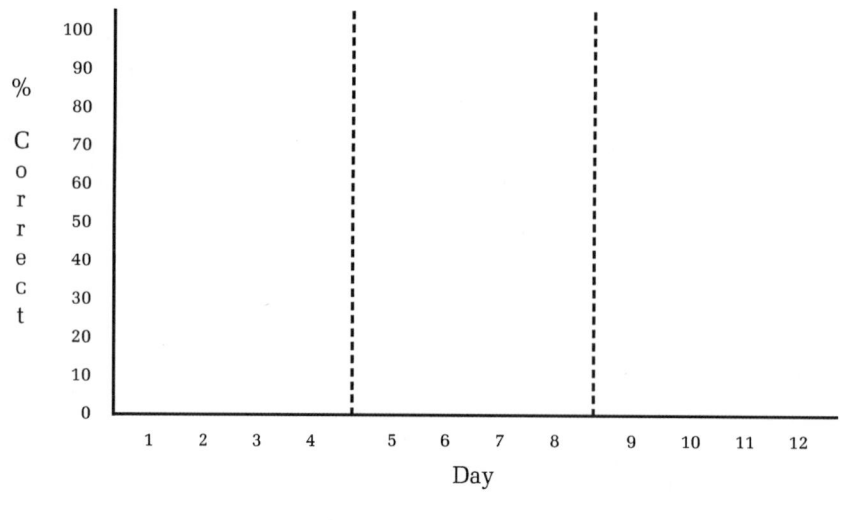

without the use of specific accommodations gives good individual data concerning the effects of the accommodations.

An example of a chart format to keep track of the effects of accommodations is shown in Box 5.8 (also refer to Chapter 9 on instruction). A case study in which these kinds of data are tracked is provided in Box 5.9. As you will note, data are collected first before any accommodations are used, and then again after the introduction of an accommodation on which the student has received instruction. Finally, data are again collected with the student not using the accommodation. In this way, you have a specific documentation of effects—and therefore, information about the student's need for the particular accommodation.

BOX 5.9

Case Study on Tracking the Effects of Accommodations

Ms. Jones decides that Mao needs to use accommodations during the state test. She already uses several accommodations for Mao during instruction, but Ms. Jones has never checked them out in any systematic way. Because she knows about the tendency to over-accommodate and recognizes the finding that over-accommodation sometimes impedes performance, she has decided to check some of the accommodations that she uses with Mao during instruction to see whether they really would have an effect during the statewide assessment.

Ms. Jones checks the three accommodations during the next three weeks. Every day except Friday, she has Mao take a short two-minute math calculation test. During the first four days (week 1), she has Mao take the test with no accommodations. Then, during week 2, she has Mao take the test under unlimited time conditions. Finally, during week 3, she has Mao take the test with no accommodations.

The following chart shows the results of Ms. Jones' tracking study. Clearly, the accommodation makes a difference in Mao's performance. The percent correct that she obtains is much higher when she is tested under unlimited time conditions. The difference is not quite as dramatic as one would initially think, however. By reinstituting testing without accommodations, Ms. Jones sees that Mao's performance is higher the second time without accommodations than the first time. This information suggests that Mao's performance is increasing simply because of the practice she is receiving taking the test (an important point: practice and instruction are as important as accommodations).

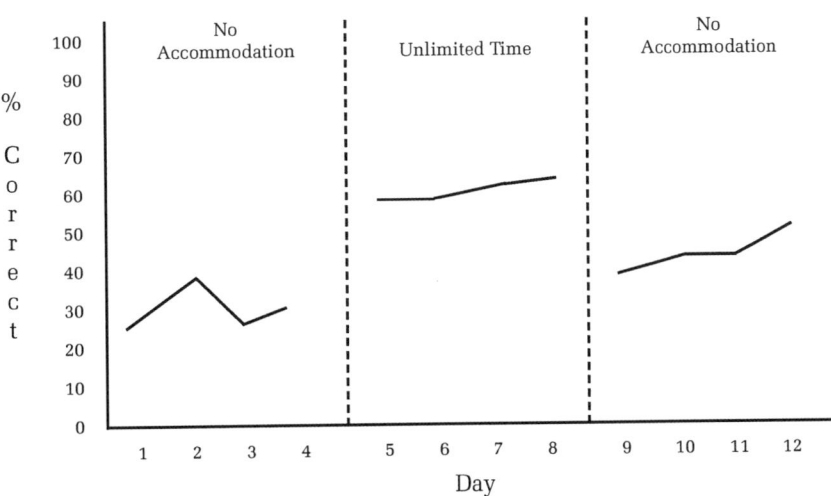

Ms. Jones could gather even more information by tracking more accommodations over a longer period of time. By extending the duration of her tracking, Ms. Jones could also get a better feel for the potential impact of simply providing Mao with practice on test formats and content.

*Rolling Classroom Accommodations into District
and State Assessments*

The information that you gathered through quick administration measures provides useful evidence of the need for an accommodation to carry from the classroom into district and state assessments. As well as having evidence of the need for an accommodation, you (and anyone who is questioning the need for an accommodation) will find it helpful to document the accommodations that a student is receiving and will need during state and district assessments. We recommend using a simple form, something like what is provided in Box 5.10, to show where a student is receiving which accommodations. Thus, as shown in the example in Box 5.10, a student might receive the same accommodation in instruction, classroom assessment, district assessments, and state assessments. Or, alternately, a student might receive a specific accommodation in all situations except the state assessment. Whenever a discrepancy in the alignment occurs, we recommend that you document the reason for the discrepancy among the situations in which an accommodation can be used.

Despite your documentation of accommodations and the alignment in where they are used, it is still possible that questions will be raised about certain accommodations. If the test publisher or others raise questions about whether an accommodation gives the student an advantage that other students do not receive, and in your opinion it is essential that the student should use the accommodations, then you will need to enlist the aid of evaluation or assessment personnel within your district.

Evaluation or assessment personnel in your district potentially can engage in collecting data from comparison students who also are provided the accommodation, although they do not need it. The purpose of performing this task is to determine whether the effect of the accommodation for the student who needs it is different from the effect of the accommodation for students who do not need it. A differential effect is typically taken as evidence of the need for the accommodation for the student who has the disability.

Remember, asking for help to have someone double check the effects of an accommodation really is needed only to carry questionable accommodations into state or district assessments. For these tests (both norm-referenced tests and criterion-referenced tests), you will have to be able to support the need for specific accommodations.

A Word About Technology Accommodations

Technology is expected to solve many of today's problems. This statement is true for instruction and assessment, just as it is true for business. We already are making use of more common technology, such as tape recorders, self-timers, communication boards, and word processors.

BOX 5.10

Form to Determine Links Between Classroom Accommodations, Classroom Testing Accommodations, and District or State Testing Accommodations

Accommodation	Instruction	Classroom Assessment	District Assessment	State Assessment	Reason for Discrepancy among Columns
e.g., frequent breaks	X	X	X	X	
e.g., read text to student	X	X	X		Policy does not allow in state test

Much of the expectation about the benefits of technology for assessment surrounds the idea of computer-adaptive testing. In this type of testing, the items that a student receives are individually selected based on how the student performs on earlier items. Thus, through computer programming, determining where a student should begin items of varying difficulty levels is relatively easy. Furthermore, you will find it relatively easy to know when to stop presenting items to the student, because all of these actions are based on how the student is performing. This kind of approach certainly would reduce concerns about student frustration, because the student is only being testing on items that are in an individually determined range between too easy and too difficult.

Lately, researchers have begun to realize that computers can aid test-taking in other ways—by providing accommodations through the computer medium. In a press release, Dr. Martha Burk (a researcher and software developer) stated, "We have . . . shown that computers are capable of producing the types of accommodations that are often recommended for these students, and such accommodations can also raise test scores." Among the accommodations that the computer version of a test could easily provide to students were large print, extra spacing, and sound. In addition to better performance, Dr. Burk reported that the computerized testing helped students feel "more confident in taking the tests—even when their computer experience was limited or non-existent."

The possibilities are blossoming. We now see computer presentation of some instruction opening tremendous possibilities for providing students who have disabilities access to the general education curriculum. This goal is achieved, for example, by incorporating definitions of terms, explanations of assumed background information, and a variety of other avenues within the text in order to widen access to the curriculum. The possibilities for likewise opening testing to provide access to students who have disabilities are soon to be explored through collaborative work of the National Center on Educational Outcomes and the Center for Applied Special Technology (CAST).

Out-of-Level Testing: A Special Case

One of the major concerns that emerges when students who have disabilities need to be included in district and state tests is that the tests are way above the level at which the students are functioning. In other words, the tests are perceived by the student to be too difficult. The assumption is that if students are functioning below their grade level, they are not likely to perform well on a grade-level test.

Out-of-level testing is seen as an answer to this problem. This solution is sometimes found listed among the accommodations that might be considered for a student who has a disability. We believe that this accommodation is not appropriate (and should not even be used as a "non-approved" accommodation). Out-of-level testing is probably appropriate for instructional decision-making when you need to determine the specific skills that a student has mastered and the skills that still need to be taught. This use of out-of-level testing would be useful to inform classroom instruction.

Out-of-level testing is not an appropriate approach to district and state tests for several reasons. We make this statement despite what some of the testing companies and psychometricians will tell you. The reasons for this stance are based on what we know is the purpose of state and district tests and what we know about expectations.

The purpose of district and state tests is to measure what students know and what they are able to do, in contrast with what they are expected to know and to be able to do at their grade level. These tests are not designed to measure what a student knows and what he or she is able to do at a grade level through which they have already passed, then have their score on that other content equated to what it would be if they had taken the grade-level test. As Maggie McLaughlin, a well-known researcher, says, "He may read at the second grade level, but that doesn't mean he thinks at the second grade level."

The effects of expectations are another reason why we strongly argue against the use of out-of-level testing. Too often, low expectations for a student cloud our views of what the student can do. We have talked to teachers who were certain that a student who had a learning disability would only get about 50 percent correct on a state assessment. They were ready to change the passing-level requirement for this student so that the student would not be too frustrated by the testing experience. When the test results came back, they were surprised to find that the student had obtained 90 percent of the questions correct, which was way above the teacher's expectations and the accepted passing level for the test. Stories such as these have been repeated to us many times.

The National Center on Educational Outcomes (NCEO) has prepared a policy paper on the topic of out-of-level testing. In this paper, NCEO summarizes several of the arguments for out-of-level testing and rebuttals to those arguments. This material is reproduced in Box 5.11. NCEO also provides a list of the assumptions for out-of-level testing and objections to those assumptions.

Facing Reality: Accommodations Needed Might Not Be Allowed

As if making decisions about accommodations was not tough enough, several complications exist that surround the use of accommodations. We identify and address three of these complications here: IEP documentation issues, non-approved accommodations, and an appeals process. We provide this information primarily to alert you. The specifics for each of these topics will vary with your district and state policies.

BOX 5.11

NCEO's Arguments For and Against Out-of-Level Testing

Pro Arguments	Rebuttals to Pro Arguments
Avoids student frustration and emotional trauma. This is the humane approach for students not performing well in school.	Can instruction that does not address needed grade-level material be thought of as humane? Trauma will be a non-issue if instruction is consistent with the difficulty of the assessment.
Improves accuracy of measurement.	How can a test that does not address "grade-level" materials be more or less accurate than chance scores?
Better matches the student's current educational goals and instructional level.	Is it honest for a test to conform to where it is perceived that a child is, rather than to match what we want the child to know and be able to do?

SOURCE: This table is reproduced with permission from NCEO's *Policy Directions 9*: Thurlow, M., Elliott, J., and Ysseldyke, J. (1999). "Out-of-Level Testing: Pros and Cons." Minneapolis, MN: University of Minnesota, National Center on Educational Outcomes. For further discussion of these issues, refer to Elliott, J., and Thurlow, M. (1999). "Out-of-level Testing" in *The School Administrator* (November, Vol. 56, No. 10, pp. 24–29).

IEP Documentation Issues   Documenting accommodations to be provided in instruction is no longer an option. This information is required by IDEA 1997 to be documented on the IEP. The accommodations to be provided during district and state assessments also must be documented.

Because IEP teams typically meet in the fall, in the late spring, or sometimes even year round, decisions are often made far from the time of district and state assessments. Much can happen during that time period, and one of the things that typically does happen is that different accommodations needs emerge or are identified. In other words, the IEP team must meet again so that the proper accommodations are documented.

No easy ways exist to get around this requirement. Simply indicating that the student can have every accommodation that is allowed by the district or the state policy is not an appropriate action to take. We already know that over-accommodation should be avoided, in large part because the use of accommodations that are not needed might actually interfere with the student's best performance.

The requirement to document accommodations on IEPs and to reconvene when changes need to be made actually heightens the importance of making good accommodations decisions at the beginning. Also, this requirement emphasizes the need to base these decisions on data, as suggested in our discussion of instructional accommodations.

Non-Approved Accommodations   Every district and state assessment has policies that identify accommodations that are not acceptable to use during the assessment, because it has been determined that those accommodations change the meaning of the test, the score comparability, or some other important test characteristic. Some policies refer to these unacceptable changes as "modifications," while others simply refer to them as non-approved accommodations. The specific accommodations that are included in these unacceptable lists vary; different districts and states disapprove different accommodations. We know that one state might recommend an accommodation that another state specifically disapproves.

The critical question is, "What are you supposed to do if the student really needs one of these non-approved accommodations in order to even have access to taking the test? Should you force the student to not use the needed accommodation so that the student's score will count? Should you provide the needed accommodation and not worry about whether the student's score counts? And, if counting means not graduating, can you legally perform this action?"

We would argue that what you do has to depend on the purpose of the test. If the test has implications for system accountability only, it seems unfair to not permit the student to use the needed accommodation. But, you should make sure that if the student uses the accommodation, that student's score still counts. If the score will not count even if the student does not use the accommodations (which is true in all too many places), then the student should use the needed accommodation. You have to make the decision, however, to demand that you will still receive information about how the student performed. Ideally, you should obtain aggregated data for all students whose scores are not reflected in the district or state reporting system.

When it comes to student accountability, the decisions might need to be different. If the use of a particular accommodation is not allowed and the student's score will not count toward passing a graduation exam if the accommodation is used, then the student and the student's parents need to make some tough decisions. Among their choices are the following: (1) file a lawsuit claiming unfair disadvantage because the accommodation is not allowed, (2) do not use the accommodation and determine whether performance is at a passing level, (3) do No. 2, then if necessary, do No. 1. Another option which might or might not be available in your state or district is to proceed through an appeals process.

Appeals Process   Many states and some districts now have an appeals process in place for those students who have not been successful in passing a test. Sometimes this appeals process also applies to the use of specific accommodations. Finding out about the appeals process in your district or state and knowing what procedures must be followed to file an appeal is essential. You must also know what options a successful appeal provides to you and to the student.

Appeals processes should exist for both graduation exams and for promotion tests that determine whether a student moves from one grade to the next. In reality, because promotion exams are only recently becoming more common, the appeals processes that do exist have been developed for graduation decisions. A fairly common approach to an appeals process is to have a criterion for when a student can begin the process (for example, having not passed the graduation exam at least three times). Then, the student typically has to provide alternative evidence of having met the graduation standards. Sometimes this alternative evidence is a portfolio that contains an array of independent student work that shows that the student is meeting these standards. Other times, the alternative evidence is an oral presentation, either to a panel or to an administrator (principal or superintendent) who then makes a recommendation to the school board or other authority.

Sometimes it takes a bit of digging to find information about an appeals process. Assessment programs do not relish the thought of appeals. They are a challenge to the assessment system. An appeal, particularly a successful appeal, indicates that the test cannot accurately measure everyone. Thus, the existence of an appeals process is often not advertised or even placed in easily accessed locations. If an appeals process is needed, however, it is well worth the effort taken to find out about it.

Summary

Accommodations are often an emotional and highly charged issue. Students have the right to appropriate and reasonable accommodations, but each person has a different perspective of what is appropriate and what is reasonable. Recognize the controversy is important, but you should not not let it impinge on making the best decisions for students. In this chapter, we have highlighted many of the major considerations to keep in mind, as well as the specifics of starting from instructional accommodations and proceeding to those that are to be used during classroom testing—and those that are to be used in district and state tests. (Refer to Box 5.12 for a case study that exemplifies many of these considerations.) As research continues on what is appropriate and reasonable, we must continue to make good decisions for individual students and to implement those decisions well. We hope that this chapter has provided you with steps along this path.

BOX 5.12

**Case Studies on Making Accommodations Decisions
for Instruction and Testing**

Roberto is a third-grade student who has recently moved into the state from a state that has extremely different educational supports. He now faces school daily with a certain amount of trepidation, because everyone in the school seems to be emphasizing what he cannot do, rather than what he can do. This situation is almost directly opposite of what was happening in his prior school, so he is beginning to question whether he can do what is expected of him. He is personalizing the concerns of teachers and administrators in his new school about his need for a reader (for the math test), extended time (for the reading test), and a spell-checker (for the writing test). Also, as a result, when first asked about what he needed when taking the state test, he indicated that he needed nothing. Nothing is what he got.

His performance was lower than any test score he had ever gotten before. Despite his excellent math skills, he barely finished any items, and those he did complete were mostly wrong.

Luckily, his math teacher had recently attended a seminar on instructional accommodations. There, he learned about what accommodations are, about the controversy that surrounds them, and why they are an important part of providing students who have disabilities with access to instruction. He began making sure that Roberto either worked with a peer—sharing the reading of directions and word problems—and then answering questions on their own. He also provided Roberto with tape-recorded homework assignments. With these instructional accommodations, Roberto's math performance soared. He was showing what he knew and could do without the impediment of his reading disability.

Test Your Knowledge

Testing your knowledge is a good way to determine what you might need to review before proceeding. Complete the following fill-in-the-blank statements, rereading parts of this chapter when necessary:

1. Making good accommodations decisions is a _____ that can be improved by information and practice.

2. Research on accommodations has revealed that the effects of accommodations are _____, varying as a function of the test, the characteristics of the student, and attitudes about what accommodations should accomplish.

3. Accommodations that are used in instruction should not be determined by the student's disability _____.

4. The availability of accommodations should not be a consideration in determining the accommodations that a student will receive during _____.

5. Changes in students' skills and greater maturity both probably play a role in possible changes in whether a student needs_____ _____.

6. Using a checklist to determine what accommodations a student needs fosters _____.

7. A critical step in accommodations decision making is to _____ the student how to use accommodations.

8. To document that accommodations are having intended effects, it is necessary to _____ _____ on their effects.

9. Out-of-level testing is probably appropriate for _____ decision-making when you need to determine the specific skills that a student has mastered and the skills that still need to be taught.

10. If different accommodations needs emerge during the year, the _____ _____ must meet again to discuss accommodations for assessment.

Answers

1. skill (p. 75)

2. complicated (p. 77)

3. category (p. 78)

4. assessments (p. 79)

5. accommodations (p. 80)

6. over-accommodation (p. 83)

7. teach (p. 89)

8. collect data (p. 89)

9. instructional (p. 95)

10. IEP team (p. 96)

Resources

Beattie, S., Grise, P., and Algozzine, B. (1983). "Effects of test modifications on the minimum competency performance of learning disabled students." *Learning Disabilities Quarterly*, 6 (1), 71–77.

Benderson, A. (ed.). (1988). "Testing, equality, and handicapped people." *Focus* (ETS Publication; Princeton, NJ), 21, 1–23.

Bennett, R. E., Ragosta, M., and Stricker, L. J. (1984, August). "The test performance of handicapped people." (ETS Research Report RR-84-32). Princeton, NJ: Educational Testing Service.

Bennett, R. E., Rock, D. H., and Jirele, T. (1987). "GRE score level, test completion, and reliability for visually impaired, physically handicapped, and nonhandicapped groups." *The Journal of Special Education*, 21 (3), 9–21.

Bennett, R. E., Rock, D. A., and Jirele, T. (1986, February). "The psychometric characteristics of the GRE General Test for three handicapped groups." (ETS Research Report RR-86-6). Princeton, NJ: Educational Testing Service.

Bennett, R. E., Rock, D. A., and Kaplan, B. A. (1985, November). "The psychometric characteristics of the SAT for nine handicapped groups." (ETS Research Report RR-85-49). Princeton, NJ: Educational Testing Service.

Bennett, R. E., Rock, D. A., and Kaplan, B. A. (1987). "SAT differential item performance for nine handicapped groups." *Journal of Educational Measurement*, 24(1), 44–55.

Bennett, R. E., Rock, D. A., and Kaplan, B. A. (1988). "Level reliability and speededness of SAT scores for nine handicapped groups." *Special Services in the Schools*, 4(3/4), 37–54.

Braun, H., Ragosta, M., and Kaplan, B. (1986, October). "The predictive validity of the scholastic aptitude test for disabled students." (ETS Research Report RR-86-38). Princeton, NJ: College Entrance Examination Board, Educational Testing Service, Graduate Record Examinations Board.

Braun, H., Ragosta, M., and Kaplan, B. (1986, November). "The predictive validity of the GRE general test for disabled students." (ETS Research Report 86-42). Princeton, NJ: Educational Testing Service.

Burk, M. (1999). *Computerized Test Accommodations: A New Approach for Inclusion and Success for Students with Disabilities*. Washington, D.C.: A. U. Software.

Burns, E. (1998). *Test Accommodations for Students with Disabilities*. Springfield, IL: Charles C. Thomas.

Elliott, J. (2000). Accommodations: Making the Instruction and Assessment Connection. (videotape recording). Alexandria, VA: National Association of State Directors of Special Education.

Elliott, J., and Thurlow, M. (1999, November). "Out-of-level testing." *The School Administrator*, 56 (10), 18–23.

Elliott, J., Ysseldyke, J., Thurlow, M., and Erickson, R. (1997). "Providing accommodations for students with disabilities in state and district assessments." (NCEO Policy Directions 7). Minneapolis, MN: University of Minnesota, National Center on Educational Outcomes.

Fuchs, L. S., and Fuchs, D. (1999, November). "Fair and unfair testing accommodations." *The School Administrator*, 56 (10), 24–29.

Fuchs, L. S., Fuchs, D., Eaton, S. B., Hamlett, C., and Karns, K. (in press). "Supplementing teacher judgments about test accommodations with objective data sources." *School Psychology Review*.

Henry, S. (1999, November). "Accommodating practices." *The School Administrator*, 56 (10), 32–38.

Thurlow, M., Elliott, J., and Ysseldyke, J. (1999). "Out-of-Level Testing: Pros and Cons." (NCEO Policy Directions 9). Minneapolis, MN: University of Minnesota, National Center on Educational Outcomes.

National Association of State Boards of Education. (1999). *Reaching to the Sky: Policy to Support the Achievement of Students with Disabilities*. Alexandria, VA: NASBSE.

National School Boards Association and Office of Special Education Programs. (1997). *Technology for Students with Disabilities: A Decision Maker's Resource Guide*. Washington, DC: United States Department of Education.

Tindal, G., and Fuchs, L. (1999). *A Summary of Research on Test Changes: An Empirical Basis for Defining Accommodations*. Lexington, KY: University of Kentucky, Mid-South Regional Resource Center.

Tindal, G., Heath, B., Hollenbeck, K., Almond, P., and Harniss, M. (1998). "Accommodating students with disabilities on large-scale tests: An empirical study of student response and test administration demands." *Exceptional Children*, 64 (4), 439–450.

Trimble, S. (1998). *Performance Trends and Use of Accommodations on a Statewide Assessment*. (NCEO Assessment Series, Maryland/Kentucky Report 3). Minneapolis, MN: University of Minnesota, National Center on Educational Outcomes.

Willingham, W. W., Ragosta, M., Bennett, R. E., Braun, H., Rock, D. A., and Powers, D. E. (eds). (1988). *Testing Handicapped People*. Boston: Allyn & Bacon.

Internet Resources

Center for Applied Special Technology: http://www.cast.org

Council for Exceptional Children: http://www.cec.sped.org/

Educational Testing Service: http://www.ets.org/

Mid-South Regional Resource Center: http://www.ihdi.uky.edu/msrrc

National Association of Test Directors: http://www.natd.org

National Center on Educational Outcomes (NCEO): http://www.coled.umn.edu/nceo

National Center for Education Statistics (NCES): http://nces.ed.gov

National Information Center for Children and Youth with Disabilities (NICHCY): http://www.aed.org/nichcy

Parents Engaged in Educational Reform (PEER): http://www.fcsn.org/peer/

6

Preparing Students for Testing

"Give me a fish, and I will eat today. Teach me to fish, and I will eat for a lifetime."

—Chinese proverb

"Preparing for these tests should enrich learning, not reduce it."

—Grant Wiggins

Hot-Button Issues

- Is it ethical to use student instructional time just to get students ready to take district and state tests?

- What if these students' scores do not count in our district's accountability system? Should I really worry about getting them ready to take the tests?

- I have to teach the curriculum. I do not have time for this test-taking skills stuff.

Test-taking strategies are just one aspect of preparing students to take district and state tests. A number of ways are available to prepare students for tests that also result in their being better students and self-advocates and that will benefit them as they move out of the K–12 system and into the world of work or other post-secondary settings. In addition, preparing students for district and state assessments and working with parents, families, and others to support students to do their best (refer to Chapter 7) also benefits the educational system as a whole.

Preparation for district and state tests is an important aspect of improving students' test performance. Some studies have suggested that scores can improve significantly just from simple instruction in how to prepare for testing. The expectation exists that these types of gains from test preparation will be even more pronounced for students who have disabilities. While many test-preparation skills come naturally to students who do not have disabilities, these skills need to be taught to students who have disabilities.

Furthermore, for students who have disabilities who need accommodations during testing, there are some specific strategies that must be addressed. Particularly, it is important that as students who have disabilities mature, they must come to understand not only their disabilities but also their accommodation needs. They need to know how to advocate for their need for specific accommodations, as well as how to use their accommodations effectively during a testing situation. Helping students become self-sufficient in these skills is an important part of the instruction that these students receive to help them in their transition through school and into post-school life.

Of course, there is more to being prepared for testing—there are strategies for learning content in the first place. Many of these strategies involve mnemonics, or learning tricks, for memorizing facts (although not the desired type of test items, they still exist). These strategies are not the focus of this chapter, however. Refer to Chapter 9 for more information about instructional issues.

In this chapter, you will learn about the importance of knowing more than just the content or type of tests for which students need to be prepared. This knowledge includes getting to the nitty-gritty of how many items of what type (and so on), so that the exposure you provide to students reflects the emphasis that is given to certain content and skills on the test. You will see an example of a test matrix and will find out how to use it, and you will also learn about setting goals (and expectations) and the significant impact that this effort can have on student performance. After providing you with many specific ideas to use with students in order to convey skills in test preparation, test taking, and dealing with the consequences of the test, we will provide you with activities to help students become strong and appropriate self-advocates of their own test-taking and test-preparation needs, including accommodations. Finally, we will alert you to many useful resources for you to explore in greater depth.

Assessment Literacy

The term *assessment literacy* is relatively new in the educational community. Its use has been spurred by the tremendous vocabulary and methodology that has arisen around assessments, particularly district and state tests. While you do not need to become a psychometric expert in order to understand tests and to help prepare students to improve their performance on these exams, you should have some knowledge of the basics of assessment terminology and philosophy. This knowledge will help you know what to emphasize and what to ignore as you help students improve their test performance.

Some basic terminology, which you might or might not already know, appears in Box 6.1. These are some of the terms that can be used to describe the tests that your students are required to take. As we use some of the terms of assessment in this chapter and in others, you can refer back to these definitions.

As you work with your students to help them understand state and district tests that they will be taking, you should check that they are understanding what you are saying. They will need assessment literacy, just as you do. In addition, you need to make certain points about state and district assessments so that students understand their purpose, the meaning of scores, and the implications of how they perform when they take these tests.

Discuss the purpose of tests.　Primary points to remember about district and state tests is that they might have either high-stakes consequences (those that have a significant impact) or low-stakes consequences (those that have relatively minimal impact), and the consequences might apply to either the student, the educational system (districts, schools, administrators, and staff), or both. Of course, the way in which you explain these concepts will vary with the age of the students with whom you are working. Nevertheless, even students in early elementary grades need some explanation of these concepts.

When discussing the purpose of district and state tests, the points that you cover should give answers to the "why" questions—questions that address the why various purposes are important. In Box 6.2, we provide you with some general ideas for discussions of the "why" questions with elementary, intermediate, middle, and senior high-level students. As you will note, regardless of the level, the gist and tone of the discussions should be matter-of-fact and non-threatening.

Discuss the nature of the test.　Students must be prepared for the test by having a sense of familiarity with the test, although they have never seen the test. To provide them with this sense of familiarity, you will need to know the test well. In other words, you need to know more than just the content area tested or that the test is norm-referenced or criterion-referenced.

Nearly every test developed today conforms to a test matrix that describes the types of items and nature of content that is included in the test. A couple of typical test matrixes are presented in Boxes 6.3 and 6.4. Obtain one of these for the test for which you are preparing students. You should be able to get one from your district research and evaluation division, from the state department of education, or from the test publisher.

BOX 6.1

Selected Assessment Terminology and Definitions

Glossary of Commonly Used Terms

Alternate Assessment

A substitute approach used in gathering information about the performance and progress of students who do not participate in typical state assessments. Under the reauthorized Individuals with Disabilities Education Act (IDEA), alternate assessments are to be used to measure the performance of a relatively small population of students who are unable to participate in the regular assessment system, even with accommodations.

Alternative Assessment

A generic term that is typically applied to a variety of different assessment activities. These assessments provide an alternative to multiple-choice tests that require students to select one response. Writing samples, portfolios, and performance-based assessments might all be considered forms of alternative assessment.

Assessment

The process of collecting data for the purpose of making decisions about individuals, groups, or systems

Authentic Assessment

Often used synonymously with performance assessment, this term can also mean an assessment that only uses real-world tasks as the basis for information about how well an individual can perform certain tasks.

Confidence Interval (CI)

A numerical range that shows the interval around a score that one would expect a person or group of persons to obtain if they were to take the same test again. A CI of 95 percent indicates that one can be 95 percent confident that if the person or group was retested, their average score would fall into the same range.

Criterion-Referenced Test (CRT)

Criterion-referenced tests are measures that are used to examine student performance relative to state and/or district criteria or standards. Instead of comparing students' scores to a national normative standard, scores are interpreted in terms of various performance standards—usually set at the district or state level (e.g., mastery versus non-mastery; low proficiency, moderate proficiency, and high proficiency within a particular subject area).

BOX 6.1

Selected Assessment Terminology and Definitions (Continued)

Glossary of Commonly Used Terms

Norm-Referenced Test (NRT)

Norm-referenced tests are those that provide a comparison of individual performance to that of a state or national comparison (standardization) sample. A norm-referenced test measures the performance of a student against the performance of other individuals. Use of the norm sample enables raw scores to be converted to grade-equivalent scores, percentile scores, and standard scores.

Normal Curve Equivalents (NCEs)

NCEs are standard scores that are generated from a normal distribution. You begin with a set of raw scores, convert them to percentile ranks, and then use a z-score table to convert the percentile rank to a z-score. The resulting z-scores are usually transformed by using a linear transformation to a new scale (such as the SAT, where the mean equals 500 and the standard deviation equals 100.) NCE scores can only be used for students who are similar in age or grade to those in the norm sample.

Percentile Scores

These scores tell the percent of people in the normative sample that scored at or below a student's score (e.g., a percentile rank of 80 means that 80 percent of the normative group earned a score at or below that student's score).

Performance Assessment

A form of testing that requires the creation of an answer or a project, rather than the selection of an answer (as in many traditional multiple-choice tests). In many cases, such assessments are intended to represent or simulate real-life situations that require problem solving. The term is often used synonymously with authentic assessment.

Portfolio Assessment

A collection of student-generated or student-focused products that provides the basis for judging student accomplishment. In school settings, portfolios might contain extended projects, drafts of student work, teacher comments and evaluations, assessment results, and self-evaluations. The products typically depict the range of skills of the student or reveal the improvement in a student's skill level over time.

Raw Scores

These scores are simply the scores that are obtained when you sum the score on each item. If items are scored dichotomously (1 or 0), then a raw score represents the total number of items answered correctly.

BOX 6.1

Selected Assessment Terminology and Definitions (Continued)

Glossary of Commonly Used Terms

Standards-Based Assessment

An assessment instrument, battery, or system that has been constructed to measure the achievement of individual students or student populations in attaining certain standards, which are generally established by local districts or state educational agencies. Most state-level standards-based assessment programs that are currently in place measure student performance against articulated standards in core academic content areas, such as reading, mathematics, writing, science, and social studies.

Standard Error of Measurement (SEM)

An index of reliability that essentially converts reliability data from a test into a confidence interval around a given score. Knowing the standard deviation, the reliability, and a person's score, you can estimate a confidence band within which you would expect the individual to score (in typical cases, 95 percent of the time) if that individual repeatedly took a parallel version of the test.

Standard Scores

These scores are linear transformations of raw scores and are considered the easiest to interpret. With standard scores, the mean and standard deviation of any distribution can be placed onto a similar scale. Common examples of standard scores are the SAT, which has a mean of 500 and a standard deviation of 100, or a typical Intelligence Quotient (IQ) test with a mean of 100 and a standard deviation of 15.

Reliability

Reliability is the extent to which a test measures what it purports to measure time after time. Reliability also refers to the accuracy, precision, or stability of a measuring instrument.

Rubric

A scoring guide that facilitates the consensus of the people who are rating the students' performances on assessment tasks. A rubric provides criteria from which those students who are assessed can learn to improve their performance.

Validity

Test validity, simply stated, refers to a test that measures what is says it measures.

SOURCE: The definitions in this paper were adapted from the definitions used by Drs. Elliott and Thurlow in their work at the National Center on Educational Outcomes.

BOX 6.2

Points to Make in Discussing the Purpose of State and District Assessments

Topic	Elementary (Grades 1–3)	Intermediate (Grades 4–5)	Middle (Grades 6–8)	Senior High (Grades 9–11)
School Consequences	This test will determine what you have been taught and will help decide how our school is performing. You should do your best so that our school earns high marks.	This test is used to determine what you have been taught in this school. This test will help determine whether this school has taught you what you need to know. You should do your best so that our school will earn high marks.	This test is used to measure what you know so that the state department of education (or the appropriate decision maker) can decide whether our school is doing what is necessary in order to educate you. You should do your best on this assessment so that our school will earn high marks.	This test is used to measure what you know so that the state department of education (or the appropriate decision maker) can decide whether to give our school extra funding. You should do your best on this assessment.
Student Consequences	This test will determine what you have been taught and will help us know that you have learned what you need to learn in this grade in order to be ready for the next grade. Do your best.	This test is used to determine what you have been taught and is used to determine whether you have learned what you need to know in order to move to the next grade. You should do your best.	This test is used to measure what you know so that we can determine whether you have the skills needed to move to the next grade level (or to graduate from high school). You should do your best.	This test measures what you know so that the school board can verify that you have the skills necessary to move to the next grade level (or to graduate from high school). You should do your best.

BOX 6.2

Points to Make in Discussing the Purpose of State and District Assessments (Continued)

Topic	Elementary (Grades 1–3)	Intermediate (Grades 4–5)	Middle (Grades 6–8)	Senior High (Grades 9–11)
School and Student Consequences	This test determines what you have been taught and helps decide how our school is doing. This test also helps us know that you have learned what you need to in this grade level, in order to be ready for the next grade. You should do your best.	This test is used to determine what you have been taught in this school and will assess whether this school has taught you what you need to know. The test is also used to determine whether you have learned what you need to know in order to move to the next grade level. You should do your best.	This test is used to measure what you know so that the state department of education (or the appropriate decision maker) can decide whether our school is doing what it needs to be doing to educate you. This test is also used to determine whether you have the skills that you need to move to the next grade (or to graduate from high school). You should do your best.	This test is used to measure what you know so that the state department of education (or the appropriate decision maker) can decide whether to give the school extra money. This test is also used to measure what you know so that the school board can verify that you have the skills that you need to move to the next grade (or to graduate from high school). You should do your best.

Often, the test matrix is provided in the test's manual. You will find it well worth your effort to obtain this matrix, because its contents can both help provide the familiarity that is needed and guide practice sessions and worksheets that you will provide to your students. The percentage of time that you spend on different types of concepts, skills, and strategies can directly correspond to the percentage of these types of items that will

---

BOX 6.3

Example of a Test Matrix for a Typical Standards-Based State Test

Mathematics Problem Solving

Makeup of Test

	Multiple Choice	Short Answer	Percentage of Test	Multiple Choice Points	Short Answer Points
Research	6	3	20	6	6
Geology	6	3	20	6	6
Biology	10	6	30	10	10
Physical Science	10	6	30	10	12

SOURCE: This matrix was adapted from one level of a state test blueprint. The content areas and numbers have been changed for illustrative purposes.

---

appear on the test—if you have the test matrix to guide your preparation activities.

A test matrix can be further expanded to directly show the links to needed instruction. Long Beach Unified Schools has performed this task to take the Stanford 9 test matrix a step farther (refer to the partial analysis in Box 6.5). By taking this action, teachers know not only what content is tested but also how it is tested, what specific types of items are used, and what prerequisite skills are needed.

Knowledge about the state and district tests and about the characteristics of students who have disabilities is now generating renewed interest in how to ensure that these tests accurately measure what students know and can do. For example, educators who are working with blind and visually impaired students have generated several principles that can guide the review and development of state and district tests for these students (refer to Box 6.6). The National Center on Educational Outcomes is similarly developing a Bias Review Manual for individuals to use when reviewing test items and other aspects of state and district assessments.

Setting Performance Goals (and Expectations)

Psychology is well known for its identification of expectation effects. The Pygmalion effect described the strong influence that expectations had on how students performed and behaved. This theory suggested that, like the

BOX 6.4

Example of a Test Matrix for a Typical Norm-Referenced Test*

Mathematics Problem Solving

Test Levels

	1	2	3	4	5	6	7	8	9	10	11	12	13
Whole Number Computation			X	X	X	X							
Number Sense and Numeration	X	X	X	X	X	X							
Geometry and Spatial Sense	X	X	X	X	X	X							
Measurement	X	X	X	X	X	X	X	X	X	X			
Statistics and Probability	X	X	X	X	X	X							
Fractions and Decimals			X	X	X	X							
Patterns and Relationships	X	X	X	X	X	X							
Estimation					X	X	X	X	X	X			
Problem-Solving Strategies			X	X	X	X	X	X	X	X	X	X	X
Number and Number Relations							X	X	X	X			
Number Systems and Theory							X	X	X	X			
Patterns and Functions							X	X	X	X			
Algebra							X	X	X	X	X	X	X
Statistics							X	X	X	X	X	X	X
Probability							X	X	X	X	X	X	X
Geometry							X	X	X	X			
Functions											X	X	X
Geometry—Synthetic											X	X	X
Geometry—Algebraic											X	X	X
Trigonometry											X	X	X
Discrete Mathematics											X	X	X
Calculus Concepts											X	X	X

*Prepared by the Long Beach Unified Public Schools for the Grade 3 Reading—Language Arts Stanford 9.

BOX 6.5

Partial Test Matrix Analysis*

Test Cluster	Number of Items and Sample Format	Content Domain	Tested Skills	Prerequisite Skills
Synonyms Recognize a synonym from a printed word	**18 items** A filly is a kind of • turtle • rabbit • horse • frog	Parts of speech, verbs, nouns, some adjectives	1) To be able to discriminate between at least one close synonym and the precise definition. 2) To be able to discriminate between words that make sense in the sentence and the one that captures the same meaning.	• Ability to show conceptual understanding by discriminating between close approximations of meaning and precise meaning. • Be able to answer questions and give examples that are not just close enough but right on.
Multiple Meanings Use context to determine meaning of a known word with multiple meanings	**6 items** I cannot bear to tell my mom I skipped school. In which sentence does the word **bear** mean the same thing as in the sentence above? • I saw a bear eating my picnic lunch. • The bridge will bear 10 tons. • My brother bears well in school. • He bears up well under pressure.	Words that change their meaning depending on what part of speech they are or depending on the context of a sentence; words can be one year below, at grade level, or one year above grade level.	1) Recognize that a word that is issued in a sentence (part of speech) can sometimes change its meaning. 2) Recognize homographs. 3) Recognize that context might change the meaning of a word.	• Understanding what context is. • Understanding that meaning resides in use, not just in the word itself. • Ability to write sentences using the same word to mean different things. • Awareness of spelling patterns and homographs.

BOX 6.5

Partial Test Matrix Analysis* (Continued)

Test Cluster	Number of Items and Sample Format	Content Domain	Tested Skills	Prerequisite Skills
Context Use context clues to assign the meaning to an unknown word	**6 items** Use the other words in the sentence to help you figure out what the underlined word means.—After the earthquake, the dog dug through the **rubble** until he found his master. • yard • house • broken concrete • tunnel	Verbs, nouns and adjectives that would not likely be encountered in third-grade literature but that could occur in upper-elementary grades.	1) Ability to get main ideas from sentences. 2) Ability to test hypotheses about language meaning and select best guesses.	• Ability to predict answers to questions without complete information. • Wide experience with a variety of above-grade level text that might be difficult but still comprehensible with guidance. • Large vocabulary • Word-attack skills (prefixes, root words, etc.)

*Prepared by the Long Beach Unified Public Schools for the Grade 3 Reading—Language Arts Stanford 9.

ancient sculptor who brought clay to life, what we expect of a person is what we get. Another effect, the Hawthorne effect, is well-known for its explanation of what happens when attention is given to one individual but not to another. Differences in performance and behavior are substantial between the attention and no-attention individuals—an effect that can be large enough to account for all of the differences between the two. This effect is not unlike the placebo effect, where a patient might respond to a sugar pill simply because it looks like medicine. We humans are subject to all kinds of laws of nature, but the effects of expectations are among the more interesting, surprising, and significant in terms of their effects on life-important outcomes.

As you probably know, these effects can also have tremendous effects on test performance. A wise educator keeps these effects in mind. At a minimum, you should not interfere with performance because of an ill-

---

BOX 6.6

Considering the Unique Needs of Students
Who Are Blind or Visually Impaired

- Analyzing test items and format for appropriate production into Braille and large print (for example, a test item might contain an entire table of contents and a question about the table of contents on one page. The table of contents might need to be shortened in order to fit on the Braille page).

- Assuring that items on the test are testing the intended competency and that the completion of the test item is not based on visual perception, visual experience, or understanding based on visual experience

- Reviewing test items for applicability to students who have visual impairments. For example, a test item that requires drawing a shape would be inappropriate for a Braille reader and might be a difficult task for students who have low vision.

- Reviewing multiple-choice items to insure that answer choices are still appropriate after the test item is altered. For example, items testing a student's ability to estimate might include graphics that are no longer viable answer choices when enlarged.

- Considering the use of alternative test items that are meaningful for students who have visual impairments (for example, substituting a test item where the student describes the layout of a building, rather than reproducing the layout).

- Considering the use of testing procedures to limit or eliminate the need for accommodations or modifications for individual students who have visual impairments (for example, providing an untimed test for all students, so that students who need extended time are accommodated without concern for test reliability).

- Providing practice materials that will enable visually impaired students to become proficient in the use of test formats.

- Reviewing tests with graphics to ensure that lines can be detected and that diagrams are labeled in the appropriate places.

SOURCE: Reprinted with permission from NASDSE (1999). *Blind and Visually Impaired Students: Educational Service Guidelines*. Alexandria, VA: National Association of State Directors of Special Education.

---

spoken phrase occasionally. Researchers have found that simple statements can have significant influences on the test performance of youngsters. For example, when girls were informed that they typically performed worse than boys on a test that was about to be administered, they indeed did perform worse. This situation occurred although the boys and girls had been picked because they had demonstrated the same level of knowledge and skills on the content and format of the test.

We mention the effects of statements that create expectations because we also want to talk about setting goals for performance that are based on the scoring procedures and cut-off points on tests. We want to perform this task, however, without creating any negative effects from what might come across as expressing expectations for what students are able to do or how they are able to perform on tests.

Today, almost all tests that are used for accountability purposes are linked to some kind of proficiency-level score—so that when reporting scores, they can be meaningfully tied to concepts such as "proficient," "beginner," and "beyond proficient." This way, districts and states can report on the number and percentage of students who are falling in each proficiency level. Even when proficiency levels are not defined, there are typically cut points where scores that are above the points are acceptable and scores below the points are not acceptable.

The first step in being able to define what a student has to do in order to perform adequately on a test is to know the relationship between the number of items on the test and the way in which the test is scored. For example, many state and district tests have anywhere from 30 to 50 test items. These items might be translated into scores such as 560 or 1120, however. Scores are often derived by using complex statistical formulas that actually serve a useful function in developing good, defensible tests. But translating a complex score into a concrete plan, such as, "You need to get 16 of the 30 items right in order to get a passing score" can do a lot to ease the anxiety that might be created when you and the student have no concept of what the student really has to do in order to perform adequately.

Having this kind of information at hand can also be extremely useful when the purpose of the test is determining whether the student moves from one grade to the next or whether he or she earns a high-school diploma. These student-accountability decisions are determined primarily by test scores. This knowledge becomes even more critical if the student must retake the test. Being able to define the number of additional items that the student needs to answer correctly is often helpful and calming to the student.

When the purpose of the test is school accountability—with consequences being assigned to schools, staff, or administrators—the motivation for simply doing one's best might be lacking. By transforming the test taking into an effort to increase the score, however, the student can become more self-motivated. One way to accomplish this goal is to give students a practice test that you score, then derive a percentage correct score. Setting a slightly higher level of performance as a goal for the student to achieve is one way to increase motivation for doing well on the test. Link this performance to class grades or to student rewards in order to ensure not only that the student is motivated and scores as well as possible, but also as an avenue to teach students about how to develop their own reward systems. Students can use this reward-producing skill in various areas of their lives, so this kind of effort is well worthwhile for both the educator and the student.

Knowing how the student has performed in the past (or how he or she is performing now) on content that is similar to the test content can help identify realistic goals. If your state or district gives its assessment yearly (or even every other year), information concerning past test performance should be directly relevant to your goal-setting activities. In this situation, you should review past test performance to help guide current test performance. Because you have more than one student about whom you need to be concerned, you will find it helpful to put this information into a chart. An example of such a chart is provided in Box 6.7.

While not absolutely necessarily, rechecking the IEP of each student who has a disability for information about accommodations that the student needs is often beneficial. Be sure that the accommodations that you are using in class are reflected in the IEP. Check to see that you are providing all of the accommodations during instruction. If needed, amend the student's IEP.

Preparing for the Test

While better understanding the test and its requirements and setting goals are both important steps in preparing for the test, they are not the bulk of the activities that need to be undertaken in order to be sure that students are prepared for the test. In this section, we delineate some specific ways to prepare your students for test taking. Next, we will delve into some approaches for ensuring that the actual test taking is done to the best of the student's ability and skills. As you will see, all of these techniques are ones that support the educational effort. They really do not take time away from instruction, and they support instruction in ways that make future teaching more efficient and effective. What a bonus—test scores improve and learning improves.

The strategies and techniques that we present here assume that you have already reviewed the test matrix, that you have planned to cover the topics reflected in the matrix with about the same degree of emphasis, that you have looked at the past performance of students, and that you have set realistic goals for test performance with the student. Given these background steps, what else needs to be done? The answer is "lots." You can pick and choose among the strategies and techniques based on your informed judgment about student needs and the time that is available.

Review General Test Vocabulary Terms   Few of the more recent resources on test taking refer to test vocabulary as an essential part of preparing to take tests. Yet, there are key words that are used in tests, and it is usually dangerous to assume that students know what these words mean in the testing situation. You should make sure that they do know

BOX 6.7

Charting Past Test Performance

Past Test Information

Class _____

Upcoming Test Content and Date _____

Student	Last Test Date	Content Area	Type of Score*	Score	Accommodations and Other Notes

*Percentile rank, raw score, or proficiency level. If there is more than one type of score noted, select and list the one that is most like the score that will be given on the state or district assessment.

these words. Words and phrases such as "contrast," "most accurate," and a host of others often have special meaning in testing situations. Several of the key words to include in a review of test vocabulary terms are included in Box 6.8.

Review Specific Content-Area Terms   While teaching the vocabulary of a content area is a natural part of instruction, you should review key terms prior to taking tests in the content area. Having a broad and well-established vocabulary is clearly an advantage when taking tests. This reason is why almost every test preparation course or text emphasizes the need to stress vocabulary. The fact that a student might receive an accommodation (such as having someone read the test or clarify the test directions) does not negate the need for ensuring that students know the content-area terms.

The best way to ensure that students have a broad vocabulary, of course, is to have them read frequently, to read to them often, and to make sure that they know the words that they are reading or hearing. Likewise, it is important to include in every lesson some time to ensure that the vocabulary in the lesson is understood. Making vocabulary a part of everything in and out of the classroom is helpful. For example, if students are learning spelling, they should learn not only how to combine the letter in order to get the word, but also to define what the word means and to show how to use the word in a sentence.

BOX 6.8

Common Test Vocabulary Terms

Analyze	Estimate	List	Pattern
Best	Evaluate	Most accurate	Point of view
Categorize	Explain	Most appropriate	Predict
Classify	Fact	Not	Reasonable
Compare	Group	Not like	Sequence
Conclude	Identify	Only one	Summarize
Contrast	Justify	Opinion	Transform
Describe	Least true	Order	Verify
Discuss	Like	Outline	

Address the Administration of Tests   When students take district and state tests, especially those tests that are high-stakes in some way, the tests themselves are handled differently from the way in which most classroom tests are handled. To the extent that students are aware of these special administration procedures, the less likely the procedures themselves are to create stress and anxiety for the student who is taking the test. Overtly discussing these procedures and experiencing them can go a long way toward improving test scores. At the same time, these procedures familiarize students with the need to know what is going to happen in any special situation and how to prepare for these unique situations.

Some of the specific administration procedures that might be encountered in testing situations include bubbling in, stopping at certain points, not turning pages, and knowing whether to work fast or to work methodically. Many other administration procedures exist that might be unique to the test that the students are about to take. You must be sure to know what the specific administration procedures are that might be new to your students and to make sure that the students know about these procedures (and are exposed to them as they take practice tests).

Provide General Strategies for Different Types of Items   While some state and district tests might use performance items or even portfolios, the most common types of items are those with which we are all familiar: true/false, multiple-choice, fill-in-the-blank, short answer, and essay. These types of questions have been and continue to be the substance of testing, although the amount of emphasis given to each type ebbs and flows with changes in perceptions about what learning should be like and about what particular types of items really test.

You should not plan to give students information about types of test items that the students might never experience. But, given your knowledge about the makeup of your state or district test (from the test matrix), you should provide students with brief instruction on approaches for various item types. The kinds of information that you might want to provide to students are shown in Box 6.9. Remember, however, that the type of item in a test should not completely determine the focus of instruction. Some evidence exists that students who prepare for essay tests, regardless of the type of test administered, do better than students who prepare for the specific type of item in a test. Similar information exists that can assist students with preparing for tests in specific content areas. In their text, *Teaching Test-Taking Skills: Helping Students Show What They Know*, Scruggs and Mastropieri provide excellent examples of these types of strategies.

Provide Practice Tests   While the old adage "practice makes perfect" might be carrying things too far, practice is important when it comes to taking tests. The more familiar students are with the format, procedures,

---

BOX 6.9

Suggestions for Answering Different Types of Questions

Item Type	Suggestions for Students
True/False	Do not be concerned with expected patterns of responses (e.g., do not try to make the number of true responses and the number of false responses equal).
	Attend to absolute statements—ones that contain words such as "never" or "always"—and realize that these are almost never true (but they can be true sometimes).
Multiple Choice	Treat each answer option as a true/false statement (i.e., determine whether each option is true or false), then respond to the stem demands.
	Mark out absurd items so that you are only choosing among the more likely options.
	Proceed through items relatively quickly, going with your first guess, and changing later only if you are certain of a different response.
Fill-in-the-Blank	Make a best guess based on content knowledge, but look for cues in the structure of the sentence.
	Be sure that the word(s) you choose fits the grammatical structure of the item.
Short Answer	Recognize short answer questions as such, and do not write too much.
	Respond directly to the point of the question; assist yourself in performing this task by underlining the key elements requested.
Essay	Write enough to be convincing.
	Keep your answer organized. To achieve this goal, take notes beside the item or jot notes onto a separate piece of paper.
	Be neat.
	Use strategies to help guide the writing process (for example, SNOW—study the question; note the important points; organize your thoughts; write to the question; Scruggs and Mastropieri, 1992).

and mechanics of testing, the more likely they are to perform better—even if nothing different has been done to the instruction that they receive.

Obtain practice tests from your district or state assessment office. Develop your own practice items that are similar to those items in the tests. Depending on the ages of your students, you might even have them attempt to develop items of each type that they will be taking. By performing this task, the student begins to understand how tests relate to the content of a topic—thereby making it easier for them to study the "right stuff" in preparation for a test.

Give the Student One or More Test-Taking Strategies   Today, there are many test-taking strategies available in books and journals and even on the Internet. The teaching of such strategies almost always has been proven worthwhile. For example, a strategy developed just for test taking is called "SCORER":

S—Schedule your time
C—Clue words
O—Omit difficult questions
R—Read carefully
E—Estimate your answer
R—Review

This strategy was developed by Ritter and Idol-Maestas and is explained nicely in the book, *Tools for Learning: A Guide to Teaching Study Skills* by M. D. Gall et al. By providing students with strategies such as SCORER, they have a systematic and stable way to approach tests. This feeling of control over what they must do goes a long way toward bolstering the confidence with which students with face tests—particularly, students who have disabilities.

A variety of mini strategies can also be useful. These strategies are found scattered throughout various sources and range from simplistic advice such as, "Read the test directions carefully" to tricks such as, "Answer the easy questions first." Many of these mini strategies are picked up by good students on their own. Other students, particularly students who have disabilities, typically do not pick up such strategies. Therefore, the strategies need to be taught to these students. Not doing so provides other students with an unfair advantage.

Most learning strategies have been developed for instruction, rather than for testing. Yet, many of the learning strategies could be adapted in order to apply these strategies to testing situations, depending on the needs of individual students.

Taking the Test

Numerous books and chapters have been written on the topic of how to help students take tests successfully. Some of these have even focused on the test-taking skills of students who have disabilities. Several of these sources are listed in the resource section of this chapter. Our purpose here is to reiterate some of the basic concepts of good test-taking skills and to focus primarily on those that have particular relevance to students who have disabilities.

Personal Strategies   Test anxiety is a common reaction experienced by test takers, especially when they think that they will be affected in important ways by how well they perform on the test. Negative reactions to having to take a test in the past were often cited as one reason why students who have disabilities should be excluded from state and district assessments. We know today that this reason is a weak reason for excluding students who have disabilities from tests. They should be prepared to take tests, to be alerted to the ways to cope with tests, and to know how to perform their best. Think about this issue as an adult. Why would you get test anxiety? Were you not prepared for the test? Were you not familiar with the test format? These reasons can be addressed. Traumatic reactions to test taking should be eliminated.

What are some of the key personal strategies that test takers, especially test takers who have disabilities, need to learn? Self-regulation during testing, especially if the test is timed, and the related skills of time management are skills on which students should receive instruction in preparation for participating in a state or district test. This preparation can be as simple as setting a kitchen timer and having the student work to complete tasks within a time limit. Finally, coping with potential stress during tests, positive thinking about test performance, and visualization of good test performance are additional personal strategies that others recommend. These techniques certainly cannot hurt and most likely will significantly benefit students when they are taking tests.

Time management and self regulation of behavior are related strategies that are frequently mentioned in test-preparation books. These, of course, are particularly key skills for students who have disabilities—many of whom suffer from poor skills in these areas. Some of the major recommendations in these areas are shown in Box 6.10.

Helping students identify ways in which to cope with stress when it occurs and getting back to a calm and productive state is another critical personal strategy that students, especially students who have disabilities, will need to be taught. Again, books about test-taking strategies often include these techniques among their test-taking hints. A first step in helping students to be able to perform these tasks is to help them recognize when a calm and productive state is disappearing. They need to know what these signs are, and when these signs begin to occur, they need to know to do certain things. Those things will be individualized, so it will be necessary to determine with each student what things are indicators of increased stress (e.g., biting nails, extreme fatigue, etc.) and what strategies work to reduce that stress (e.g., self-talk, a moment with closed eyes, etc.).

You should realize that some of these strategies might actually be accommodations for the student who has a disability. Thus, indicating that

---

BOX 6.10

Self-Regulation and Time Management

Recommendations for Self-Regulation and Time-Management Strategies

---

Be wise in the use of time. Use strategies that help you go through certain steps, rather than getting bogged down by specific items.

Practice monitoring your own time on-task. Perhaps start by having an alarm clock set at intervals of five minutes. Each time the clock rings, mark on a log whether you are on task. Hone your on-task-skills to the point that you can maintain on-task behavior for the entire duration of a test. If the inability to do so is related to your disability, explore accommodations that might help your on-task behavior.

Have everything that you need at your fingertips so that no unnecessary time is spent looking for or retrieving needed items (e.g., erasers, spare pencils, tissues, etc.).

During practice tests, figure out good pacing strategies for you and for completing the test in a reasonable amount of time.

---

the student needs to listen to music while taking tests for extended time periods might be the basis for an accommodation that should be written on an IEP. The sooner that you and your students can figure out specific needs for coping and reducing stress, the more that you will know and the easier it will be to get these important strategies into the IEP in case they are viewed as accommodations, rather than as test-taking strategies.

Positive thinking and visualization are also often identified as among the important strategies for reducing stress and improving test performance. Positive thinking, for sure, is aided by adequate test preparation—by knowing the content. Research has demonstrated that positive thinking in and of itself can help boost test scores. Therefore, even off-handed comments that you or other adults make can affect the thinking of students and whether that thinking is positive. Comments about the test being too hard, or noting that a student really should be taking a different test, can easily translate into negative thinking when overheard by the student—resulting in poorer performance on the test than need be. This situation represents a self-fulfilling prophecy at work.

Visualization is another strategy that athletes often mention, but this technique is equally applicable to testing situations. Helping students see themselves as good test takers, sitting up straight with a smile on their faces, is an example of visualization strategies. Encouraging them to visualize a rewarding experience after their best effort on the test is another example. Many other ways to produce good visualization skills exist and are often worth the time to help students learn how to perform this task on their own.

Using Accommodations Well   Although students have accommodations noted on their IEPs and have been using them during instruction, there are almost always ways to improve the way in which these accommodations are used. One important aspect of accommodations, especially as students get older, is to make sure that the students know why they need the accommodations that they use and that they are not embarrassed by their use (of course, this process involves making sure that classmates also understand the need for accommodations). Evidence has been gathered that this situation is not always the case and that students who need accommodations (and whose performance would certainly benefit from their use) might opt not to use them, simply because they have not been helped to understand their importance.

Howard Eaton, an individual who was diagnosed with significant developmental dyslexia, provides lessons on self-advocacy that can be helpful in aiding student understanding of the importance of using accommodations and advocating for these accommodations. While his small book is designed to assist students with making the transition from high school to college, many of his lessons are valuable for students in the K–12 system, as well. One such lesson titled, "Do your own academic work" concludes with the statement, "Do not ask your parents or teachers [to type papers, spell check, etc.]. Instead, learn how to ask your teachers for *accommodations*. Do your own academic work."

Letting students know that how they perceive the use of accommodations might be different from how their classmates perceive them might also be important. Surveys of classmates of students who have disabilities have revealed that the majority of these students are supportive of the use of accommodations by students who have disabilities. Their concerns about fairness are raised only when students who have disabilities are held to different standards for the same grades (for example, having to get fewer items correct).

In a related vein, certain accommodations are subject to malfunction. Despite the wondrous nature of various mechanical and technological accommodations, the possibility always exists that they will not work at the time of the test. These kinds of glitches have to be prepared for so that if they should occur, a backup is available (or as a last resort, that plans have been approved for movement to a different testing site—e.g., another school that has a computer not being used, etc.).

Finally, in considering accommodations, you should know the test and the policies about accommodations that apply to them. Sometimes, techniques exist to help students get the benefit of what might be non-approved accommodations. For example, having someone read all of the directions to students is viewed as inappropriate for many tests. This reading is deemed to change the meaning and comparability of scores of students who have this accommodation provided to them. On the other hand, in these same tests, it is considered appropriate for someone to read directions to a student if the student has raised his or her hand and has asked that the directions be read. Thus, it would be helpful to explain this point to the student, and if needed, agree with the student that he or she will raise his or her hand every time a new set of directions are encountered—so that they can be read to the student.

Physical and Mental Readiness Students who take tests, particularly when they have high stakes attached to them, should be physically and mentally ready for the test that they are about to take. We have already touched on several points that will help students in this endeavor, such as developing coping and calming strategies. The need for physical readiness is also important, but this skill is one that is generally pushed back to the home. The home (parents) is not the only place that has ownership of this responsibility, however. Tests should not be scheduled after physical education activities or even perhaps after lunch. Fresh air in the testing site—air that is neither too cold nor too hot—is another important avenue to ensuring physical readiness.

You can identify several factors in your school that have an impact on physical and mental readiness. Identify these factors on paper and indicate what will be done to address each one of them.

Helping Students Become Advocates for Their Own Testing Needs

Students must become advocates for their own testing needs, especially as they become older. This skill is critical for them to have as they make the transition to high school, to post-secondary education, and later into the world of work. The skills that are needed, however, are not just being able to ask for what is needed. Of course, this skill is the most critical. But beyond that, the student should know how and when to ask for accommodations in the most appropriate manner possible. This action involves developing interpersonal skills that some students lack. This skill should be a focus of instruction, because hopefully they are among the IEP goals that are set for students who lack appropriate skills when advocating for themselves.

Summary

This chapter has given you lots of ideas about preparing students for testing. We have covered the need for you and your students to understand the basics of assessment—its purpose and the nature of tests that students will take. Setting performance goals and placing test taking within a reasonable set of expectations fits within the larger scheme of preparing for test taking. The array of ways to prepare students for tests and strong test-taking skills, beyond the prerequisite good instruction, are ones that you can use and expand upon as you see the benefits of these for improving the performance of students.

Because accommodations are unique to students who have disabilities in most places (but not all), and they have both emotional and logistical issues attached to them, it is particularly important to pay attention to using them well during testing. Making sure that the correct accommodations appear on the IEP and that those accommodations on the IEP are occurring in instruction and during assessments are the important basics of using accommodations well.

Test Your Knowledge

Complete the following fill-in-the-blank statements. Reread parts of this chapter if the words that go in the blanks are not obvious to you.

1. It is important that as students who have disabilities mature, they come to understand not only their disabilities but also the _____ needs that they have.

2. Although you do not need to become a psychometric expert to help students improve their test scores, it is important to have basic assessment _____.

3. To help you and your students understand the nature of a district or state test, you should get a test _____ to help with planning and preparation.

4. _____ can have a significant effect on how students perform on a test, although they are not directly related to the test's content or to the student's skills.

5. Before testing, the student's _____ should be reviewed for information about accommodations.

6. Having a broad and well-established _____ is an advantage for students when taking tests.

7. Treating each answer option as a true or false item is a strategy for taking _____ items.

8. In addition to obtaining practice items from your district or state assessment office, you can _____ some of your own items for students to take.

9. _____ anxiety is a weak reason for excluding students from state and district tests.

10. Time management and self-_____ are related strategies that are frequently mentioned in test-preparation books.

11. Physical readiness is just as important as _____ readiness when taking a test.

12. Students must become _____ for their own testing needs.

Answers

1. accommodation (p. 104)
2. literacy (p. 104–105)
3. matrix (p. 105)
4. Expectations (p. 111)
5. IEP (p. 117)
6. vocabulary (p. 117, 119)
7. multiple-choice (p. 121)
8. develop (p. 121)
9. Test (p. 123)
10. regulation (p. 123)
11. mental (p. 126)
12. advocates (p. 126)

Resources

Abbamont, G. and Brescher, A. (1997). *Test Smart: Ready to Use Test-Taking Strategies and Activities for Grades 5–12.* Upper Saddle River, NJ: Prentice Hall.

Bigge, J. L. and Stump, C. S. (1999). *Curriculum, Assessment, and Instruction for Students with Disabilities.* Belmont, CA: Wadsworth Publishing.

Eaton, H. (1996). *Self-Advocacy: How Students with Learning Disabilities Can Make the Transition from High School to College*. Santa Barbara, CA: Excel Publishing.

Fry, R. (1996). *Ace Any Test*. Franklin Lakes, NJ: Career Press.

Gall, M. D., Gall, J. P., Jacobsen, D. R., and Bullock, T. L. (1990). *Tools for Learning: A Guide to Teaching Study Skills*. Alexandria, VA: Association for Supervision and Curriculum Development.

Gamsby, L. H. (1987). *Coping with School: Organizational and Learning Techniques for Parents, Teachers, & Students*. Concord, NH: Parent Information Center.

Gilbert, S. D. (1998). *How to Do Your Best on Tests*. New York: Beech Tree Books.

Klingner, J. K. and Vaughn, S. (1999). "Students' perceptions of instruction in inclusion classrooms: Implications for students with learning disabilities." *Exceptional Children*, 66 (1), 23–37.

National Association of State Directors of Special Education. (1999). *Blind and Visually Impaired Students: Educational Service Guidelines*. Alexandria, VA: NASDSE.

Polloway, E. A., Bursuck, W. D., Jyanthi, M., Epstein, M. H., and Nelson, J. A. (1996). "Treatment acceptability: Determining appropriate interventions within inclusive classrooms." *Intervention in School and Clinic*, 31 (3), 133–144.

Pressley, M. and Woloshyn, V. (1995). *Cognitive Strategy Instruction that Really Improves Children's Academic Performance* (2nd ed.). Cambridge, MA: Brookline Books.

Ritter, S. and Idol-Maestas, L. (1986). "Teaching middle school students to use a test-taking strategy." *Journal of Educational Research*, 79 (6), 350–357.

Scruggs, T. E. and Mastropieri, M. A. (1992). *Teaching Test-Taking Skills: Helping Students Show What They Know*. Cambridge, MA: Brookline Books.

Internet Resources

Council for Exceptional Children: http://www.cec.sped.org/
Educational Testing Service: http://www.ets.org/
National Association of Test Developers: http://www.natd.org/
Scholastic Testing Systems: http://www.testprep.com/

Parent Support for Testing

A stumble may prevent a fall.

—English proverb

As parents of children with and without disabilities, we expect to be active partners involved in all levels of educational decision making. We require quality, accountability, and proof that our children are learning from our public education systems.

—Debbie Johnson
Parent

Hot Button Issues

□ What do parents really need to know about testing? Is there nothing that they can do that will really help their child do better?

□ Even if you let parents know what they can do to help their child perform better, they won't really do it.

□ Giving parents too much information is dangerous; they will just have stuff to use in lawsuits.

Parents and families are important players in the attempt to improve student performance, yet their potential is rarely capitalized upon, probably for many reasons. One reason may be that we don't trust them to do what we think needs to be done. Another reason is that we don't think that they know enough to be able to do what needs to be done. And, perhaps more common yet, it takes time and effort to help parents understand what they can do to help improve student performance. Some educators are concerned that the time and effort devoted to parents takes away from the time and effort that we can devote directly to students. However, the time and effort almost always have significant benefits for students.

In this chapter, we show you the many ways that parents can indeed help improve the test performance of students with disabilities. First, we discuss the need to inform parents about testing. This includes presenting the reason for administering district and state tests as well as their characteristics (such as multiple-choice math questions, short-answer reading questions, and long-answer writing tasks). Next, we address the issue of who has the last say about whether a child takes a test, and the responsibility of schools not to encourage inappropriate recommendations to parents about this decision.

We also address in this chapter the important topic of how to equip parents with the knowledge and resources to make good decisions about test participation and accommodations. Then we provide ways to help parents understand what test results mean, both in general and specifically in relation to how their child performed on the test.

In addition to the resources that we provide at the end of each chapter, we identify several resource centers for parents and other family members as well as specific materials that have been developed to inform parents about district and state assessments, accommodations, and a variety of related topics.

Informing Parents About Tests

To help parents make good decisions and to help them learn how to support their child so that the child performs optimally, it is essential that they know about the test. This means that they need to know about the purpose of the test, the content areas tested, the types of items that are included on the test, how long the test or each part of the test usually takes, where and how the test is usually administered, and what the consequences of the child's performance on the test are.

We again recommend that a test matrix be developed. Starting with the one developed in Chapter 5, "Accommodations—How to Make Sound Decisions for Instruction and Assessment," is helpful. The matrix may need to be simplified or rearranged for parents. We provide in Box 7.1 an example of a test matrix that was developed specifically for parents.

Another strategy that usually is helpful to parents, and in turn to their children, is to give parents a sample test. If your district or state releases items each year, then you have available to you many possible items to pull from to develop a sample test for your parents. Make it special by sending it in an envelope to the parents of your students. Ask them to look the items over to see what their children will be doing when they take the test. Suggest that they try some of the items. Encourage them to work on some of the items with their child.

BOX 7.1

A Parent Version of a Test Matrix

Topic	# Items	Sample Item	What My Child Has to Do
Synonyms: Recognize a word that means the same as another word	18 items	A filly is a kind of ▪ turtle ▪ rabbit ▪ horse ▪ frog	Your child will have to tell the difference between the correct word and one that is fairly close in meaning to it. The more you can help your child increase his or her vocabulary the better, especially when you can note differences between words that are close in meaning to each other.
Multiple Meanings: Determine the meaning of a word that has multiple meanings	6 items	I cannot bear to tell my mom I skipped school. In which sentence does the word bear mean the same thing as in the sentence above? ▪ I saw a bear eating my picnic lunch. ▪ The bridge will bear 10 tons. ▪ My brother bears well in school. ▪ He bears up well under pressure.	Your child will need to get the exact meaning of a word from the sentence in which it is used. Words that are pronounced the same but that have different meanings are what is being testing. The more you can highlight these for your child, the better.
Context: Pick the best word to use, given a sentence or paragraph	6 items	Use the other words in the sentence to help you figure out what the underlined word means. After the earthquake, the dog dug through the <u>rubble</u> until he found his master. ▪ yard ▪ house ▪ broken concrete ▪ tunnel	Your child will need to pick out the best word just from having read a sentence in which a word meaning approximately the same thing is included. The more you can help your child increase his or her vocabulary, the better. Also playing games in which your child guesses at the missing word are also helpful in preparing for these types of test items.

SOURCE: This material was adapted from a test matrix analysis prepared by the Long Beach Unified Public Schools for the Grade 3 Reading - Language Arts Stanford 9.

As an alternative, you could organize a parent test night. Give parents not only the opportunity to see what the test is like, but also to discuss with other parents ways in which they can help their children perform well on the test. By bringing parents together in this way, you also increase the possibility of collaborative efforts by groups of parents. Sometimes these collaborative efforts result in support for those parents unable to help their own children (because of lack of time, skills, or English language skills, for example). Promoting discussion among parents is a nearly sure-fire way of raising consciousness about what can be done to help students do their best.

We recommend that you do not put pressure on the parent to take tests or work with their children on them. The purpose in sending items to parents is to introduce the parents to the tests, so that they know what is expected of their child. A parent who knows even a little about what the child will be doing is a much better support for the child than a parent who knows nothing about the test.

Equipping Parents to Make Good Participation and Accommodation Decisions

Making sure that the parent knows about the test is the first step in equipping parents to make good decisions about district and state tests. The two decisions to which parents must contribute (according to IDEA 1997) are (1) the decision about which test the student will take, and (2) the decision about the use of accommodations during testing. To be able to make these decisions wisely, it is critical that parents have good information about the implications of each of the decisions as well as what the options are.

The excerpt in Box 7.2 is from a report produced by the Federation for Families of Children with Disabilities. It provides a strong rationale for why it is important to have students with disabilities participate in district and state assessments.

In the past, the only decisions that parents of students with disabilities had to make about the test participation of their children was whether they were going to take the test or be exempted from it. Of course, the IEP teams made those decisions and often parents weren't even provided the option to assist in that decision.

Since the reauthorization of IDEA, however, parents are to be partners in making decisions about *how* students participate; whether they take the same assessment as most other students in the state or they take an alternate assessment designed for those students unable to participate in the regular assessment even if provided with accommodations to give them access to that assessment.

Parents need to be given enough information to make good decisions about the assessment in which their child will participate, be it the regular assessment or the alternate assessment. The key kinds of questions that

---

BOX 7.2

Excerpt from Federation of Families Report

Benefits to Students

Statewide assessments have enormous ramifications for students with disabilities. Benefits to students include

- **A Key to High Expectations:** The overall goal of our nation's many education reform initiatives is to raise the level of learning for all students, including students with disabilities. The goal is grounded in the belief that all students are capable of meeting much higher standards than have been expected of them in the past. Historically, expectations for students with disabilities have been appallingly low, as these students have been discouraged from participation in general curriculum studies. Students with disabilities must participate in assessments to ensure meaningful access to the same high curriculum and standards that drive education for all students.

- **School Accountability for All:** Participation in assessments sends the message that schools are accountable for all students reaching higher levels of learning. The higher expectations placed on schools can result in increased usage of accommodations or adaptations and other strategies to help students with disabilities reach higher standards.

- **A Role in Shaping Policies and Programs:** To help students meet higher standards, state and local education agencies are developing new instructional methods and technologies. Data from assessments can be used to gather information about promising practices and to improve programs. If students with disabilities are included in assessments, their needs will be considered in shaping education policies, programs, and practices.

- **High Stakes for Individual Students:** For individual students, the importance of assessments may be even more direct and critical. Increasingly, assessments are used as the basis for awarding diplomas or for gaining access to post-secondary opportunities. Students with disabilities must have equal opportunities to demonstrate their competencies in order to have full and equal access to future opportunities.

SOURCE: Reprinted with permission from J. K. Landau, J. R. Vohs, and C. A. Romano's *All Kids Count: Including Students with Disabilities in Statewide Assessment Programs*, Boston, MA: Federation for Children with Special Needs, Parents Engaged in Educational Reform, 1998, pp. 1–2.

---

they need to be made aware of and that you need to help them answer are as follows:

- *What is the purpose of the regular assessment?* It is especially important for parents to understand that there are specific reasons for their child to participate in assessments whether the purpose is for system accountability or student accountability. The reasons just differ.

  For system accountability, their participation helps to ensure that the system is held accountable for their performance. If schools or districts are not meeting the needs of all students, then this needs to be evident. Students with disabilities have the right to perform well, just like all other students; therefore, their performance also needs to be made evident.

For student accountability, the reason to have students participate is to ensure them access to diplomas. In many states (but not all), having the student not take a graduation exam may mean that the student will not receive the same kind of diploma as other students.

- *What are the characteristics of students who should be taking an alternate assessment?* States and districts are required by IDEA 1997 to have guidelines for making decisions about who participates in the alternate assessment. These guidelines should make it fairly evident to those making decisions what the characteristics are of students taking each kind of assessment. Parents need to be familiar with these guidelines and how the characteristics defined in them (or implied by them) correspond to their own child's characteristics.

- *What kind of accommodations does my child need to be successful in school and in other situations? Can these be provided during assessments and still produce scores that have meaning?* Parents need to be aware that they have insights about their child that no one else may have. They may see the child providing himself or herself with accommodations during home life or during homework situations. Parents may provide accommodations to the child in the home that would be useful in the school environment as well. It is important for parents to understand what accommodations are and their purposes. Parents should also provide input to school personnel about what they know about accommodations needed and those used from the parent's perspective.

- *What will the impact of participating in testing (either regular assessments or alternate assessments) be on my child? Will it be harmful to his or her motivation to learn or self-esteem?* Parents naturally have concerns about the potential impact of testing on their child. This is true whether or not the child has a disability, but the concern seems to be elevated for students with disabilities because we start with low expectations for them. The effect of this is compounded by the fact that low expectations often have resulted in instruction that has not pushed the student forward enough, with the inevitable result being continued low performance.

Adding to the negative impact attributed to testing is the fact that teachers, parents, and administrators do not (perhaps because they do not know how) provide the information and support to students before they sit down for an exam. Students need to be told the purpose of testing, just like teachers and parents are told. Students also need to be given details of what the testing is like, how long it lasts, where it is given, and a variety of other characteristics. They need to be provided with practice so that they are comfortable with the testing situation and procedures. In addition, they need to be informed about accommodations that are available to them, the importance of their performance, and other relevant characteristics that may apply to their specific locations.

All school personnel have a responsibility to ensure that students do their best, that they recognize the importance of the test, and that they are not made to feel that their participation is a negative thing for anyone. Parents should be supported and never be pressured to keep their child at home on the day of district or state testing.

Helping Parents Understand Test Results

In the past, many district and state educational assessments were notorious for the incomprehensible information that they provided to parents. This should no longer be the case since most (but not all) district and state tests now use common words (such as below basic, basic, and proficient) to define student performance levels. However, we should realize that the use of common words doesn't necessarily make the meaning comprehensible. There is a great need for better communication about test results. No matter what the testing company may do to try to make the results of state and district assessments more comprehensible, it is educators who are ultimately responsible for ensuring that parents understand test results.

Several things need to be communicated to parents to ensure that they understand the results of testing. It is important for parents to be informed about the meaning of test results in general and the meaning of test results specifically for their child. Each of these is addressed here.

Understanding General Test Results

Because almost every district and state has its own testing program, it will be important for you to flesh out the information that we provide here and make it specific to your own testing environment. This should take only a little bit of time to do and will be well worth the effort. On the other hand, districts and states should be able to request that their testing programs provide the kinds of information that we present here. Generally, this will happen only if it is required in the contract set up with the test's developer.

Parents need to be provided with four essential pieces of information to have a basic understanding of overall test results: (1) the purpose of the test, (2) the content of the test, (3) the format of the test, and (4) how the test was administered. To this must then be added information on what is expected; how should students be performing? Several questions and answers for parents on these topics are provided in Box 7.3.

The *purpose* of the test needs to be addressed in terms of two aspects: (1) whether the test will compare students to a standardization group or assess whether they have met a standard, and (2) whether there will be consequences for the school system (or aspects of it, such as teachers), for the student, or both. The first topic focuses on norm-referenced testing (NRT) and criterion-referenced testing (CRT); the second topic focuses on accountability.

Parents should be helped to understand the basic distinctions between NRTs and CRTs. Ways in which these differences can be explained are included in Box 7.4. A primary reason for making sure that parents have an understanding of the differences among test types is that whether a test is an NRT or a CRT often affects accommodation policies.

The consequences of the test need to be clear, defining what specifically will happen if students perform or do not perform in a specific way. It may be that teachers will lose their retirement benefits if at least 60 percent of the students' scores are below basic. It may be that the principal will get a raise if at least 50 percent of the students are proficient and not more than 15 percent are below basic.

When there are consequences for the student, it may be that the student will not receive credit for a course if a certain percentage of correct answers is not reached. Or it may be that the student will not get a regular graduation diploma if he or she does not earn a certain score on the test. It is important to be very specific about the purpose of the test.

The notion that the purpose of district and state tests is to improve instruction probably will make little sense to the parent (and to others as well). Improving instruction directly for individual students is rarely a result of state or district assessments. Rather, the improvement of instructional programs is a more realistic effect of these assessments. This in turn may have a direct effect on the instruction provided to individual students.

The *content* of the test also must be clearly defined for parents. Here we mean more than just the subject matter covered (such as reading, math, and writing). We also mean the nature of that content. For example, are high standards being measured, are basic standards, or is the content based on what students nationally are learning (such as in norm-referenced tests that use a pool of items that can be taken by students in any state)? Is the content directly related to what students are learning in class, or is it pushing the limits of what they are taught? Does the content reflect the minimum that students should know?

BOX 7.3

Parent Questions and Answers About State and District Assessments

Question: Why do I need to know whether my state or district assessment is a norm-referenced assessment?

Answer: Norm-referenced tests (NRTs) are developed to enable a student to be compared to other students, or for a group of students (say, those in a school) to be compared to a group of students nationwide. This feature enables schools, districts, and states to know how they are performing in comparison to other schools, districts, or states. Although this seems to be important, NRTs have several limitations, one of which is that they do not directly assess standards; they assess a broad set of objectives that are not directly related to any one student's curriculum. In addition, they have many limitations for students with disabilities. One of these is that most NRTs have been developed without considering students with disabilities; items have not been checked by these students or educators who know the characteristics of students with disabilities. Furthermore, because of the importance placed on everyone taking the test in the same way, NRTs enable few accommodations to be used.

Question: Why is it important for my child to be included in assessments if their purpose is just to decide whether the school gets a reward for student performance? One student won't make a difference.

Answer: It is important that the school knows that every child counts. Although it is true that the score of one student may not make a big difference in the overall rating a school gets, it is very easy for one student to multiply into many students, and these students generally are those expected to perform less well on the assessment. Once a student is not included in the assessment, there is not the urgency to worry about whether they are mastering the skills that will be on the test. And if there is no urgency to worry about them, then it is easy to forget about them. Furthermore, when decisions are based on data, the missing data from students who didn't take the test will have no influence on the reforms that are generated as a result of student performance. All of these together produce a situation in which students not only are excluded from the assessment, but also from the indirect benefits of reform and often also from the direct benefits of instruction.

Question: How can I tell whether the test my child is taking is based on standards, basic skills, or something else?

Answer: The best way to determine what is being measured is to ask. Often this information is provided in information about the test, but not always.

Question: My student has a learning disability. What kinds of test items are going to be easiest for my child, and what kinds of test items do I need to have him work on at home?

Answer: There is no simple answer to this question. The research does not give easy answers. Most likely, the "easiness of items" is going to be related to things other than simply whether they are multiple choice, essay, or performance events. Because of this, it is important that your child's teacher knows exactly what kinds of items are included in the test, and that practice on these items is provided. The item types should not drive instruction, however. There is some research evidence that preparing the student to answer essay questions will also better prepare the student to answer multiple choice questions.

BOX 7.3

**Parent Questions and Answers about State and District Assessments
(Continued)**

Question: How can I help the IEP team make good decisions about the accommodations that my child will need during the state or district assessment?

Answer: Making decisions about accommodations should be a collaborative effort. You should provide information that supports the information that your child's teacher and other educators bring to the IEP team meeting. It is best to keep your input to what you know. Based on your knowledge of your child's learning experiences, you have a lot to say. Think about what helps your child get things done at home. Does he or she need to be in a distraction-free environment to finish tasks? Does he or she need frequent breaks to do a good job on household chores? Think about recreational activities, household chores, and skill learning and bring information about these things to the IEP meeting.

BOX 7.4

NRTs Versus CRTs and Standards-Based Assessments

Norm-Referenced Tests: These tests are developed to measure a student's performance in comparison to the performance of other students. These tests are developed to create a spread of scores, so that some students will score poorly and others will score well. A national sample of students takes the test, and the scores of students are compared to the scores of this national sample. Because the goal is to have all students take the test under the same conditions, very few accommodations are allowed.

Criterion-Referenced Tests: These tests are developed to measure a student's knowledge and skills, which are held up to a level of acceptable performance to indicate whether the student has reached the desired criterion. These tests also measure the student against a criterion, not against other students. Because having all students take the test under exactly the same conditions is not a goal of criterion-referenced tests, many more accommodations are allowed in criterion-referenced testing.

Standards-Based Assessment: These are tests (or other measures) that are criterion-referenced where the criterion is composed of standards identified by the state or district. Thus, the measurement is directly tied to instruction, if instruction is directly aligned to the standards. Like criterion-referenced tests, many accommodations are allowed during these assessments.

The *format* of the test may be a traditional multiple choice test, multiple choice plus short answer and/or extended response, a performance event, or a portfolio. The names of these formats should be translated for parents so that they are hearing both the current terminology and the terms with which they may be more familiar. Box 7.5 provides a quick guide for translating terminology for parents.

Information on *how the test is to be administered* is also important for parents to understand, so that they know the conditions under which their child will take the test. The first part of this is to describe the requirements of the testing situation. The second part is a discussion of the accommodations that may be used during the assessment.

The *requirements* of the testing situation include whether the test is timed, whether it involves group work or individualized responding, whether it is completed over time (such as on three days during a week) or on one specific day, and whether it is administered in the regular classroom or somewhere else. It also includes whether the test is a paper and pencil test or is provided through other media (such as via computers). All of these kinds of requirements are important to include because they set the stage for understanding the accommodations that may be used during the assessment.

Understanding the *accommodations* is another important part of preparing parents to understand the test results. It is critical for parents (and students, as they mature) to be aware of accommodation needs. It is also important for them to understand how these needs relate to what the test allows, and what happens if the student uses accommodations that the test does not allow.

Many excellent brochures have been developed by states to explain accommodation policies to parents. Many of these can be viewed on state Web sites (the end of this chapter lists specific sites). What is much less clear (and rarely explained to anyone) is what happens when a student needs something other than what is allowed.

Most district and state tests do not allow the reading test to be read to the student. Why? Because, it is argued, reading the test to the student confounds the construct being assessed, namely reading ability. But what if a student truly cannot read but can understand text that is read to him or her? Some would argue that if you allowed this, you would really be testing listening comprehension, and therefore the student must be excluded because the test would no longer be evaluating reading skills. Thus, parents and schools end up with no information on the child. In our opinion, it is better to have the student participate in the assessment, using the accommodations that the child needs, and then disaggregate the data of that student (as well as other students using "non-allowed" accommodations) so that there is some evidence about their performance. This is better than having no data at all.

Another approach, now embraced in only a few locations, would argue that for a student who truly is dyslexic it is important to assess how proficient the student is at obtaining information from written text. How this

BOX 7.5

Guide for Translating Testing Terminology for Parents

Testing Term	Alternate Term	Explanation
Aggregate	Combine	The aggregation of test scores is the process of putting the scores from many students together to form a total picture. It is simply a process of combining scores, albeit sometimes in very complex ways.
Alternate assessment	Different assessment	Alternate assessments are mandated by federal law for those students unable to participate in the general assessment. The alternate assessment is simply a different assessment. It may or may not look at all like the general assessment that it is an alternate to. In many states, the alternate assessment is a portfolio, while the general assessment is a paper and pencil test.
Disaggregate	Separate	The disaggregation of test scores is the process of separating out the scores of a group of students. Federal law requires that the scores of students with disabilities be disaggregated from the scores of other students and be aggregated with them.
Large-scale assessment	State or district test	Large-scale assessment simply means that the test was developed to be administered to large numbers of students, usually in groups. District and state tests are large-scale assessments.
Reliability	Consistency	Reliability is a psychometric term used to indicate the extent to which a score is (in very general terms) stable over time, the same if scored by two individuals, or the same if broken into two parts.
Rubric	Rules	Rubrics are descriptions of a test performance that support scoring guides, which are used to indicate the closeness of a student to a standard. The rubrics define what kind of a performance is Below Basic and what is considered Proficient.
Validity	Accuracy	Validity is the accuracy of a measure derived from a test. It indicates that the test measures what the test developer wanted it to measure.

information is taken in by the student is not as important as determining whether it is. Thus, in this view, allowing the reading test to be read to the student is okay.

Parents also need to be helped to engage in more long-range thinking about accommodations and their child. For example, they need to realize that the need for accommodations can change over time. This can happen as the child gains skills that take over for previously needed accommodations. Nearly all students also go through a period during which they do not want to use any accommodations; they don't want to be set apart from their peers by their need for accommodations. Recognizing this ahead of time can help parents talk to their child about this, about the consequences of not using an accommodation that is needed, about talking to their peers about their accommodations, and so on.

Parents should also be aware of the need to assist their child in recognizing accommodation needs and in advocating for their own accommodations. As children get older, there is a tendency for teachers and others to rely more on what the student says than on what may be on a piece of paper. When the child enters middle school or high school, teachers often have less access to IEPs and other documents that describe the student's accommodation needs. Thus, the student must be aware of his or her own needs and must know how to ask for accommodations to meet those needs. This is an essential skill that should be a part of every transition program (see Chapter 8, "Integrating Transition Needs with Accountability Requirements").

Understanding Their Child's Test Results

Not long ago, we were listening to a group of parents talk about their children's scores on the tests that their school districts administered every spring. One parent mentioned that her son had received three scores in reading and three in math. None of them made any sense. He remembered that they were all percentages, but the reading ones were 25 percent, 55 percent, and 40 percent. He remembered that there were three more scores for math. One score was the same, 55 percent, but the others were completely different (90 percent and 75 percent). No one had explained the tests or their scores to the parent.

It turned out that the district used a nationally and locally normed reading test and a criterion-referenced mathematics test. The score that the parent was seeing in reading reflected three elements: (1) how the student did compared to other students in the same grade in the district, (2) how the student performed compared to other students in the same grade in the nation, and (3) the percentage of items attempted that were correct. The math scores, on the other hand, reflected (1) the percentage of items correct, (2) the percentage of items attempted, and (3) the percentage of students obtaining the same score or lower. This example demonstrates why it is important for parents to know about the tests and to be provided with clear-cut, easy-to-remember scores.

Another example is very different. This parent could only remember that she saw a lot of letters on the test (such as SS or M) and that they were defined in footnotes. But the footnote just contained words like "scale score" and "mean" without telling what those words meant. The results, according to the parent, were meaningless.

Even parents who get test results that come back with words like "basic," "proficient," and "beginner" do not understand what they really mean unless they are defined. In addition, parents should be given examples of what those scores mean in actual performance.

Several excellent Web sites and parent booklets provide this type of information in clear and concise ways. Even though these materials are useful, we think that it is important to apply that clarity to the actual scores that parents see. This must be done either by the test development company, by the state department, or by the district or school itself.

What kinds of information do we think parents need? In addition to the student's scores (with explanations and examples attached), they need to know the content of the test, the nature of the items, and whether the district's scores reflect performances on basic standards, high standards, or some other entity (such as criterion or norm-referenced tests). They also need to know the consequences of the test, and any challenges that existed during the testing or scoring (such as accommodations that the student was not able to use or that produced a score that was considered non-aggregable).

Working with the test developer to produce appropriate materials is probably the best and most efficient approach to meeting the need for parent information. Putting it on the Web is good but does not yet meet the needs of all parents. Thus, if neither of these exist, it is critical to get together with parents to define what kind of information they need, and then to either hire a contractor to develop the materials or to do it yourself. There should never be an excuse for not providing parents with enough information about testing programs, tests, what scores mean, and their consequences. See Box 7.6 for more information on parent centers and other resources.

States and districts often develop reports that portray in one way or another the scores that students earn on tests. Recently, there has been an increased interest in reporting so that parents can understand what test results mean. Box 7.7 contains an excerpt from a recent report for parents in Washington state. It would serve educators well to provide these kinds of explanations for parents or, if they do not exist, to develop them.

BOX 7.6

Resource Centers and Materials for Parents

Several parent centers now produce information directly relevant to district and state tests. In the past, these centers generally knew only about testing for eligibility determination or for re-evaluation purposes. Here are some centers that are worth connecting with:

Families and Advocates Partnership for Education (FAPE), a federally supported project within PACER Center (4826 Chicago Avenue South, Minneapolis, MN 55417; Voice: 888-248-0822 or 612-827-2966; TTY: 612-827-7770; Fax: 612-827-3065)

Parents Engaged in Educational Reform (PEER), a federally supported project within the Federation for Children with Special Needs (95 Berkeley Street, Suite 104, Boston, MA 02116; Voice/TDD: 617-482-2915; Fax: 617-695-2939)

The Alliance, Technical Assistance Alliance for parent centers, a federally supported project within PACER Center (4826 Chicago Avenue South, Minneapolis, MN 55417; Voice: 888-248-0822 or 612-827-2966; TTY: 612-827-7770; Fax: 612-827-3065)

BOX 7.7

Example of Information Presented in State Report

Putting Scores in Context: Looking at the Big Picture

As we step back and look at the results from these tests, there are several important points to remember:

- These are **higher** standards. For example, reading means not only being able to understand words, but being able to analyze and interpret texts. Mathematics means not only computation, but being able to apply mathematical skills to create equations, solve problems, and explain how results are derived.

- Students that didn't meet the standards didn't "flunk." Their performance has been measured against **higher** academic standards that reflect the challenges they will face in our complex world.

- Only by looking at the data over time will we begin to see patterns emerge. In the meantime, we can be confident that steady progress will be made as we sharpen our focus on essential academic learning requirements.

- Schools in Washington are accountable for improvements. Schools should be measured by the progress they make over time in increasing the number of their students who meet the state's academic standards rather than being compared to other schools. Student work should be evaluated against clear academic expectations and standards of achievement.

SOURCE: Reprinted from *Reaching Higher: A Parent's Guide to the Washington Assessment of Student Learning* (prepared by the Office of Superintendent of Public Instruction), p. 6.

Summary

In this chapter, we have highlighted several things that parents/guardians need to know, and that you as an educator are responsible for helping the parent to learn. Included in this chapter is information about testing in general and the tests administered by the state or district in particular.

This chapter probably has given you lots of ideas about what parents need. You may be questioning whether it is really your responsibility to provide this to parents. We answer this question with an unqualified "Yes," if not for the parents themselves, then to protect yourself. Parents who do not understand the test that is being given to their children are more likely to question the results and the test itself. They are more likely to cast blame for low scores than are those parents who really understand the assessment and who have worked to assist their child in preparing for the test. And, as we all know, angry parents often turn to lawyers to relieve their feelings of frustration.

Test Your Knowledge

Complete the following "Fill in the Blank" statements. Re-read parts of this chapter if the words that go in the blanks are not obvious to you.

1. _____ need to know about the purpose of the test, the content areas tested, the types of items that are included in the test, how long the test or each part of the test usually takes, where and how the test is usually administered, and the consequences of the child's performance on the test.

2. A strategy that is usually helpful to parents is to give them a sample _____.

3. A test _____ can be simplified or rearranged to help parents better understand skill and item emphasis of the assessment.

4. Making sure that the parent knows about the test is the first step in equipping parents to make good _____ about district and state tests.

5. Parents are partners in making decisions about *how* students _____ in district and state tests.

6. In the past, district and state educational assessments were notorious for the _____ information that they provided to parents.

7. Districts and states should be able to request that their testing programs provide good _____ for parents.

8. There are excellent examples of _____ that states have developed to explain accommodation policies to parents.

9. Even parents who get test results with words like "basic" and "proficient" may not understand what they really mean unless they are _____.

10. Working with the _____ _____ is probably the most efficient approach to meeting the need for parent information.

Answers

1. Parents (p. 131)

2. test (p. 131)

3. matrix (p. 131)

4. decisions (p. 133)

5. participate (p. 133)

6. incomprehensible (p. 136)

7. information (p. 136)

8. brochures (p. 140)

9. defined (p. 143)

10. test developer/company (p. 143)

Resources

Bigge, J. L., and C. S. Stump (1999). *Curriculum, Assessment, and Instruction for Students with Disabilities.* Belmont, CA: Wadsworth Publishing.

Cookson, P., J. Halberstam, K. Berger, and S. Mescavage (1998). *A Parent's Guide to Standardized Tests in School.* Norwalk, CT: Learning Express.

Goldberg, M., B. Guy, and J. A. Moses (1999). *Education Reform: What Does It Mean for Students with Disabilities?* (NTN Parent Brief). Minneapolis, MN: University of Minnesota, National Transition Network.

Landau, J. K., J. R. Vohs, and C. A. Romano (1998). *All Kids Count: Including Students with Disabilities in Statewide Assessment Programs* (PEER Project). Boston, MA: Federation for Children with Special Needs.

McGinn, D. "The big score." *Newsweek*, 134 (10), September 6, 1999, pp. 46–51.

Thurlow, M. L., J. L. Elliott, and J. E. Ysseldyke (1998). *Testing Students with Disabilities: Practical Strategies for Complying with District and State Requirements*. Thousand Oaks, CA: Corwin Press.

Internet Resources

Parent Alliance: http://www.pacer.org/index.html

Parents Engaged in Educational Reform (PEER): http://www.fcsn.org/peer/

Chapters 4–7
Self Check:
Where Do I Stand?

Review the following statements as a personal survey of where you stand in relation to the information presented thus far. Base your responses to each survey on the topics that are presented in this book and what you think that you already know and are doing.

- I have a clear understanding of what the alternate assessment is, its purpose and importance. I know where my district is going with its development of our alternate assessment (Chapter 4).

- I understand the importance of having the alternate assessment linked to standards. I am familiar with my district's standards and have an idea of which standards will work and others that will need to be extended or even added (Chapter 4).

- Like any other assessment, I understand the importance of using the results to improve instruction and programs for students. I am prepared to do that for my students (Chapter 4).

- I understand the need and purpose for providing accommodations. I am familiar with those permitted on my district's and my state's assessments. I teach and reinforce those identified for students throughout my instruction with them (Chapter 5).

- I understand that in the past there has been the tendency to overaccommodate students. When I am in question about those students who truly need a specific accommodation, I collect and chart performance data on the student. That is, I let the student use the accommodation and keep track of how the student uses the accommodations and how well the student performs (Chapter 5).

- I am familiar with my district's appeals process. I know this is especially important for students who may fail a district or state test or be denied graduation or promotion due to the denial of a needed accommodation (Chapter 5).

- I have a plan for helping the students with disabilities in my class prepare for the district assessment. It involves both preparing for the test and providing information and practice on test-taking strategies (Chapter 6).

- I know ways to encourage students to do well on tests and I know how to avoid expectations that are damaging to students' self-concepts and to their test performances (Chapter 6).

- I know how to promote strong but pleasant advocacy skills in my students with disabilities and am encouraging them to assert themselves in appropriate ways so that they will receive needed accommodations as they become more independent (Chapter 6).

- I realize that parents, guardians, and other family members are an important part of improving the test performances of students with disabilities. I have a plan for engaging parents in the testing process, from encouraging participation in decisions at the IEP meeting, to providing awareness materials about the nature of the test, to helping them understand the results of testing (Chapter 7).

- I know how to explain the test, the testing terms, and the results to parents and have a set of materials to also convey this information (Chapter 7).

- I encourage parents to help their students prepare for tests in whatever way they can, realizing that this may vary widely among the parents/guardians of students for whom I am responsible. I respect this variation and create innovative strategies for students whose parents cannot be as involved as other parents (Chapter 7).

8

Integrating Transition Needs with Accountability Requirements

Begin with the end in mind.

—Stephen Covey

The most basic obligation of educators is to meet the needs of students as we find them.

—Art Coleman, Office of Civil Rights

Hot Button Issues

- *Why should students working in vocational programs have to meet the same requirements that students do who are in our school all day?*

- *There is no way those vocational kids are going to be able to pass the required district and state tests; they are in a different program.*

- *How can students who are enrolled in vocational programs be included in accountability and assessment systems when they are learning different stuff?*

- *Kids with disabilities will always be dependent upon adults. Why work so hard at creating transition plans?*

- *More and more it appears schools have to take on the role of the family. Now we have to make linkages to agencies.*

Schools are full of many students for whom learning in the traditional environment is ineffective and even inappropriate. This should come as no surprise, especially in light of the fact that several laws promote the development of individual students according to needs. In this chapter, we explore the federal laws governing quality and equity for youth with disabilities, such as those who are exiting school to enter a job or go to college. We describe what transition means, what it looks like, and how it is connected to standards-based reforms, including the assessments associated with those reforms. We also identify how you can make sure that students both meet their transition goals and improve their performances on district and state tests. This includes providing students with skills to attain their own independence and be masters of their own transitions.

Too Many Laws, Too Little Time

Over the past decade much has happened in the field of school-to-career, transition, and general career preparation. Most of the activity has revolved around federal laws that have made clear the rights of youth with disabilities to equitable participation in high-quality school-to-career systems. These laws fall into two basic categories. The first category includes career preparation laws, such as the School-to-Work Opportunities Act of 1994 and the Carl D. Perkins Vocational Technical Education Act of 1998. The second category includes civil rights laws such as Section 504 of the Rehabilitation Act of 1973, the Americans with Disabilities Act (ADA) of 1990, and the Individuals with Disabilities Education Act (IDEA), reauthorized in 1997.

Our purpose here is not to bore or overwhelm you with laws, laws, laws. Rather it is to make you aware of what exists and the driving forces behind the need to integrate vocational training programs and district accountability and assessment systems.

School-to-Work Opportunities Act of 1994

Also known as "school-to-work," this law was created to facilitate the development of programs that integrate school- and work-based learning, vocational and academic education, and secondary and postsecondary education. Its goal is to create quality school-to-career transition systems for students. Included in this act is the requirement that students meet the same academic standards set by the state for all students, and that schools adequately prepare students for postsecondary education.

The Carl D. Perkins Vocational and Technical Education Act of 1998

The purpose of this act is two-fold: (1) to integrate vocational and academic education so that students develop strong basic and advanced academic skills in a vocational setting, and (2) to assist students in understanding all the aspects of the industry they are studying and preparing to enter. The Perkins Act explicitly requires that students in vocational education programs be taught the same challenging academic standards and proficiencies that all other students are taught.

Section 504 of the Rehabilitation Act of 1973

This act prohibits discrimination on the basis of disability in federally funded programs. For school-aged students, this prohibits discrimination on the basis of race, national origin, and gender. Students who are limited in speaking English are also protected. The act requires educational agencies to take action to overcome language barriers that impede equal participation by students in instructional programs. A youth with a disability automatically qualifies under Section 504 and is also protected against discrimination.

The ADA of 1990

The most relevant part of this act in terms of transition is its prohibition of discrimination by public entities regardless of whether they receive federal funds. Such entities include state education agencies, local school districts, public technical schools, community colleges and four-year colleges and universities, as well as all other employment activities. The ADA specifically states:

> No qualified individual with a disability shall, by reason of such disability, be excluded from participation in or be denied the benefits of the services, programs, or activities of a public entity, or be subjected to discrimination by any such entity.

The IDEA 1997 Amendments

A close examination of the School-to-Work Act, the Perkins Act, Section 504, and the ADA reveals sketchy guidance on how to design accommodations, modifications, and support services needed to enable all students the opportunity for meaningful participation. IDEA goes much further than these other laws in providing guidance. IDEA provides a clear path for individualized planning and service design. The provisions of IDEA (evaluations, IEPs, transition planning and services) forge strong links for accomplishing what all the other laws require.

So Where to From Here?

We hope it is clear that the bar has been raised for vocational education and other transition programs. Its transformation into career development education infused with high expectations and strong academics is timely for today's standards-based reforms. For a very long time, vocational education and transition programs were seen as programs for low-track students considered unable to compete in general academics. In the same way, special education was deemed to be a program for the academically inferior, resulting in diluted curricula and little opportunity to develop higher order thinking skills or skills needed for higher education. Thus, students in both of these programs (vocational and special education) in the past often were channeled into poor quality programs because of, quite frankly, discriminatory assumptions about intelligence and disability. Contrary to the civil rights laws, the education of these students has been guided by low expectations simply because they have a disability.

The amended IDEA of 1997 is changing the tide of this past practice. It clearly indicates that students with disabilities must be given meaningful opportunities to acquire the knowledge and skills and to attain high academic standards expected of all students.

The Breakdown

All of these laws create a strong opportunity to ensure high expectations and quality outcomes for students with disabilities. By now, some of you are wondering how and where all these laws fit into the picture (or any picture for that matter). The big picture of this chapter is to reorganize efforts to integrate the transition needs of students with disabilities into assessment and accountability systems, and to use this as a basis for improving their performances.

Often a separation exists between special education and vocational or school-to-career programs within a school. IEP teams gather to plan a student's year. Beginning no later than age 14 (and younger if determined appropriate), a mandatory part of the IEP is to ready students for transitions into post-secondary environments. It is required that each student's IEP include a statement of needed transition services (see Box 8.1). As a part of the transition IEP, parents must be notified of the purpose of the meeting and be informed that the school is formally inviting the student and the public agency to which the student will be transitioning when leaving high school. Too often, however, it is common for this to happen without someone from a school-to-work program or a vocational program in attendance at the IEP meeting. Besides being out of compliance, people attending are usually unfamiliar with vocational programs, expectations, and curriculum. A required participant at every student's IEP is a school district representative who has both the expertise and knowledge about designing specialized instruction for students with disabilities. That means, for students who are at the age of transition planning, someone at the table must have knowledge about the district standards and requirements, as well as those needed for the environment or the vocation the student is being prepared to transition into.

BOX 8.1

Transition Services Defined

Transition services means a coordinated set of activities for a student with a disability, designed within an outcome-oriented process, that promotes movement from school to post-school activities including but not limited to post-secondary education, vocational training, integrated competitive employment (including supported employment), continuing and adult education, adult services, independent living, or community participation. The coordinated set of activities must be based on the individual student's needs, taking into account the student's preferences and interests, and shall include needed activities in the following areas: (1) instruction, (2) community experiences, (3) the development of employment and other post-school adult living objectives, and (4), if appropriate, the acquisition of daily living skills and functional vocational evaluation (34CFR 300.18).

This lack of cross-fertilization between environments and programs often results in IEP goals and objectives that are inappropriate or unrelated to those people who will ultimately be responsible for the implementation. The result can be that students are denied meaningful participation in educational programming and services, a big no-no! Without delving into the legal jargon, this in essence is a violation of Section 504, the ADA, and IDEA.

Issues Confronted When Transitioning From the Current Education System

Many issues have created the breakdown between school and vocational programs. These directly affect transition planning for students.

The Lack of Non-Academic Standards

An analysis of states' content standards quickly reveals two findings (1) many states lack vocational or career-oriented standards, and (2) although some states have non-academic standards, they don't necessarily emphasize or assess them. For the most part, states have focused on academic standards. Curricular frameworks developed by school districts follow the same suit but may be more likely to have some broad non-academic standards.

The Lack of Coherence Between General Education Programs and Vocational Programs

As noted earlier, it is not uncommon for students who attend vocational programs or are in need of vocational training to be seen as less capable students. School districts have not placed equal emphasis on vocational or career tracks in school programs. The general belief that these students are less capable of achieving the regular requirements has translated into less attention to quality programs and, in turn, less concern about student achievements within these programs. Therefore, little collaboration has occurred between vocational programs and school districts. This has resulted in districts not monitoring what students in these programs are actually learning and whether what they are learning is linked to what all students are expected to know and be able to do.

Everyone Is Going to College

The unrealistic or narrow perspective that all students should be going to college is another reason for the lack of coordination of programs. Look at any post-graduation statistics kept by school districts and you will find those that tout the percentage of graduates who entered institutions of higher education. Very few boast the numbers of students who went into apprenticeships or trades. An interesting statistic that is usually missing is one that shows how many students remain in post-secondary schools after one or two semesters of their freshman year. This statistic is just another indication of poor transition planning for students.

Lack of Linkages to Post-Secondary

In general, a lack of coordination and collaboration exists between secondary and post-secondary institutions of learning. Consider the number of students who enroll in post-secondary schools and are automatically slotted to take remedial classes for mathematics or English, another indication of the lack of collaboration between secondary and post-secondary institutions. Then think of the general complaint of the business community about the number of graduates who are unprepared to compete in the work force, yet another indication of poor communication. Nationally, very little ongoing communication takes place between either institution for the sake of improving programs and preparing students for their next environment, work or higher education. Is the picture becoming clearer?

The Lack of School District Accountability for Students Attending Vocational Programs

Out of sight is out of mind. Little accountability exists for what students learn in relation to the standards all students are required to meet. In addition, it has been these students who have been traditionally exempted or excluded from district assessments. Why should they take the assessments if they are attending different vocational schools or programs? The answer should be clear. These schools are required to meet the same standards as any other school. However, the general lack of collaboration between home schools and vocational programs has left a wide gap in accountability for all students.

We recognize that some of you may be in a state or school district that has addressed all these issues, but for the most part this is not common practice. With the changes in the recent laws, especially IDEA 1997, any student with a disability must be assessed and accounted for in the standards no matter where schooling takes place and no matter what program the student is enrolled in. If your state or school receives money from School-to-Work, the Perkins Act, and IDEA (which is most schools and states), then you are required under law to account for student learning and assess using the same assessments, regular or alternate, that all other students take.

A recent publication by the American Federation of Teachers (AFT) highlighted the need for dramatic improvements for students who traditionally have been left unprepared or ill-prepared by high school. The document made several recommendations for creating educational experiences that set the foundation for the future success of students:

- Provide all students with a strong academic foundation prior to high school regardless of their ability.
- Expose all secondary students to rigorous academic coursework in all core subjects, and remedial or general-level courses for non-college-bound students.
- Use effective engaging teaching methods with a heavy dose of applied learning.
- Expose students to the workplace. Reinforce and show the relevance of academic learning.
- Make the high school diploma count. Create incentives for students to study and achieve.
- Provide sustained, quality professional development.
- Evaluate program effectiveness on a regular basis. Use student achievement data.

According to the AFT, students, especially those not likely to be enrolled in rigorous college-prep programs, need to be provided with the opportunity to see the connection between their school learning and the jobs they hope to someday hold. Some students cannot see that far into the future, and this is all the more reason to provide lots of applied learning and experiences in the work of work.

What Role Do Transition Plans Have in All This?

Transition through school or out of school occurs regardless of whether there is good assessment or accountability. For a long time, educators were not required to document a plan for students' movement throughout school to a post-school environment of work, post-secondary education, or other activity. In fact, it is the poor post-school outcomes of students with disabilities, the lack of planning for the transition of these students, and the failure to define what the important outcomes of education are for these students that probably best explain why planning, assessment, and evaluation are so important during transition.

Before 1990, when transition plans were first required for all students with disabilities, transition was discussed almost exclusively in relation to students with low-incidence disabilities (such as significant cognitive delays or multiple disabilities). However, findings of poor post-school outcomes made it evident that students with learning disabilities were also having difficulties after completing school, with few graduates finding adequate employment or assuming adult responsibilities. In fact, these students were found to be among the most likely to leave school before graduating, joining the ranks of dropouts and leading to many questions about the appropriateness of secondary school programs for students with learning disabilities.

Regardless of the label or type of disability, it is now very clear that the traditional curriculum of basic skill remediation, while perhaps necessary, is not sufficient to prepare students to meet the challenges of society. Within the past decade, the concept of accountability has come to the forefront in education. It is critical that a transition plan include an assessment of both district/state standards and program effectiveness. In turn, evaluation of a transition program is also important. But program effectiveness. Is the student ready for the ultimate transition: entering the post-secondary community? Is the program doing what it was intended to do? How do we know? And how is it linked to the standards all students should know and be able to do?

Evaluation of Transition Programming

One of the most difficult steps in evaluating a program is deciding where to begin. This difficulty is actually two-fold (1) program instruction should align with the standards required of all students, and (2) the program should effectively meet the individualized goals of each student. Both aspects need to be assessed.

As discussed in Chapter 3, "Standards-Based Instruction: The Backbone of Educational Accountability," and Chapter 4, "Improving the Performance of Students in the Alternate Assessment," states and districts are examining standards, especially in light of the federal requirement for the alternate assessment. Part of evaluating a transition plan is examining the extent to which a student's IEP goals and objectives align with standards identified as important for students to know and be able to do. In some states, standards are the same for all students. In others, standards have been expanded or bridged to include students with significant cognitive disabilities.

Throughout the evaluation of transition programs, never lose sight of what the process is about—preparing an individual student for high school exit. Although it is important to be sure students are working toward standards that are aligned with the standards for all, it is critical to plan for the success of each student. Based on the current levels of performance and future goals, planning for transition should remain focused on the individual student's needs. When evaluating transition programs, it is important to evaluate for the integration of an aligned program of instruction that reflects the strengths and needs of individual students.

Creating Seamless Transitions

Most people think of transition services primarily for students with more significant disabilities, but the law indicates transition services must be planned for all students with IEPs. Since students with disabilities are individual and unique, so should transition plans be individualized and unique. Although the law indicates transition planning should begin no later than age 14, some states start preplanning or screening as early as age 12. Not only do age requirements vary state to state, so do the levels and kinds of assessments. Regardless of the specific requirements, in order to maximize planning and available instructional time, instructional content and activities need to be coordinated among elementary, middle, and secondary programs.

Between-School Transitions

If you are a classroom teacher, you know this scenario only too well. It happens at transition points when students move from preschool to kindergarten, elementary to middle school, and middle school to high school. It is common for these students to show up with IEPs that do not reflect the new environment. Although IEPs may meet individual goals, they aren't necessarily connected to the standards that are required. When this happens, IEP addendum meetings must be held, and goals and objectives must be rewritten or added. Valuable instructional time may be lost while folks figure out what the student needs to be learning that aligns with district standards.

The way to avoid this is simple—hold transition IEPs. When students are moving from elementary to middle school, it makes sense that someone from the middle school attend the IEP meeting. Alternatively, middle school and elementary school special education teachers can meet to mutually communicate and familiarize themselves with the IEP process and, more importantly, with the standards and curriculum. Elementary teachers can share what they have taught and write IEPs that will reflect the next learning environment of middle school. In the same manner, middle school teachers can learn a lot about their new students and begin forward thinking for the upcoming school year.

Within-School Transitions

Consideration must be given to the level of support a student needs in both current and future environments. For example, a student with a learning disability or speech/language impairment may require a different level of assessment and a different planning timeline than a student with a moderate or more significant disability. Post-school environments (social, vocational, community, employment, and education) will vary from student to student regardless of skill and ability. Therefore, it is important to assess not only the vocational programs students may be participating in currently and in the future, but also the linkages between district and state standards.

For example, Jordan is a student working at a local cafe as a dishwasher kitchen aide. What standards is Jordan working on? How are these standards integrated into his current vocational setting? How do we know this job site is working for Jordan? Who is evaluating program effectiveness?

Then there is Julie, soon to be an incoming freshman at a community college, who has mobility needs. Julie needs to know how to use the city bus line including where to get the bus, transfer, what to do if she misses her bus. How is Julie being prepared for this post-secondary school environment? Is it reflected in transition plans? It should be! It can be as simple as Box 8.2.

The notion of conducting an evaluation of the planning process may seem monumental, but then so was the idea of transition when it was first required. Unfortunately, despite the need for evaluation, especially evaluation of the transition planning process, efforts to conduct such evaluations have not been done, unless conducted in response to compliance requests. We continually need to be able to answer the following questions:

BOX 8.2

Planning Inventory for Campus Mobility Skill

---

1.   **Yes**   **No**   **Needs Improvement**

   Julie can use the city bus line to get to campus with minimal assistance.

2.   **Yes**   **No**   **Needs Improvement**

   Julie is able to obtain exact change for her round-trip bus fare.

3.   **Yes**   **No**   **Needs Improvement**

   Julie knows how to dress appropriately for inclimate weather in anticipation of waiting at the bus stop.

4.   **Yes**   **No**   **Needs Improvement**

   Julie is able to read a city bus line schedule in order to catch the bus from home or campus at varying times throughout any given day.

5.   **Yes**   **No**   **Needs Improvement**

   In the event Julie misses the bus, she can read the bus schedule for the next bus time.

- How do we know whether community-based instruction and mobility training has led to productive employment and on-time arrival at the job site or other setting?
- How do we know whether students indeed have learned to advocate for themselves and make their needs known in a post-secondary setting?

The bottom line is that we need to evaluate whether instruction is producing the results we said or thought it would, and we need to do this for individual students.

Several principles should be kept in mind when beginning to plan for an evaluation of the transition process:

- Evaluate only a few indicators of quality at a time.
- Examine linkages between standards and programs. Are there connections? Do instructional programs and planned experiences incorporate standards defined for all students?
- Collect information from all those involved; the student, parents, teachers, agency personnel, and administration. What are their per-

ceptions of the program? What do they know about student outcomes for programming?

- Examine how transition students are included in district and state assessments? What are these decisions based on?

Back to Jordan, the student dishwasher kitchen aide. How can we be sure he is learning the skills he needs to be successful in his next environment. Are we evaluating to see whether he is developing independent skills? How much prompting or guidance does he require? Has there been growth, moving from many to fewer prompts or reminders? We have another simple way to check for student performance (see Box 8.3). The results of the observations of Jordan provide evaluative data directly related to whether he is progressing toward his transition goals and whether instruction and the opportunity to learn are improving his achievement.

Transition planning is good for all students, whether they are in general education or special education programs. For many, leaving one environment and entering the next is not a natural transition. Many unknowns must be dealt with. Just as every student could have an IEP, so should they have transition plans. For example, many students, like Marla, could use coaching on interpersonal skills that will generalize to different settings and situations. A transition goal for her could include the following:

- Marla will correctly use the appropriate tone of voice (not too loud, not too soft) when addressing an adult, 100 percent of the time.

- Marla will speak using correct grammar, free of slang, when addressing customers, 100 percent of the time.

Among other skills that Marla needs, these are the ones that she needs to work on most intensely. These objectives can be monitored in the school environment as well as the work environment by using a simple observation checklist (see Box 8.4).

Since transition planning is a process that takes place over several years, we suggest that both formative and summative evaluations be considered. For example, some areas of informal or formative assessment could include the following:

- What do the student's parents, guardians, or other significant family members think about the transition process? Do they see the transition goals and objectives as being on the right track? What are these perceptions based on?

- What suggestions or feedback do these folks and teachers have about the progress the student is making toward the identified outcomes?

BOX 8.3

Observation Checklist for Jordan's Kitchen Aide Position

Name: Jordan   **Job Site:** Fred's Fishery/Kitchen

Date/Time: November 18

Outcome Objective: Upon arrival to job site, Jordan will perform the following skills independently with 100 percent accuracy for no less than three consecutive observations.

Skills performed as follows: **M**-model, **V**-verbal, **I**-independently	Date of Observation	Date of Observation	Date of Observation
1. Greets coworkers			
2. Hangs coat			
3. Punches in			
4. Locates and adorns apron			
5. Checks dish room for dirty dishes			
6. Loads dirty dishes			
7. Rinses off with sprayer			
8. Pushes through machine			
9. Stacks clean dishes			
10. Checks pot area			
11. Washes dirty pots			
12. Stacks pots to dry			
13. Continues with #6-13 until complete			
14. Checks with boss for other duties			
15. Takes 15-minute break when directed			

- What does the student think (what a concept — ask the student!)? How are the transition plan and goals working for the student? What suggestions or input can the student offer?

BOX 8.4

Marla's Communication Skills Checklist

Name: Marla				Setting: School Library

Area: Communication Skills

Interpersonal Skills

A	B	C	D	**1.** Tone of voice age appropriate, not too loud, not too soft
A	B	C	D	**2.** Establishes eye contact when speaking
A	B	C	D	**3.** Spoken grammar is free of slang and profanity
A	B	C	D	**4.** Listens to questions/directions and follows through with request

A = Outstanding
B = Satisfactory
C = Marginal
D = Not Satisfactory

Post-School Transitions

When students age-out, graduate, or leave, more formal or summative questions need to be asked. Ask the student how the transition planning process worked. Did it help prepare him or her? Follow-up to find out how students have adjusted to their targeted post-secondary school settings. What are the indicators of success? What are the indicators or areas of difficulty?

It is critical to keep track of these summative evaluations. They provide valuable information for proactive planning for other students who may be headed for similar transition experiences. We certainly want to avoid information that comes too late. So evaluate early and in an ongoing manner.

The evaluation questions are endless. We recognize that the nature and scope of individual students' transition plans will vary substantially. Ongoing evaluations of the overall transition planning process is the key to improving student performance. Assessment data should drive instruction. The two are inextricably linked. The process of collaboration, assessment, planning, and the development of transition goals and objectives for any student will most likely follow a similar routine. It is the format or framework for transition planning and the transition plans themselves that require evaluation. Is it effective? How do you know? Does it allow for the best possible transition planning for each student? If not, what needs to change?

IDEA, among other laws, has provided students and educators with the responsible mandate of transition planning for post-school life. We encourage you to think of evaluation of the transition process as more than an externally mandated activity. The notion of evaluation goes well beyond the issue of legal compliance. It provides us with an avenue toward improving the performance of students. We have some data about how students do once they leave high school; it has been nothing to write home about. It is imperative that we continually evaluate whether the transition-planning process meets the needs of students and that we are providing them the instruction and support to meet their intended outcomes.

Transition and Diploma Options

With some educational reforms has come a new emphasis on making sure that students know what they should know before moving on. Graduation from high school has become a high-stakes event. Depending on your state, graduation may include specific course requirements and successfully passing a graduation assessment. Actually, several assessments will be important for some students with disabilities. The transition age assessments are used to verify the successful completion of programs, determine acceptance into new programs, and certify the attainment of skills needed for some jobs. Perhaps the most common assessments in which transition age students with disabilities participate are as follows:

- Graduation or GED exams

- Entrance exams

- Certification exams

How are your students being prepared for these exams? Is preparation part of students' transition plans?

The type of high-stakes exam that is probably most familiar to you and your students is the graduation exam. To date, more than 20 states require students to earn both course credits and pass a graduation exam. These states have taken a variety of approaches to diploma options. In addition to the standard diploma, some of these states provide a certificate of attendance, while others provide an IEP diploma. Yet other states provide additional honors diplomas and other special diplomas (such as occupational, GED, and career readiness). In general, four basic options exist for awarding diplomas. Each has its own advantages and disadvantages (see Box 8.5)

We bring this information to your attention because improving student performance and thorough transition planning may have a significant impact on your students. If you are in a state where students must meet course requirements to graduate, it will be imperative to be sure students are working toward the standards needed to pass these courses and the

BOX 8.5

Advantages and Disadvantages of Four Diploma Types

Diploma Options	Advantages	Disadvantages
Standard Diploma. It is available to all students with or without disabilities. Must meet the same requirements for earning the diploma.	▪ Familiar to post-secondary institutions or employers ▪ Clear meaning due to one set of criteria	▪ Does not consider different learning styles of students with disabilities ▪ Can result in significant numbers of students not receiving any kind of exit document from high school
Standard Diploma, Multiple Criteria. Students with disabilities are allowed to meet requirements for the standard diploma in ways different from other students (different courses, meeting IEP goals).	▪ Recognizes differences in students' learning styles and skills that may not align with set criteria ▪ Enables more students to receive a diploma than would a single set of criteria	▪ More variability in student knowledge and skills leaving school ▪ Creates a non-standard set of knowledge and skills among students receiving the same diploma
Completion Options. They are certificates of attendance, completion, achievement, attainment, etc. Requirements vary considerably.	▪ Upholds the integrity and meaning of the standard diploma ▪ Creates other exit options for students unable to meet standard diploma requirements	▪ Little knowledge or evidence about students' knowledge and preparedness for post-secondary schooling or employment
Special Education Diploma. It is a certificate available for students with IEPs. This diploma is usually in addition to options available for non-IEP students.	▪ Aligns curriculum and skills with different or expanded standards for students with more significant disabilities	▪ Makes known those students receiving special education services

SOURCE: Reprinted with permission from the National Center on Educational Outcomes

end-of-course exams attached to them. If you are in a state that requires both course requirements and passing a graduation exam, then it should be very clear what you will need to do to ready your students for T-day (test day). Finding ways to improve student performance becomes very clear when stakes are attached to them. Unfortunately, it shouldn't be so. We should strive to push students to all they are capable of, regardless whether high stakes are attached.

Making Connections among Standards, Transition Plans, and Accountability Systems

It all starts with standards. The current of the connection is directly wired to the standards that all students should know and be able to do. Regardless of the disability, program, or post-secondary school plans, students' IEPs must reflect the identified district or state standards. Only then can we begin to narrow the divide between vocational programs or special education programs and accountability for all students. The problem causing a disconnection is the general lack of knowledge both special educators and vocational program educators have about the standards. This is not to point fingers or place blame, but to elevate a need. The importance of standards and students with disabilities has come to the forefront since IDEA 1997. The reality is that states and districts have already written both content and performance standards and have trained teachers and administrators on them. Sadly, most of this development and training did not include special educators.

Being the bright capable professionals they are, special educators are now jumping on the standards wagon, not because of IDEA, but because it is good for kids. The bottom line is that special educators must get caught up to speed on the standards, and then impart this knowledge to people in vocational programs so that students' IEPs reflect them. This is a relatively easy thing to do. Remember our backmapping discussion in Chapter 3? The same process can be used here. Identify the areas of need and link them to the standards. Then map out the instruction needed for the student to meet the objectives. Your assessment should reflect the cognitive level you instructed (e.g., Bloom's Taxonomy).

You may also want to review Chapter 4 on alternate assessments. You may find it easier to identify domains for students and then back fill them with standards that have been developed for all students. You may also find the need to expand some of the standards to fit the needs of some of your students. Once the domains are filled, you can write IEP goals and objectives directly linked to standards. The nature of transition needs for some students may require the consideration of a special set of vocationally based standards. As we have mentioned previously, many states lack these standards or have them but don't assess them. So dig around; you may be surprised what you'll find. For many of our students, these standards will be the meat of their transition plans.

Share the district standards with vocational program members, community agencies, and employers. Be sure they are aware that students are on a diet of standards and are working with purpose. Once these people become more knowledgeable about the standards and/or domains, it will become that much easier to integrate them into transition plans that make sense for everyone—the student, the parent/guardian, the employer, and those evaluating student performance.

Now you are ready to decide what assessment the student will participate in. Based on the ultimate outcome of schooling, the IEP team must decide whether the student will take the regular assessment or the alternate assessment. Remember the decision generally is based on the severity of the disability in addition to the course of study, such as regular courses versus life-skill curriculum (see Chapter 4 for a review). In some states and districts, however, the criteria are different, so know what these criteria say. Always include students in these decisions since they often are capable of providing valuable input on their current program as well as their future.

Creating Student-Centered Transition Programs

The key to success for students working on transition plans is teaching them self-determination throughout their school life. Students can and must be taught to take responsibility for their educational experiences and post-school lives that hinge on independence. Never forget, as early as kindergarten, students can be taught and learn how to set goals, solve problems, and make decisions. They are able to learn to work with their own unique learning characteristics. Therefore, it is really important that students be a part of the IEP process, participating and even directing their IEP process. Students need to be provided the opportunity to explore the career options they would like, work with mentors, and prepare for postsecondary schooling if appropriate. Involvement is empowerment.

It is also critical to involve family and other supporters in the transition planning process. While students work on developing needed skills for post-high school life, family involvement and empowerment must not be overlooked. These elements are important for helping students advocate for their involvement and participation in agencies. Families can help find agencies that have similar philosophies and approaches for developing a student's independence.

Teaching students responsibility for their future and current learning environments should be integrated into IEPs. Strategies such as having students set goals based on their understanding of their interests and limits, as well as breaking down goals into smaller pieces or tasks to be obtained over a period of days or weeks, are effective in teaching students responsibility and self-determination (see Box 8.6). Holding frequent evaluative meetings with teachers or employers provides students the opportunity to process and monitor their progress and revise as necessary. After all, this is about readying students for life.

BOX 8.6

Problem-Solving: Just Do It!

D	Define the problem I am faced with.
O	Outline and think out my options.
I	Identify the outcome of each option.
T	Take action.
!	Get excited about your effort and perseverance!

SOURCE: Adapted from Kohler (1998)

Be sure students understand their disabilities and the gifts they have. Empowering students to self-advocate is a lofty but necessary goal for most students (see Box 8.7). Here we want students to be able to ask for assistance and accommodations they know they need without hesitation or embarrassment. Connecting students with disability networks allows them the choice and opportunity to find support and peers to socialize with.

Expecting youth with disabilities to emerge from high school ready to fly on their own may in itself be unrealistic. Training and family networks are critical to the success of students' transition through school and out of school. For many students, parents/guardians will need to start early in making arrangements and finding future funders or support for students. Nothing replaces student-centered transition planning. So start early, be thorough, communicate, and collaborate with all parties involved—students, parents/guardians, employers, post-secondary institutions, and state agencies.

BOX 8.7

A Self-Advocacy Plan: I PLAN

I	Inventory my strengths, my areas to improve or learn, and my goals for learning and accommodation.
P	Provide the results of my inventory.
L	Listen and respond to feedback.
A	Ask lots of questions.
N	Name my goals.

SOURCE: Adapted from Kohler (1998)

Summary

We hope we have made it very clear throughout this book that students with disabilities need to participate in district and state assessments and be accounted for the systems that use the results of those assessments. And, yes, this includes students taking courses in vocational programs. Whether students are spending part of their day at a job site or taking career development classes on the school campus, these courses must be linked to the standards for all.

Transition planning will look and sound different for different students. The premise must remain the same—meeting the needs of students with disabilities while providing them access to the general curriculum with needed accommodations. One of the first steps in transition planning is making sure all parties involved are aware of the standards and how they will be assessed for each student. Some students will participate in the regular assessment and others the alternate assessment. Regardless, students' performances must be accounted for. Results must be used to drive instructional and program improvement. How else will we know whether the instruction and transition plans we have in place will work to improve the performance of students with disabilities?

Test Your Knowledge

So how did you do? Try your skill below.

1. At least _____ laws address youth with disabilities and vocational programs.

2. Transition plans must be addressed on students' IEPs beginning no later than age _____.

3. Many states lack _____ standards.

4. Historically, there has been a lack of collaboration between school districts and _____ programs.

5. There has been a lack of _____ for students attending vocational programs.

6. Poor post-school outcomes are documented for both low incidence and students with _____ _____.

7. It is critical to _____ whether or not a student's transition plan is doing what it is intended to do.

8. Making the connection: It all starts with _____.

9. Teaching students _____ for their future and current learning environments should be integrated into IEPs.

10. Training and family networks are critical to the success of a student's _____.

Answers

1. five (p. 151–152)
2. fourteen (p. 153)
3. vocational or career-oriented (p. 154)
4. vocational (p. 155)
5. accountability (p. 156)
6. learning disabilities (p. 157)
7. evaluate (p. 157)
8. standards (p. 158)
9. responsibility (p. 167)
10. transition (p. 167)

Resources

American Federation of Teachers (1999). *Reaching the Next Step: How School to Career Can Help Students Reach High Academic Standards and Prepare for Good Jobs.* Washington, DC: AFT.

Center for Law and Education. *Ensuring Access, Equity, and Quality for Students with Disabilities in School-to-Work Systems* (1999). National Transition Network. Minneapolis, MN: University of Minnesota.

Council for Exceptional Children (1999). Student-centered transition programs critical for post-school success. *Today,* 6(3), 1–15.

Eaton, H. (1996). *Self-Advocacy: How Students with Learning Disabilities Can Make the Transition from High School to College.* Santa Barbara, CA: Excel Publishing.

Guy, B., H. Shin, S. Lee, and M. Thurlow (1999). *State Graduation Requirements for Students with and Without Disabilities (Technical Report 21).* Minneapolis, MN: University of Minnesota, National Center on Educational Outcomes.

Kohler, P. (1998). "Implementing a Transition Perspective of Education: A Comprehensive Approach to Planning and Delivering Secondary Education and Transition Services," in *Beyond High School: Transition from High School to Work,* edited by F.R. Rusch and J. Chadsey. Bristol, PA: Taylor and Francis.

Thurlow, M. and J. Elliott (1998). "Student Assessment and Evaluation," in *Beyond High School: Transition from High School to Work,* edited by F.R. Rusch and J. Chadsey. Bristol, PA: Taylor and Francis.

Thrulow, M. and S. Thompson (1999). *Diploma Options and Graduation Policies for Students with Disabilities (Policy Directions 10).* Minneapolis, MN: University of Minnesota, National Center on Educational Outcomes.

Wehmeyer, M. (1998). "Student Involvement in Transition-Planning and Transition-Program Implementation," in *Beyond High School: Transition from High School to Work*, edited by F.R. Rusch and J. Chadsey. Bristol, PA: Taylor and Francis.

Internet Resources

American Federation of Teachers: http://www.aft.org

Institute on Community Integration: http://www.ici.coled.umn.edu/ici

National Transition Alliance for Youth with Disabilities: http://www.dssc.org/nta

National Transition Network: http://ici2.coled.umn.edu/ntn

Transition Research Institute: http://www.ed.uiuc.edu/sped/tri/institute

Instruction: The Bottom Line in Improving Test Performance

" . . . perhaps there are teachers who think they have done a good day's teaching irrespective of what pupils have learned."

—John Dewey, 1933

"Good teaching is good teaching. There are no boundaries or borders in which it can occur."

—Bob Algozzine

Hot Button Issues

- Can all students really learn?
- Why are states and districts reducing the numbers of days allotted to professional development opportunities at a time they are needed most?
- If we take credit for our successful students, who takes credit for the unsuccessful ones?
- What really works for teaching diverse learners in our classrooms?
- How can I be sure students are learning and making real progress in the curriculum?

Does instruction really matter or do we just drive all kids through the curriculum and hope for the best? In this chapter, we will take a close look at where instruction fits in the national push for accountability and assessment. We will also look at what instruction should look like in order to improve student performance and, more importantly, to insure that students learn.

In late 1980, the business community and post-secondary institutions of learning hoisted a flag. They announced that they were tired of receiving high school graduates who were unable to compete in the global work force or to go to college without first receiving remedial coursework. In fact, high school graduates could not always read or complete simple math. The Business Roundtable was a group that made public its grave concern over the quality of the education of students in America's schools. Business corporations started conducting academic boot camps in an effort to raise the basic skills of new hires. Many consider the actions of the business community, in general, a major push behind public discussion and national concern over academic accountability.

At a specially convened meeting in 1989, the nation's governors and the U.S. president together agreed upon six education goals. Reworked into eight education goals by Congress, they became a major piece of legislation in 1994 known as Goals 2000: Educate America Act. During the development of the law, national groups began to gather to establish standards in major areas such as mathematics, social studies, and science. Many of these national standards served as guideposts for beginning the task of establishing content standards for states and districts.

Where the Rubber Meets the Road

" . . . Perhaps there are teachers who think they have done a good day's teaching irrespective of what pupils have learned." "I represent that remark," thousands of teacher's could answer. Those of us who have taught many students want credit for our successful students, but not for unsuccessful ones. After all, teaching is hard work and on top of that many students come to school from broken homes and low socioeconomic backgrounds. Yet other students who come to school may be chemically dependent or are in other psychological states that are not conducive to learning. Still others have not mastered fundamental skills or have poor or nonexistent work habits. The reasons (and excuses) for unsuccessful learners, in other words, are not hard to find.

However, we know more about teaching, and about how to teach special needs and at risk students, than ever before. Yet many teachers are not aware of this knowledge. Even more tragic, this knowledge and years of extensive research about what works for kids is not always present or apparent in classrooms. How many of you know of teachers who "babysit" their students or give them little work or only easy work to do? This can happen for lots of reasons. One of the most prevalent reasons is the level of expectation (or the lack thereof). We are talking of those folks who really believe that students with special needs can't learn what other kids are learning. And we must point out that this belief is prevalent in both general and special educator camps.

Consider this scenario: a special education teacher was at the school building's copy machine, making copies of pages from the Grade 9 Algebra book (of course, this was because she had no books for her students!). A general education teacher looked over her shoulder and said "*Your* kids can do that?" We bet this sounds remotely familiar to some of you and needs little elaboration.

Over the past 25 years, since the inception of landmark special education law, educators have created a dual system of teaching: one for general students and another for special education students. Although many thought a separation seemed appropriate given the diversity and differences between general and special education students, professionals, parents, and students have come to know only too well the unanticipated outcomes of such a system. For the most part, society has done a good job educating students with special needs. Take a minute and think about the curriculum and materials used in special education classrooms. We bet you, like most educators, especially special educators, immediately said to yourself "What curriculum? What materials?"

With today's push for accountability and assessment, one would think the curriculum and materials issues would be a situation of the past. More than ever before, the use of effective instruction connected to standards, curricular frameworks, and aligned assessments is vital to maximizing the performance of all students, including students with special needs.

What Do We Know about Current Student Assessment Practices?

In most cases, when a student does not progress through the curriculum at the expected rate, the child is placed under a microscope. That is, the student is usually referred for psycho-educational evaluation that almost always focuses upon what skills the student lacks. Seldom does the evaluation examine classroom factors that may in fact be directly linked to the student's lack of progress. What is often missing is evaluation of the instructional environment. Variables that are explored in such an analysis are those known to be directly related to academic success, such as academic engaged time, opportunities to respond, teacher presentation style, teacher-student monitoring procedures, academic learning time, and teacher expectations, to name of few. Without a comprehensive evaluation of the student within the context of the instructional environment, it is often impossible to validly indicate the real cause of poor student progress.

Teachers today are expected to raise the test scores of an increasingly diverse group of students, teach huge amounts of content, and manage a wide range of disruptive behaviors with limited resources. Teachers don't always act upon what they know. They are working in an educational system where time is the constant and learning is the variable. Think about it. Students either get it or they don't. They are tested and results reported. They either pass a test or benchmark or they don't. In high-stakes systems, failure may mean students aren't promoted to the next grade, or they don't graduate. In low-stakes systems, scores are simply reviewed and documented in student files. This raises serious questions about assessment and accountability systems. Do we really believe and support the notion of "all students learning to high standards?"

Preparing for Instruction: The Planning Pyramid

Teaching is complex. Teachers make thousands of decisions everyday. (No wonder you drag yourself home every night!) Deciding what to teach and how to teach for each student makes teachers' jobs even more tricky. Consider the basic components of the instructional planning pyramid. There are lots of ways to think about instruction. Not all of them lead to structured, thorough planning. Introduced by Schumm, Vaughn and Leavell (1994), the concept of a pyramid provides a visualization of the context, topic, and instructional practices that are needed by students (see Box 9.1). It also enables you to consider the information or curriculum that all students should learn, what most students will learn, and what some students will learn.

One of the strengths of the pyramid is that it provides a way to think of instruction within the context of students' abilities. That is, some students will naturally need extensions or more in-depth coverage of topics. And there will be others who will work to learn the basic elements of a concept or strategy.

Whether a student learns at the base, middle, or top of the pyramid is not determined by a student's ability. Unlike some current practices where students with disabilities are sentenced to a particular curriculum or set of teaching methodologies, the instructional planning pyramid takes into consideration a student's prior knowledge. That is, student's skills and interests will vary by the topic introduced. For example, some of us are more excited than others to learn algebraic equations, biophysics, or mythology. In the same manner, students' interests will influence their excitement and ease with which they learn topics. Knowing this can help you plan your instruction differently. The context is also important. Consider learning mythology on the steps of one of the ruins in Greece. That could make it at least tolerable, don't you think? In the same manner, students need a context of where and how the learning will be important and useful. Context matters. Instructional practices should reflect the student, topic, and context of instruction. Thus we offer some orienting questions for use with the planning pyramid concept (see Box 9.2).

The instructional planning pyramid is just one way to look at the breadth and depth of what you teach and its relevance for all students. It is important that you decide the bottom line for all students. What do you expect all students to master? Most? Some?

BOX 9.1

Components of the Instructional Planning Pyramid

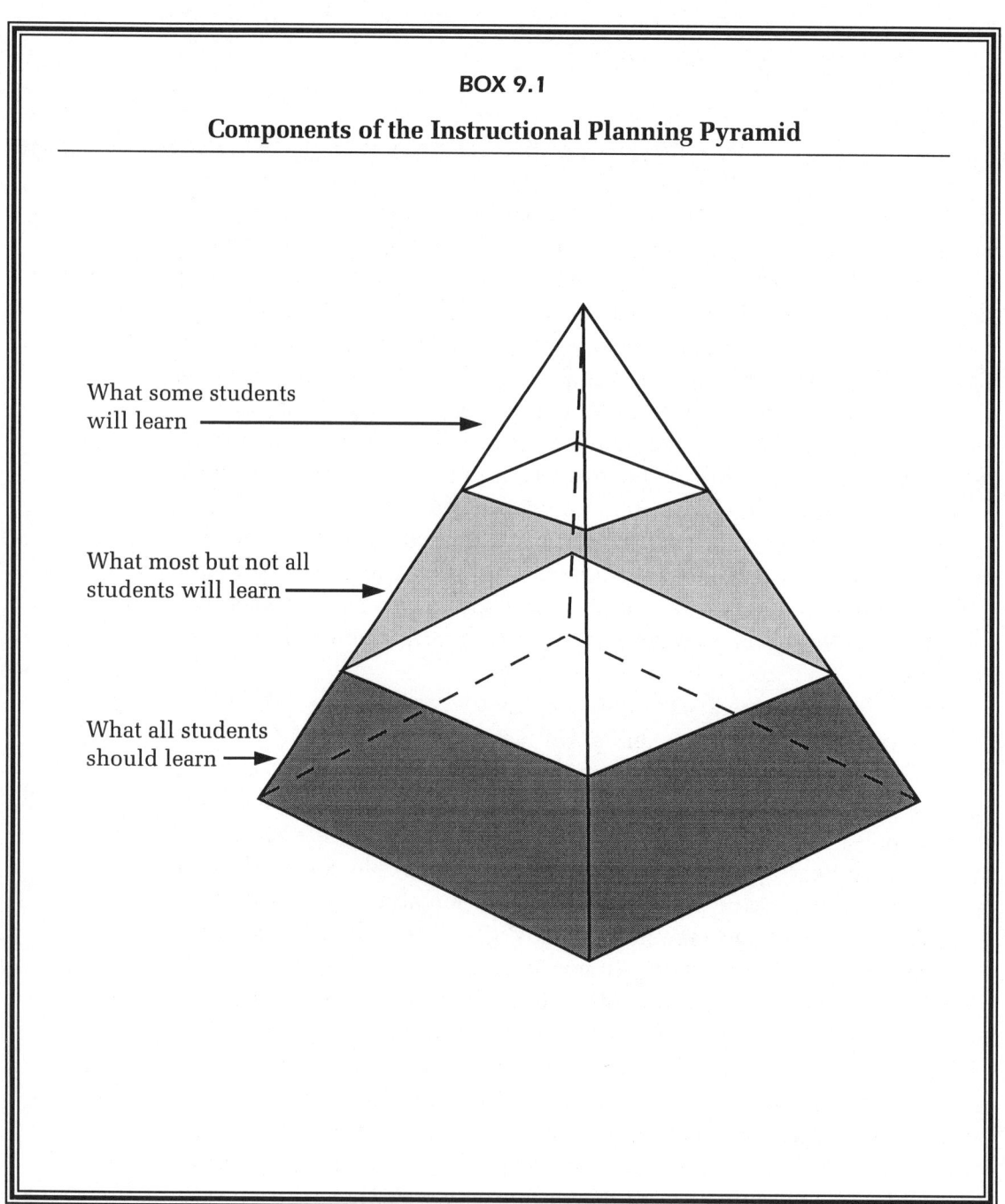

What some students will learn

What most but not all students will learn

What all students should learn

BOX 9.2

Guiding Questions for the Instructional Planning Pyramid

The following questions can be used in a self-questioning process to guide decision-making when considering topics of instruction, readiness to teach the material, and student readiness to receive the instruction.

Questions Pertaining to the Topic

- Is the material new or review?
- What prior knowledge do students have of this topic?
- How interesting is the topic to individual students? To me?
- How many new concepts are introduced?
- How complex are the new concepts?
- How clearly are concepts presented in the textbook?
- How can this material be connected to previous instruction? Can it?
- How important is this topic or parts of the topic for students to learn?

Questions Pertaining to the Teacher

- Have I taught this material before?
- How can I evaluate whether students are learning what I am teaching?
- How interesting is the topic to students? To me?
- How can students' cultural and linguistic backgrounds be connected to the topic?
- How much time do I have to plan for the unit and individual lessons?
- What resources do I have available to me for this unit?

Questions Pertaining to Students

- Will students' communication skills make comprehension of a particular topic or concept difficult?
- Will students with reading difficulties be able to work independently while learning about the concept from the text?
- Will a student with behavior or attention problems be able to concentrate on this material?
- Which students will likely have high interest in or prior knowledge of this concept or be anxious to explore this topic in greater breadth and depth?
- What experiences have the students had that will relate to this concept?
- Is there some way to relate this concept to the cultural and linguistic backgrounds of the students?

What Do We Know about Effective Instruction?

Research on effective instruction has been going on for years. Most of this research focuses on general education settings. This research, over the years, has delineated a plethora of variables correlated with sound instruction practice (see Box 9.3).

Improving Student Performance: A Model of Effective Instruction

In order to maximize student learning and achievement, we believe you must first delve into instructional practices. In this section we provide a research-based model of effective instruction that emphasizes principles, strategies, and tactics. A practical model presented by Algozzine and Ysseldyke (1992) includes four components on how to plan, manage, deliver, and evaluate instruction in the classroom. Note that for each component there is a set of empirically demonstrated principles and strategies of effective instruction (see Box 9.4).

In this section, we outline each of the four components and corresponding principles. For each principle we have a THINK ABOUT IT box. This box is just one of the many ways this model can be used to deliver valuable techniques and tactics to the classroom for the improvement of student learning. For more information about strategies and tactics for effective instruction, see the Resources section at the end of the chapter.

BOX 9.3

Some Research-Based Findings on Characteristics of Effective Instruction

---

Levine and Lazotte (1990) identified research-based characteristics of effective schools. The following list is their delineation for the characteristic "Effective Instructional Arrangements and Implementation."

- Successful grouping and related organizational arrangements
- Appropriate pacing and alignment
- Active/enriched learning
- Effective teaching practices
- Emphasis on higher order learning in assessing instructional outcomes
- Coordination in curriculum and instruction
- Easy availability of abundant, appropriate instructional materials
- Classroom adaptation
- Stealing time for reading, language, and math

BOX 9.4

Components of Effective Instruction

Planning instruction	The degree to which teaching goals and teacher expectations for student performance and success are stated clearly and are understood by the student.
Managing instruction	The degree to which classroom management is effective and efficient. The degree to which there is a sense of positiveness in the school environment.
Delivering instruction	The degree to which there is an appropriate instructional match. The degree to which lessons are presented clearly and follow specific instructional procedures. The degree to which instructional support is provided for the individual student. The degree to which sufficient time is allocated to academics and instructional time is used efficiently. The degree to which the student's opportunity to respond is high.
Evaluating instruction	The degree to which the teacher actively monitors student progress and understanding. The degree to which student performance is evaluated appropriately and frequently.

SOURCE: Reprinted with permission from Sopris West, Inc. Algozzine and Ysseldyke, 1992

Planning Instruction

Principles

- Decide what to teach
- Decide how to teach
- Communicate realistic expectations

Seems reasonable and simple doesn't it? Planning for instruction is the backbone of effective instruction; the rest follows. You need to know what to teach in order to plan. A great place to start is the standards and curricular frameworks established by your district and/or state. Guess what? Instructional results are better when instruction is planned. As previously mentioned, one of the characteristics of **norm-referenced tests** (NRT) is the lack of overlap in what is taught and what is tested (the overlap has been estimated to be approximately 20 percent). Although many states now use standards-based assessments, most still also use NRTs. One sure way to plan for the ultimate fruits of instructional labor (fall and spring testing) is to examine the scope and sequence of the test and decide what must be instructed and with what kinds of emphasis. (see Chapter 3, "Standards-Based Instruction: The Backbone of Educational Accountability," for a discussion of backmapping). Three principles for effective planning exist: Deciding what to teach, deciding how to teach, and communicating realistic expectations (cf. Algozzine and Ysseldyke, 1992; Algozzine, Ysseldyke, and Elliott, 1997).

Deciding what to teach In deciding what to teach, teachers must have a firm grasp on the scope and sequence of the curriculum and skills needed to demonstrate proficiency or mastery of the content material. Effective educators accomplish this by working to match the students' level of skill development with the level of instruction. Be sure to look at beginning, middle, and end of the tasks for the hierarchy of skills, if any, needed to complete them. In addition, it is also important to take into consideration the need for instructional accommodation. Organization of the instructional environment is also important and includes things like the physical layout of the classroom, peer interactions, instructional grouping arrangements, and the like. The goal of deciding what to teach is accurately determining the appropriate content to present, matching the students' instructional levels and using high expectations to guide learning and teaching (cf. Algozzine and Ysseldyke, 1992; Algozzine, Ysseldyke, and Elliott, 1997). Think about it (see Box 9.5).

Deciding how to teach Teaching can be an experimental process. Teaching students involves gathering data or information on the kinds of things that do and do not work. Deciding how to teach involves making educated guesses about what might work with some students. Although many methods are touted as the "best" way to teach, not everything works for every student. What we do know is basic elements exist for preparing how to teach. They include setting instructional goals, selecting methods and materials, determining the pace of instruction, and deciding how student participation and performance will be monitored. The goal of deciding how to teach is finding the best way to present desired and/or required instructional content teaching (cf. Algozzine and Ysseldyke, 1992; Algozzine, Ysseldyke, and Elliott, 1997). Think about it (see Box 9.6).

Communicating realistic expectations Expectations for success must be clearly communicated. Set them high, but be sure they are attainable. Think about a time you enrolled in a graduate class. What was the first thing you were interested in? If you are like most people, you said the course syllabus. Most graduate students want to know how to get an "A", whether there will be a final or midterm, and so on. Things are no different for students in

BOX 9.5

Deciding What to Teach: Think about It

- Prioritizing standards
- Starting with skills that are needed to learn other skills
- Identifying types of knowledge needed and teaching all of them

The breadth and depth of a curriculum can be overwhelming when you think about the actual number of days of instruction within which learning must occur. Given this reality, it is critical to prioritize those standards and skills students need to acquire. Give top priority to those skills that are hierarchical in nature, those that are needed and essential to the performance of more complex skills.

Three basic types of knowledge exist: factual, conceptual, and strategic. **Factual knowledge** involves things like rote learning simple facts (H_2O is water, $20 \times 2 = 40$), verbal chains (saying the alphabet) and discrimination. Factual knowledge can be demonstrated without a student understanding how to figure out how the answer was derived ($20 \times 2 = 40$, not two sets of 20).

Conceptual knowledge involves students understanding the meaning and critical attributes. For example, what are the critical attributes of a square? What are the critical attributes of a mathematical word problem? We often lose students when we move from factual to conceptual. Try it with students; have a student explain how he got the answer to $20 \times 2 = 40$. Can he or she explain it is two sets of 20 items or 20 sets of two? Or what is absolutely necessary to solve the word problem? Or even what are the noncritical attributes or distracters in the word problem? You will be surprised what you will find out.

Strategic knowledge involves using a procedure, plan, or steps in the process to solve problems, perform tasks, or derive answers. Strategic knowledge can range from how to solve a mathematics equation to how to find Malawi, Africa on a map. How do we do that? By using a strategy, of course! So although students may be able to come up with the correct answer to simple questions, they may not have the ability to explaine how they arrived at the answer.

Identifying the types of knowledge required for specific assignments and tasks doesn't mean that a task has only one type of knowledge. On the contrary, many things we ask students to identify or produce have all three types of knowledge. For example, multiplying three-digit by two-digit numbers requires the use of facts, the concept of multiplication, and the strategy of actually solving the problem.

Think about how this fits into preparing students for assessments. We usually know ahead of time by looking at a test matrix (for district/state tests) or because we developed the test what types of questions will be asked and how many. The importance here is that you understand the types of knowledge you are teaching and are able to identify them when students have difficulties.

BOX 9.6

How to Teach: Think about It

- Identify skills that are hierarchical in nature or are foundation skills.
- Identify students' levels of proficiency.
- Monitor and adjust instruction to move students to next level of proficiency.

To plan effectively, it is good practice to identify the proficiency level at which the student is working. Three basic levels exist: accuracy, mastery, and automatically. If a student is learning new material or lacks knowledge on a task, she is at the initial phase of learning called **acquisition**. Student progress is often slow and correctness will be below 80 percent. Another student may be able to perform work correctly but at a slow rate. This student needs fluency instruction that facilitates mastery, accurate and fast. Finally, all instruction is aimed to have students use a skill independently and automatically when needed. This is called **generalization**. We know this does not happen automatically for many students. Therefore, they need to be taught how to transfer the use of skills to other related tasks or different settings.

Why is this important? Think about assessment. Often certain sections of a test are timed. Are students being taught fluency and speed skills in order to pace themselves through these sections? Do they have a sense of time? What about during instruction? Do you have a sense of where every student is in terms of acquisition of skills? Are they able to generalize and integrate information and skill to other topics? This is obviously a critical skill in essay writing and performance events. Does your instruction reflect and consider levels of proficiency?

---

schools today. It is essential that they know what is expected of them every step of the way. Think about it: do you start every lesson by telling your students what they will learn, why they will learn it, and how mastery will be shown? The goal of communicating realistic expectations is providing clear communication of high realistic expectations so that everybody is on the same page and no one's needs are overlooked or missed teaching (cf. Algozzine and Ysseldyke, 1992; Algozzine, Ysseldyke, and Elliott, 1997). Think about it (see Box 9.7).

Managing Instruction

Principles

- Prepare for instruction
- Use time productively
- Establish positive classroom environment

BOX 9.7

Communicate Realistic Expectations: Think about It

- Tell students what they will learn.
- Tell students why it is important to learn.
- Tell students how good is good enough.

Effective educators tell their students what they are expected to know and be able to do and to what level of proficiency. These educators do this at the start of every lesson. When preparing students for any assessment or test, it is imperative they know what to expect. What will be covered and how (multiple choice, performance event, and so on). Not only does it keep students accountable, but teachers as well. One of the keys to improving student performance is communicating to students what they must know and then provide them the roadmap to get there. It is like a trip. We know where we are going and the way to go, but how do we know when we arrived?

In the Algozzine and Ysseldyke (1992) model, managing instruction is not about managing student behavior per se. Managing instruction refers to how efficient and effective classrooms routines are. That is, there is a presence of cooperation, structure, and order. Effective instruction requires managing a complex mix of instructional tasks and student behaviors. This means making decisions that control and support an orderly flow of instruction. After all, it is hard to teach students anything if they aren't in their seats and/or attending to task. And how much learning can really occur in classrooms that are unstructured and chaotic? Effective managing is accomplished through three principles: Prepare for instruction, use time productively, and establish a positive classroom environment teaching (cf. Algozzine and Ysseldyke, 1992; Algozzine, Ysseldyke, and Elliott, 1997).

Preparing for instruction Effective teachers establish classroom rules and expectations, communicate them early in the year, and throughout the year. They teach students the consequences of following and not following classroom rules and procedures. Rule infractions and other classroom disruptions are handled as quickly as possible after they occur. One of the ultimate goals of managing instruction is to have students manage their own behavior. A goal of preparing for instruction is to try to anticipate, avoid, and address problems that might disrupt the orderly flow of instruction teaching (cf. Algozzine and Ysseldyke, 1992; Algozzine, Ysseldyke, and Elliott, 1997). Think about it (see Box 9.8).

BOX 9.8

Prepare for Instruction: Think about It

- Prepare students for instruction.
- Provide opportunities for students to show what they know and can do.
- Make teaching fun.

A fun instructional tactic to use with the whole class is called the Good Behavior Game, but it really isn't a game. Simply divide the class into two teams; be sure they are balanced for skill and ability. Identify one to three behaviors or skills that need improvement or will be taught. Decide on the criteria you will use to evaluate whether the behavior or skills have been demonstrated. Discuss both the target skills and criteria with students so they understand what is expected and what they need to demonstrate to get points for their team. Then let the game begin! For example, the class may need to work on responding to questions, working cooperatively, and work completion. During instruction, multiple opportunities are provided for students to demonstrate the behaviors, and tallies are kept for both sides. Teams can see who has more tallies and work to compete for the most points. What do they win? That is up to you. For most students, the satisfaction of being on the winning team is enough. Some teachers keep track of points and teams work for some incentive to be delivered after a week or so. Another example of this technique can be to list skills such as reading for comprehension, correctly solving algebraic equations, using correct strategies or steps to solve problems. Anything goes. You can work on behavior or skills in a format in which progress is posted publicly and team work is developed.

In preparing students for assessments, you can adapt the Good Behavior Game by using facts, concepts, or strategies that they will be required to know to perform well. It can be used during initial instruction or for review. This "game" is merely a technique to help students focus on behaviors and skills that need attention. Try it. Be creative.

Using time productively Effective educators make decisions that maximize the amount of time students spend actively engaged in learning. They minimize the time spent on activities not related to learning. There is evidence to suggest that students often spend more time in transition than engaged in learning. It is imperative that teachers establish routines and procedures, including transition time, and allocate time to activities that maintain an academic focus. The goal of using time productively is maximizing the time teachers spend teaching and students spend learning (cf. Algozzine and Ysseldyke, 1992; Algozzine, Ysseldyke, and Elliott, 1997). Think about it (see Box 9.9).

BOX 9.9

Use Time Productively: Think about It

- Allocate time for instruction.
- Check your instructional time for actual engaged student learning.
- Provide instruction that actively engages students in learning.

How is instruction time in your classes allocated? Allocated learning time is defined as the amount of time set aside for **engaged** student learning. Daily classroom schedules should be allocated by three basic rules of thumb: (1) The instructional day or class period should allocate at least 70 percent for student learning, (2) the amount of time students are to be engaged in learning should be about 85 percent, and (3) the rate of accuracy of students' engaged work should be around 80 percent. A quick formula to check your allocated learning time is the total amount of time in an instructional day or class period multiplied by .7. For example, 6.5 hour school day × .7 = 4.6 hours. That means that 4.6 hours of the day need to be devoted to active engaged student learning. Another example, 50-minute class period × .7 = 35 minutes should be allocated to engaged student learning.

Check your daily instructional classes to see how much time students actually spend in engaged learning. It is not enough to say social studies is taught from 1 to 1:50 p.m. everyday. We need to be able to identify how that 50 minutes of student learning is spent. What we have found in working with teachers in these areas is that more time is spent in transition than realized, or little time is allocated to guided practice with students. The connection to this and improving student performance on assessment should be clear. The more we engage students in what they should know and be able to do, the better they will perform.

Establishing a positive classroom environment   It has been said that students learn three to four times more when they are motivated to learn. Most children and youth (and adults) perform better when teachers interact positively with them. Motivation is built through supportive and helpful learning environments. Students like school more when their classrooms are pleasant, friendly places. And students will work better when they like their teachers! Effective educators are accepting and caring and strive for positive interaction that fosters active student responding. The goal of establishing a positive classroom environment is creating a place where students like to be, feel supported, and enjoy learning (cf. Algozzine and Ysseldyke, 1992; Algozzine, Ysseldyke, and Elliott, 1997). Think about it (see Box 9.10).

BOX 9.10

Establishing a Positive Classroom Environment: Think about It

- Keep a positive attitude—it's contagious.
- Teach students that one can learn from making mistakes.
- Use positive praise statements.

Did you know the more students like and respect you, the harder they will work? Think about that as adults. Do we not tend to stick it out with people, colleagues and friends, when we respect them? We can't forget that this holds true for the students we teach. Teaching is tough and sometimes we forget to let students know how much we care about them and the work they are doing. How often do you tell students how much you appreciate them? We know that some days are harder than others, but this is still a critical piece of the instructional process. Improving student performance is inextricably linked to how students feel about themselves and the support they feel, their self-concept, and their abilities to take risks.

Making personalized statements to students about their efforts and perseverance is important. Consider this statement: "Wow, Jose you did a great job!" What does this really say? Does this reflect the time and thought Jose put into the task? What about "Wow, Jose. Nice job sticking to the assignment. Look at the results of your labor!" We encourage you to think about how you recognize student efforts. In order to motivate a learner, students must see the connection between their efforts and the fruits of their labor no matter how small.

Delivering Instruction

Principles

- Present information
- Monitor presentations
- Adjust presentations

Teaching is the systematic presentation of content necessary for mastery of the subject matter (Algozzine and Ysseldyke, 1992). Good teaching just doesn't happen. It involves careful planning to decide what and how to teach as well as providing a smooth flow of classroom rules, routines, and procedures that are conducive for student learning. Delivering instruction involves presenting information while monitoring student understanding of what is being taught. This means that teachers are constantly planning how to present information while keeping track of student performance and adjusting instruction to accommodate for individual differences. Three principles exist for effectively delivering instruction: Present information, monitor presentations, and adjust teaching to accommodate the needs of students (cf. Algozzine and Ysseldyke, 1992; Algozzine, Ysseldyke, and Elliott, 1997).

Presenting information   Empirically demonstrated ways exist for presenting instruction. Effective educators interact positively with their students to gain and maintain attention, review previously taught material, provide organized lessons, and introduce new material by connecting it to students' prior knowledge. Among other things, brisk pacing and checking students' understanding are all vital to presenting information to students. When teaching thinking skills, for example, effective teachers model ways to solve problems. When motivating students, effective teachers use extrinsic incentives with enthusiasm. Teachers always keep in mind that the ultimate goal of motivating students is to get them to become intrinsically motivated or reduce the tangible incentives to a minimum. When providing practice, effective teachers provide relevant but varied opportunities to practice and provide time needed by students to do so. Teachers utilize a variety of activities when providing both guided and independent practice. The goal in presenting information is to teach students new information, or to extend or reinforce previous knowledge (cf. Algozzine and Ysseldyke, 1992; Algozzine, Ysseldyke, and Elliott, 1997). Think about it (see Box 9.11).

Monitoring presentations   When providing feedback to students, effective teachers provide immediate and frequent information that supports students efforts to derive correct responses. Effective teachers model corrective procedures and methods for making improvements. When keeping students involved in lessons, teachers find ways to regularly monitor responses and use peer-mediated activities to provide ample and varied opportunities for learning. The goal in monitoring presentations is to ensure students are learning the content as it was intended (cf. Algozzine and Ysseldyke, 1992; Algozzine, Ysseldyke, and Elliott, 1997). Think about it (see Box 9.12).

Adjusting presentations   This principle involves making decisions about how to change or modify instruction for students. Effective teachers use a variety of teaching strategies; they monitor and adjust the instructional pace to accommodate the individual needs of students, monitor student understanding, and stick with students until they have had the time to master what has been taught. Instructional information gathered throughout this process is in turn used to adjust instruction so that all students can meet with success. The goal of adjusting presentations

---

BOX 9.11

Presenting Information: Think about It

- Be creative.
- Extend students' learning and abilities in creative, fun ways.
- Provide activities that integrate students' learning.

Teachers can incorporate many different techniques to get students motivated, excited about learning, and provide opportunities to practice what they have learned. Here is a favorite: teach students how to create license plates for the topic of study they are learning. California is known for its "vanity license plates" that have snappy sayings about the people who are driving the car. You know the ones you try to figure out when you are stopped behind them; then they drive away before you can figure out what the license plate was trying to say. For instruction, try having the students create one on a specific topic. For example, students studying Civil War could create a license plate for a soldier (if he had a car!). Another example would be a license plate for a scientist who worked on the discovery of atom fusion. It sounds easier than it appears. You must have command of the subject as well as understand the facts, concepts, and strategies in order to apply it to this creative task.

BOX 9.12

Monitoring Presentation: Think About It

- Keep students actively involved.
- Find ways to assess student knowledge that don't have to be cumbersome.
- Provide lots of opportunities to show what they have learned.

Here is a technique that enables you to monitor student learning as well as provide students with a structured opportunity to expand their knowledge about a topic. We call it Chat-Check-Change. Have students stand in two concentric circles. Students on the inside circle face outward, while students on the outside circle face in. Pose a question or topic to the students and say "go." Students on the inside circle must chat for 60 to 90 seconds about the question. When the time is up say "stop" and tell the circles to move. The inside circle moves to the right, while the outside circle walks to the left. Tell students to stop and face their partner. Re-pose the same question or topic. This time the students on the outside talk for 60 to 90 seconds. After this sharing, the teacher discusses the answer to the question or topic with the entire group. In this manner, both student circles have the opportunity to chat about the subject; relearning and extending the knowledge of facts, concepts, and strategies occurs during this activity.

For the purpose of assessments, Chat-Check-Change enables the opportunity to review information for the test and it gives students the opportunity to learn information they may not have been aware of or understood. It is a great way to provide an active practice of learning.

is to make necessary instructional changes to guarantee that all students profit from instruction (cf. Algozzine and Ysseldyke, 1992; Algozzine, Ysseldyke, and Elliott, 1997). Think about it (see Box 9.13).

Evaluating Instruction

Principles

- Monitor student understanding
- Monitor engaged time
- Keep records of student progress
- Use data to make decisions

A fourth component of effective instruction is evaluating the results of that instruction. Effective instruction requires evaluating, which is the process of deciding whether the approaches, methods, and material used work with your students. As Algozzine and Ysseldyke (1992) point out, information gathered from effective evaluation is used to make decisions about whether to refer students to other student support services, change or modify interventions, and/or help determine whether a student can be exited from a program (such as exited from special education services or remedial reading programs). Evaluation completes the integral and valuable cycle in effective instructional processes and also feeds the instructional process. The evaluation of student progress should be ongoing and take place throughout instruction as well as at the end of a lesson or unit of study. Effective evaluating has four principles: Monitor student understanding, monitor engaged time, keep records of student progress, and use data to make teaching decisions (cf. Algozzine and Ysseldyke, 1992; Algozzine, Ysseldyke, and Elliott, 1997).

Monitoring student understanding The goal here is to keep track of and decide the extent to which students have benefited from instruction. This involves using a variety of ways to check with students to see if they have really understood what has been taught. The goal here is to push students beyond the superficial level of learning to make sure they can show what they know (cf. Algozzine and Ysseldyke, 1992; Algozzine, Ysseldyke, and Elliott, 1997). Think about it (see Box 9.14).

Monitoring engaged time This involves keeping track of the rate of student participation during instruction. The goal of monitoring engaged time is to determine the extent to which all students are actively and

BOX 9.13

Adjusting Presentations: Think about It

- Teaching is orchestrating what and how we teach with how students learn.
- Consider the types of knowledge and the levels of proficiency when adjusting instruction.
- Tailor-teaching strategies improve student achievement.

It is important to monitor how students are doing in instruction. It all gets tied together when we monitor students for the type of knowledge we are teaching, the level of proficiency they are at, and what instructional techniques make the most sense to improve student performance. It is about adjusting and aligning student learning and instruction. The following chart is a useful summary to help in pinpointing how to teach for student learning.

Types of Knowledge					
Accuracy		**Mastery**		**Accuracy**	
Entry Level	**Initial Advanced**	**Proficiency**	**Maintenance**	**General-ization**	**Adaption**
Absense of skill or low frequency (10% correct)	10%–25% correct / 26%–64% correct / 65%–90% correct	High rate of speed and accuracy above 90%	Fast and accurate (90%–100% correct)	Spontaneous transfer to new settings/ conditions	Higher-order thinking and problem solving
Instructional Tactics:	**Instructional Tactics:**	**Instructional Tactics:**	**Instructional Tactics:**	**Instructional Tactics:**	**Instructional Tactics:**
• Assessement	• Direct instruction • Demonstrating successful approximations • Modeling levels of cueing/ prompting • Specific directions • Feedback	• Drill practice modeling—fast and accurate • Specific reinforcement and praise	• Periodic checks and review • Direct instruction as needed	• Teach for generalization • Direct instruction in a variety of settings and conditions • Vary instructors	• Teach creative problem solving • Vary question types • Use "What if?"
Skill Identification	*Skill Acquisition*	*Skill Fluency*	*Skill Retention*	*Skill Expansion*	*Skill Extension*

BOX 9.14

Monitor Student Understanding: Think about It

- Use a variety of techniques to check for student understanding.
- Keep track of what works.
- Be certain students understand.

HDYKT! That is, How Do You Know That? This simple technique forces students not only to give an answer, but tell how they got it. Too often teachers hear the correct answer and move on without determining how students derived the answer. It isn't unusual to use HDYKT only to find out the answer is correct, but the strategy for deriving the answer is incorrect or lacking. Preparing students for short-answer or essay tests is not an easy task. This technique assists in expanding students' breadth and depth of information.

---

appropriately engaged in relevant instructional activities (cf. Algozzine and Ysseldyke, 1992; Algozzine, Ysseldyke, and Elliott, 1997). Think about it (see Box 9.15).

Keeping records of student progress   Effective teachers keep track of student achievement and performance by using a variety of evaluative procedures. In addition, they routinely share this information with students. The goal of keeping records of student progress is to stay on top of student achievement as well as to keep the students' informed about their efforts teaching (cf. Algozzine and Ysseldyke, 1992; Algozzine, Ysseldyke, and Elliott, 1997). Think about it (see Box 9.16).

Using data to make decisions   The goal here is using student data or progress to make decisions about what is or is not working. The information gathered here can assist in making decisions about what additional assistance may be needed or, even better, no longer needed for students. The priority here is to use student data to make decisions that provide more or different support and/or instruction for students (cf. Algozzine and Ysseldyke, 1992; Algozzine, Ysseldyke, and Elliott, 1997). Think about it (see Box 9.17).

Today, more than ever before, teachers are faced with the responsibility of educating increasingly diverse students. Teachers are expected to assist all students in meeting high standards across the content areas. Although empirically demonstrated principles of learning and teaching exist, difficulties can be experienced when implementing them. Teachers

---

BOX 9.15

Monitoring Engaged Time: Think about It

- Don't sit, but wander.
- Provide opportunities for students to be actively involved in learning.
- Teach—monitor—assess—teach.

All Write! Often teachers teach a lesson and don't stop to check for understanding. Although students may appear they are engaged, they may not. This technique keeps students on their toes. During a lecture, stop and do an All Write. Simply ask students to write a quick response to a posed question. Give students about a minute to jot down responses, including that they don't know. Walk around the room while students are writing. Then ask students to share responses. This technique is about identifying which students are on-track as well as identifying information that needs clarification or more instruction. It provides students with a timed response—they have to quickly respond to the question.

Improving student performance is about making sure students are learning. We can't be sure of that unless we check for understanding and monitor our instruction. This becomes a challenge given the amount of information, standards, and curriculum that must be taught. However, the time it takes to check for engaged learning and understanding is worth its weight in test scores.

---

across the nation report that they don't have the time or resources to implement such principles. As is common with anything new, comprehension and implementation of this model of effective instruction may at first glance seem overwhelming. Remember the first time you tried to read or make sense of a student's IEP? It is the same phenomenon. Overwhelming at first, but automatic after practice.

The Algozzine and Ysseldyke (1992) model of effective instruction provides a systematic and structured approach for linking research-based principles of learning and teaching to classroom strategies and tactics. Grounded in the findings of educational research, the components and principles of this model provide a structure for organizing, understanding, and applying strategies and tactics used by effective teachers. The model is a flexible instructional improvement tool that can be used to make the connections between standards, curriculum, and assessments. The best way to improve instruction is to decide which principles of instruction are the most important in your situation and work on those first. Doing this necessarily involves selecting one of the components (planning, managing, delivering, or evaluating) and working on the principle within it first.

BOX 9.16

Keep Records of Student Progress: Think about It

- Vary evaluative procedures.
- Keep assessments easy, quick, and informative.
- Use assessments to drive instruction.

Use two-minute papers. At the end of class have students complete a two-minute paper and hand it in. They simply take two minutes to respond to the following statements.

1. Something I learned, relearned, or rediscovered as a result of this lesson is . . .

2. Something I am still confused about or need clarification on is . . .

Students have two minutes to complete both sentences. At the end of two minutes, they put their pens down or may finish their thought and then stop. Collect the papers and you have an understanding of how well you did in instructing students and how well they understood. It also provides you with a planning tool for your next day's lesson—where to reteach, review, or reinforce.

This technique simply keeps you informed about how students are learning. After all, that is what counts when improving student performance and making progress through the curriculum and standards.

By initially working on only one component and respective principles, strategies, and tactics, the task of improving instruction and ultimately student achievement is more systematic and manageable.

Summary

In this chapter, we have explored the key elements of maximizing student achievement by way of effective instruction. Nationally, the focus on assessment has created heightened tensions and stress in the teaching force. Some argue that the breadth and depth of what gets taught in the classroom is directly related to what gets tested. If this in fact is true, why is it that so many students are still performing lower than expected and desired. Educators and other professionals can only blame the state/district assessments for so long; then they must direct their attention to what matters: instruction. In order to maximize the performance of all students, including students with disabilities, teachers especially must focus on what takes place (or doesn't take place) in the classroom. Although there

---

BOX 9.17

Use Data to Make Decisions: Think About It

- Don't guess, assess!
- Chart student progress.
- Use student performance to make instructional decisions about what next.

Too often we think students aren't getting it, so we change our technique or move on. And too often we continue to use a technique or method that is ineffective because that's the way we have always done it or we think students will get it eventually. It's too much of a guessing game, don't you think? This scenario happens because we don't keep progress data on exactly how students are learning.

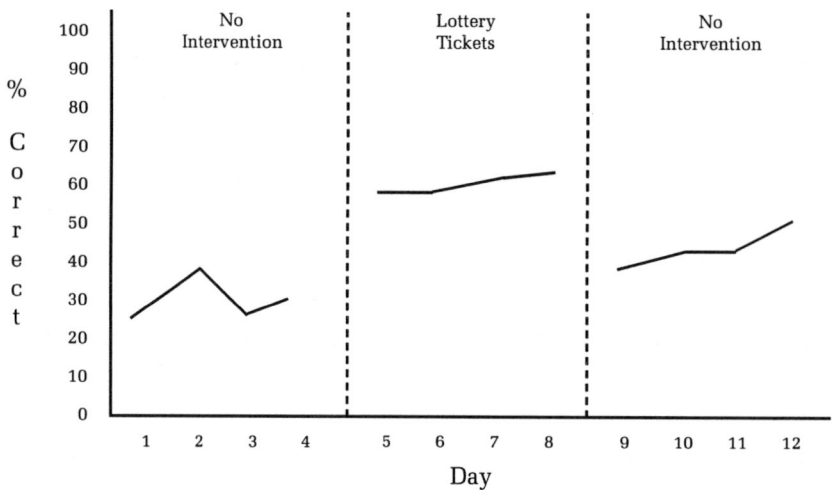

It should be clear how valuable this technique is to improving student performance. The aimline takes the guesswork out of how students are performing and the rate at which they are learning information. Aimlines may be more necessary with some students than others. Aimlines also can be used to set group or classroom goals as well. They provide both students and teachers with a visual tracking system for connecting performance to the end goal of instruction. Depending on the age of the students, they could record their progress on their own charts.

*See Elliott, Algozzine, and Ysseldyke (1998)

---

is no one right way to teach all students, empirically proven ways exist for increasing student performance through the implementation of direct and effective instructional strategies and tactics (cf. Algozzine, Ysseldyke, and Elliott, 1997).

A final note: Remember the copy machine scenario? Well, that special teacher's ninth-grade algebra class took the state-mandated end-of-course test and 12 of 16 student passed! It's amazing what can occur when components of effective instruction provide guiding principles for the strategies and tactics used in teaching all students.

Test Your Knowledge

Show what you know and learned in this chapter by answering the following questions. It's open book, so look back if you need to.

1. One of the earliest pushes to investigate accountability and student learning came from the _____.

2. An unanticipated outcome of the creation of special education is a _____ system of educating students.

3. _____ _____ connected to standards, curriculum frameworks, and aligned assessment is vital to maximizing the performance of all students, including students with disabilities.

4. One of the purposes of an assessment is to remove the focus from solely on the _____ to that of what happens in the instructional environment.

5. We are educating students in an educational system where _____ is the constant and _____ is the variable.

6. There is a research-based model of effective instruction that has the following four components: _____, _____, _____ _____, _____.

7. _____ for instruction is the backbone of effective instruction.

8. Evidence suggests that students often spend more time in _____ than engaged in learning.

9. _____ feeds the instructional process.

10. We can only blame the _____ for so long; then we must direct our attention to what matters: instruction.

Answers

1. business community (p. 173)
2. dual, separate (p. 174)
3. Effective instruction (p. 174)
4. student (p. 174)
5. time, learning (p. 175)

6. planning, managing, delivering, evaluating (p. 178)
7. Planning (p. 179)
8. transition (p. 184)
9. Evaluation (p. 189)
10. assessment or test (p. 193)

Resources

Algozzine, B. and J. Ysseldyke. *Strategies and Tactics for Effective Instruction*. Longmont: CO, Sopris West, Inc., 1992.

Algozzine, B., J. Ysseldyke, and J. Elliott. *Strategies and Tactics for Effective Instruction*, 2d ed. Longmont: CO, Sopris West, Inc., 1997.

Elliott, J., B. Algozzine, B. and J. Ysseldyke. *Timesavers for Educators*. Longmont: CO, Sopris West, Inc., 1998.

National Research Council. *Testing, Teaching, and Learning: A Guide for States and School Districts*. R.F. Elmore and R. Rothman (eds.). Washington, DC: National Academic Press, 1999.

Levine, D.U., and L.W. Lazotte. *Unusually Effective Schools: A Review and Analysis of Research and Practice*. Madison, WI: National Center for Effective Schools, 1990.

Schumm, J.S., S. Vaughn, and A. Leavell. "Planning pyramid: A framework for planning for diverse student needs during content area instruction." *The Reading Teacher*, 47 (8), 608–615, 1994.

Internet Resources

National Center to Improve the Tools of Educators (NCITE): http://idea.uoregon.edu/-ncite.

Sopris West, Inc.: http://www.sopriswest.com.

Teaching and Assessment for Shades of Gray: The Kids in Between

The pessimist complains about the wind, the optimist expects the wind, the realist adjusts the sails.

—Anonymous

Are the students gray, or have we created gray area assessment systems?

—Pat Almond

Hot Button Issues

- Some students will never reach the standards!

- That special education kid is on my class roster and I don't feel I should be responsible for her. She will never pass the district/state test.

- We should be able to filter out all students with disabilities from our assessment results before we rank our schools.

- They expect me to teach these kids. My question is "What do I teach them?"

A new term has crept into our vocabulary—"gray area students." Many definitions exist for gray area kids. It depends on who you ask. Some people don't believe they even exist. Even more important questions emerge when we ask, what do we do with them once we have agreed who they are and why they exist? In this chapter, we explore the many aspects, trials, and tribulations of educating the kids in between, those students who don't neatly fit into categories, systems, classifications, and/or assessments (know any kids like this?).

Who Are Gray Area Kids?
Do They Really Exist?

So many definitions, so little time. Gray area kids, also known as gap kids, kids in the middle, kids in between, and the no place kids, have at least two distinct definitions. For our purposes, we define gray area kids as students with disabilities for whom the general state/district assessment is inappropriate even with extensive accommodations, but for whom the alternate assessment is equally inappropriate. The kinds of kids who fall in this gray area depend as much on the state/district tests as on the characteristics of the kids themselves. In some cases, gray area kids can take the regular assessment, but the accommodations they need are those assumed to invalidate the test. The alternate assessment is inappropriate for these students because it is assessing something other than what they have been taught in the general curriculum. As a result, these students become known as gray area kids, simply because *they* don't fit the assessment system.

What's wrong with this picture? If we are truly about the business of producing students who will be contributing and successful citizens of the 21st century, shouldn't we focus on developing education and assessment systems that encompass all students? In doing so, should we enable accommodations that ultimately will be provided in society?

The Realities

It seems quite ludicrous that we expect all ninth graders to be ready to complete a required course in algebra when many arrive on the high school steps not able to do basic mathematic calculations. Why then do we have students take end-of-course exams that reflect math standards for ninth graders? We don't know, but we do know that by the ninth grade, in this example, we have colored more kids with shades of gray. All of this goes directly back to standards-based instruction and assessments.

We believe that standards-based anything should be concerned with the reality of student achievement, not time requirements. Standards-based districts are dedicated to the guiding principle that all students will read and ninth graders will learn algebra. In some cases, it is simply a matter of time. In the Long Beach Unified School District in Long Beach, California, there is a recognition that some students will complete Algebra 9 in 10 months, while others may need two years. The district has developed an expanded algebra class that enables students two years to complete the course. Adding to this, the state of California requires that all high school students pass an algebra test in order to graduate. The expanded time course makes great sense for kids.

In the same manner, while Long Beach, an urban district of approximately 93,000 students, expects all third graders to be proficient readers by year's end, they understand that some students just won't be there on time. This is not because of reading disabilities, but due to many other variables that exist, such as attendance, discipline, instruction, and poor performance in reading development. Because the district is more concerned about achievement than time requirements, it has instituted a multitude of reading institutes that occur during the school year and in summer. In one of these institutes, students attend a reading program for about eight weeks. During this time, students spend the entire day learning to read. After the eight weeks, students are returned to their regular classrooms to continue learning in the curriculum.

So the issue, as we see it, isn't whether gray kids exist, but how to build education and assessment systems that reflect students in our schools today, rather than the political landscape of the year. As illustrated, gray area kids are not necessarily low-performing students. In many cases, they are students learning the general curriculum, but whose characteristics necessitate different ways to show what they know, different from the standard pencil-paper tests. These are students who are learning the same standards under the same performance standards, but who are unable to demonstrate their knowledge in the traditional manner.

Some people define gray area kids as those students who struggle learning the general curriculum, but for whom special education support services are not appropriate. In other words, they don't qualify for special education.

We ask you, do gray area kids really exist or is the push for accountability and assessment the real culprit?

Issues and Dilemmas

Now that we are totally clear on what shade of gray a gray area student is (or was that the education system?), let's take a look at common issues and dilemmas surrounding the education of these students. No doubt you know people who have tried their darndest to get gray area students into special education. For many states and districts, the incentive is to get these kids into special education so the IEP team can have the final say as to what assessment these kids take and with what accommodations. In some states, the IEP team has the authority to change graduation requirements, including modifying coursework or the exemptions from final exams, reducing the number of credits needed, and even changing the required passing scores on state/district tests (see Box 10.1).

Policies such as these provide an incentive to push students who are underachieving or expected to do less well on accountability assessments (our second definition) into special education. Although inappropriate, it isn't hard to see why some educational systems focus their efforts here. Most often these kids are caught in the bureaucratic system that promotes high standards for all, no matter what it takes. Unfortunately, these kids are

---

BOX 10.1

Changes in Requirements for Students Allowed in Some States*

Changes	States Allowing
Modified coursework*	Arkansas, Colorado, Connecticut, Delaware, Florida, Hawaii, Illinois, Iowa, Kansas, Maine, Michigan, Missouri, Montana, North Dakota, New Hampshire, New Mexico, New York, Oklahoma, South Dakota, Texas, Utah, Vermont, Washington
Modified exam or exemption from exam	New Jersey, Minnesota, Ohio, Texas
IEP completion	Arkansas, Maine, Minnesota, Missouri, Oklahoma, Texas, Wyoming
Team decides requirement	Arizona, California, Colorado, Connecticut, Idaho, Maine, Maryland, Massachusetts, Pennsylvania, Wisconsin
No changes allowed	Alabama, Alaska, District of Columbia, Indiana, Louisiana, Nebraska, Nevada, North Carolina, South Carolina, Rhode Island, Virginia

SOURCE: Adapted from National Center on Educational Outcomes, Technical Report 24.
*Coursework may be modified as a reduced number of credits, credits approved for alternate courses, or lower performance criteria.

---

also the ones who are the casualties of such systems. That is, among other things they may not have had the opportunity to learn, they may have been caught in the middle of policy or curriculum changes, or they may have received poor instruction. Therefore, they are at great risk of failing or not graduating if they are not pushed into special education where protection is provided via the IEP. So is it a student issue or the education system of our schools?

Pushing all kids to high standards is a worthy goal, but we also recognize that this is not a one-size-fits-all world. Imagine creating the standard "All people will wear size four shoes." Some of us would have great difficulty meeting that standard, and in many cases it would cause great pain. Others would almost meet the standard by fitting half their foot in the shoe, while the rest of it hung out. The big question is what would we accomplish with the "size four shoe" standard? How valid would the performance standard really be if some folks walked (or rather hobbled) around with half a foot hanging out of their shoe? What are we really trying to accomplish—uniformity, utility, or mediocrity?

If we are genuinely concerned with educating all kids at high standards, then doesn't it make sense to allow for individual differences? Our current education system is one where time is the constant and learning is the variable. Students don't all "get it" at the same time. For example, we could all participate in a 5K running race and finish, some of us ahead of others. Some of us would be running the entire route, while others would be walking it. In the end, we would all get to the finish line. Why then is our education system so rigidly structured? Of course, there is the reality of resources (or lack thereof), teachers, time, and space shortages. After all, it is more cost-effective to have all kids take one type of test, preferably multiple choice with perhaps a few short answers, than providing kids with different individualized ways to show what they know. Isn't it interesting that the gray area kids are currently viewed as one of the most difficult groups of kids to accommodate? Although they may not be receiving special education services, they struggle in the curriculum and perform poorly on assessments for a variety of reasons. So we could say that all students, both general and special education, have shades of gray when it comes to instruction and assessments. They can learn the standards but would better show what they have learned if they are provided more time to learn and thoughtful methods of assessment.

The only difference between general education and special education groups of gray area kids is that the latter group is protected by IEPs. How fair is that? We define "fair" as each student getting what he or she needs to be successful. Be that as it may, the black hole of instruction and assessment, the kids in between, gets bigger by the day.

The Opportunity to Learn and Gate-Keeping Exams

No doubt you have heard the term opportunity-to-learn (OTL). At one point in the standard-based education movement, there was discussion of three types of standards: content, performance, and OTL. However, the last type of standard didn't stick. OTL standards indicate the resources and services that need to be provided to ensure that students have a fair opportunity to learn content standards at the desired level of performance. OTL includes, but is not limited to, the provision of quality education that is aligned with student standards, curriculum, and the demands of the assessment. Relatively little attention has ever been given to OTL standards. When we get right down to the heart of the matter, providing students equitable opportunities to learn really is what today's discussion of gray area students is about. Are we providing all students, including students with disabilities and limited English proficiency, the means to learn and show what they know? And, what if they need assessment accommodations that have been identified as those that will invalidate the test? What if you are in a state that requires the student to pass these same assessments for grade promotions or graduation? Who and what are really gray?

Recently, the U.S. Office for Civil Rights issued strong indicators of the probable forthcoming consequences of not providing students the opportunity to learn required standards needed to pass district/state assessments (see Box 10.2). Inherent in these questions is the issue of whether students are provided ample opportunities to learn. What supports or tutorial services have been provided? What accommodations? We bet you can, from the perch where you sit, answer these questions without hesitation. It takes one lawsuit to make people sit up and take a serious look at what they are doing for kids.

More and more circumstances surrounding gray area students have become civil rights issues. That is, does the test make educational sense? Based on the premise that tests should be an integral part of learning and achievement, one federal circuit court set the following context:

> If tests can predict that a person is going to be a poor employee, the employer can legitimately deny that person a job, but if a test suggests that a young child is probably going to be a poor student, the school cannot on that basis alone deny that child the opportunity to improve and develop the academic skills necessary to succeed in our society (Larry P. v. Riles, 793 F.2d 969,980).

Therefore, the education community must collectively guarantee that the establishment of high standards for all students does not unfairly result in the denial of educational opportunities for any student. As more states move their policies to high-stakes testing programs, the civil rights issues become very clear. It is not a disability issue, but an "all kids" issue. So while the decision about which test a student should take (regular assessment or alternate assessment) is important, it becomes even more critical when high stakes for students are involved.

It has become more and more common to read about test corruption across the country, such as administrators changing students' test answer sheets, teachers providing test preparations using photocopied portions of actual tests, newspapers printing subtest items bootlegged from a test, and on and on (see Chapter 2, "Educational Accountability: What Is It?" for more discussion). It appears that these corrupt practices reflect the need to improve instruction and assessments to better meet student needs. It isn't hard to see that this is *not* a special education issue or even a kid issue, but rather an accountability and assessment issue.

BOX 10.2

Six Basic Questions on the Opportunity to Learn

Six basic legal questions must be answered (Arthur Coleman, Deputy Assistant Secretary, Office for Civil Rights, presentation CRESST Conference, September, 1999):

1. What is the educational justification for using the test(s)?

   To improve the quality of schooling?

   To ensure graduates are competent?

   To establish meaningful, quantitative standards?

   To ensure a diploma is not a meaningless piece of paper?

2. What is the history of discrimination and its effects?

   Is there evidence of equal opportunities to achieve high standards?

   What is the role of educators in addressing the needs of different students from different backgrounds and equipping students with tools for success?

3. Are the requirements new?

   Is this change from prior practice?

   What is the degree of change?

   What is the notice of change to students and the public?

4. What is the time between the policy change and the consequences?

5. How is the educational program administered?

   Are there compensatory tutorials and other academic support?

   Is there intensive instruction available?

   Multiple opportunities to take the test?

   Waivers of test requirements?

6. What is the alignment between teaching and testing?

   What is the validity of the test instrument for the purposes used?

   Is there any alignment between the curriculum, instruction, assessment, and standards?

The Million Dollar Question: What Can Be Done for Gray Area Kids?

Wouldn't it be great if we had a simple answer? Sorry, we don't. Given the high-stakes nature of more and more accountability systems, a few areas really stand out, namely, standards, instruction, and assessment.

We started this chapter by defining gray area students in terms of the appropriateness of the assessment. For many students with disabilities, the regular district and state assessments are "too hard." This is usually due to at least three reasons: (1) students have not learned the content, (2) the format of the test is such that it impedes students' ability to show what they know (multiple choice tests versus performance assessments), and (3) students need accommodations not allowed on the test.

First, we must always ask, "why haven't students learned the content?" If the ultimate goal of students is to graduate with a high school diploma as a result of completing the same course requirements as all other students walking across the stage on graduation day, then why aren't they learning the same information? Currently, eight states enable students with disabilities to graduate with a diploma if they attain the goals and objectives written on their IEP. In these states, it is critical that their learning reflects the same standards that other students are learning. An unintended result of this policy is for educators to feel less pressure or responsibility for students with disabilities to learn the same general information because they will receive a diploma regardless. In the same manner, students with significant cognitive disabilities should be learning a life-skills curriculum that is linked to the same or expanded standards all other students are working toward.

The second issue of test format is perhaps a trickier one. We can impact and change the quality of instruction and OTL factors, but we can't change the format of the test. For example, there is little to be done if the mandated state test is the SAT-9 or if the standards-based test is multiple choice, which is the case in many states.

Here comes those shades of gray again. The kids don't fit the test, so the bottom line is that students are learning the regular curriculum and they should therefore take the assessment that reflects it (see Box 10.3). However, as pointed out earlier in this chapter, the issue of fair assessment of student knowledge is fast becoming a civil rights issue. So while the alternate assessment is not an appropriate assessment for these students, states and districts will need to look into the issue of alternative forms of assessing the same information.

Considerations for Addressing Gray Area Kids

Although we don't have the answer to the million dollar question, we have some considerations to think about.

Consideration One

Is the student expected to complete school by meeting the same requirements as all other students? If the answer is "yes," then the student needs to take the regular assessment with accommodations where needed. Take care not to make decisions early in the student's educational years. For example, do not peg a student for a special diploma in elementary school. This would

BOX 10.3

Tracking Student Pathways

Student	Graduation Expectation (Regular or Alternative)	IEP/504 (Yes or No)	Needed Instructional Accommodation	Needed Assessment Accommodation	Additional Instructional, Considerations, or Areas of Intervention	OTL Requirements

be a gross disservice to most students. Keep the options open until it becomes crystal clear that the student will work toward something other than the regular diploma. We recognize that this will be clear early on for some students. For most of those with disabilities, this is not the case.

Consideration Two

What assessments are required? Again, if the answer to Consideration One is "yes," then students should be taking the mandated district/state assessments required of all students.

Consideration Three

Consider the type of diploma the student is working toward. If it is the same one as all other students, then the student must be provided with the supports needed to obtain it. This necessarily includes the opportunity to learn what is required as well as accommodations and adaptations needed to meet established performance standards.

Consideration Four

Consider instructional practices. This is where the rubber meets the proverbial road. What is really going on in the classroom? What does instruction look like? Are empirically based practices of effective instruction taking place in the classroom? Do the practices include thorough planning, managing, delivering, and evaluating of instruction? We can only blame the assessment for so long, and then it's time to take a critical look at instruction.

Approaches to Gray Area Students

Consider each of the three approaches to gray area students as ways to begin thinking out of the box for this rather large population of students. We believe gray area students are the result of assessment systems that have forced students to fit one assessment or the other.

Approach 1

Use a body of evidence for these students. By this we mean don't depend on one assessment, but rather use multiple measures of performance. In this way, students could use needed non-standard accommodations, even modifications, and still provide other evidence of what they know and can do on standards.

Approach 2

Develop an alternative (not alternate) assessment for these students. This alternative assessment could provide students a different way to demonstrate proficiency on the same standards as measured by the regular assessment. So, the students will have the same standards, but a different test format (such as a portfolio or performance events).

Approach 3

Provide computer-adapted testing (CAT). CAT enables assessments to cover a broad range of items. The range narrows as students progress through the assessment. The path of items presented to the student is predicated on the performance of the student on previous items.

The means exists for addressing students who do not neatly fit into the current assessment systems. It is the system that needs to change to meet students where we find them, not vice versa.

Summary

In this chapter, we have raised issues surrounding the current dilemma of the kids who fall in the middle, familiar to most as the gray area kids. The dilemma of what to do with these kids is being wrestled with by educators across the country. The bottom line is that there may not be a bottom line. In many states, education laws have been enacted without careful consideration of the students in our schools and the contextual factors inherent in educating students in urban, suburban, and rural districts. Although we are not saying lower the bar or expect less, we are saying that each state and district context is unique in itself. Each entity has its own set of contextual factors that policy makers often overlook when mandating requirements and timelines under which schools must reform. In many cases, the result is malicious compliance.

Students, teachers, administrators, and parents can all be positively affected by accountability and assessment systems. However, it is the manner in which education policies are legislated and carried out that is problematic. Schools, districts, and states that thoughtfully take care to teach, accommodate, and include all students, including students with disabilities in their mission to educate learners may take harder hits than others who choose to educate the best and take care of the rest. The risk for sanctions and other consequences is worth its weight in gold if we can say "all our kids count in everything we do and are held accountable for." After all, what part of "all" don't people understand? Perhaps it is time we discuss holding accountable those who legislated laws that allow schools to creatively exclude those students who may jeopardize rankings and accountability indices so easily mandated by the stroke of a pen.

Test Your Knowledge

Use this exercise to review what you have learned in this chapter. There are no shades of gray in these answers!

1. Two basic concepts of gray area kids exist: (1) Those for whom the state and district _____ is inappropriate even with accommodations, and (2) students who struggle in the general curriculum, but for whom _____ _____ services are not appropriate.

2. Gray area students are not necessarily low-performing students. Sometimes they simply need a different way to show what they _____. Often they are unable to demonstrate their knowledge in the _____ manner as other students.

3. The way we see it, it isn't the kids who are gray but the _____ and _____ systems.

4. Currently, 19 states with credit requirements and graduation exams allow _____ teams to change criteria for earning a standard diploma.

5. A standards-based system is one that recognizes that not all students will " _____ it" at the same point in time. It recognizes that learning should be the constant and time the variable.

6. " . . . if a test suggests that a young child is probably going to be a poor student, the school cannot on that basis alone deny that child the opportunity to improve and develop the academic skills necessary to succeed in our society." This quote is taken from a _____ _____ _____ ruling.

7. The Office of Civil Rights issued a statement about the OTL and high-stakes assessments. The issue of providing students an alternative way to show what they know differently from the traditional paper-pencil test has become the focus of the civil rights discussion. The courts will be asking one of several questions when this issue lands in court. One is _____ _____.

8. Several states allow students with disabilities to graduate by meeting their _____ and _____ listed on their IEP.

9. If the student is learning the regular curriculum, she should take the _____ assessment.

10. We can only blame the test for so long. Then we need to look at what goes on in the _____.

Answers

1. assessment (p. 198); special education (p. 199)
2. know; traditional or same (p. 199)
3. education or accountability; assessment (p. 199)
4. IEP (Box 10.1, p. 200)
5. make or get (p. 201)
6. federal circuit court (p. 202)
7. There are several. Your pick. (Box 10.2, p. 203)
8. goals, objectives (p. 204)
9. regular (p. 204)
10. classroom (p. 206)

Resources

Coleman, A.L. (1998). "Excellence and Equity in Education: High Standards for High Stakes Tests." *The Virginia Journal of Social Policy and the Law, 6*(1), 81–113.

Guy, B., H. Shin, S-Y. Lee, and M. Thurlow (1999). *State Graduation Requirements for Students With and Without Disabilities (Technical Report 24)*. Minneapolis, MN: University of Minnesota, National Center on Educational Outcomes.

National Center on Educational Outcomes (1999). Forum on alternate assessment and "gray area" assessment (sponsored by Council of Chief State School Officers, Federal Resource Center, National Association of State Directors of Special Education, National Center on Educational Outcomes, and Regional Resource Centers). Minneapolis, MN: University of Minnesota, National Center on Educational Outcomes.

Internet Resources

National Center on Educational Outcomes: http://www.coled.umn.edu/nceo

Addressing the Assessment Needs of Students With Disabilities Who Are Learning English: The IEP/LEP Population

Excellence is never an accident.

—Anonymous

We are now at a point where we must educate our children in what no one knew yesterday, and prepare our schools for what no one knows yet.

—Margaret Mead

Hot Button Issues

- Hold on, I barely know how to work with students with disabilities. How can I possibly be expected to do anything with IEP students who don't even speak English?
- IEP/LEP makes no sense. It has to be one or the other.
- These are the kids that we really should exempt. No test can be valid for them.

Although we have raised a number of issues in this book, many have still not been addressed. One of these is the issue of students who are on IEPs and who have limited English proficiency (LEP). The number of such students varies from one place to the next, in many cases because we do not yet know how to accurately diagnose disabilities in students who are learning to speak English.

In this chapter, we intend to give you some tools for working with these students. First, we describe who these students are, how many there are, what their characteristics are, and other similar information. Then we address several key issues for improving the test performance of these students: how to make decisions about their participation in assessments, what accommodations they may need, and how their scores should be reported. We also address the instructional issues that are created by students who are learning English, issues above and beyond those created by having a disability.

It will become obvious to you that we do not have all the answers when it comes to students with disabilities who have LEP, but we do have some basic assumptions for you to consider and some starting steps for you to take as you assist these students in becoming prepared for district

Who Are They, These IEP/LEP Students?

Let's start with some terminology. We have used the term "limited English proficient" student. We selected that term because it is used in federal legislation, but many more terms are used in schools, districts, and states today. Some of the more common and the fine distinctions among them are provided in Box 11.1. As you will note in this list of words, some terms might be used interchangeably, such as English language learners (ELLs) and LEP students because they generally refer to the same group of students. Other terms have very different meanings, and they may be misused by those who really don't understand the differences among the groups. A common mistake is to equate students whose home language is other than English, commonly referred to as having a non-English-language background (NELB), and LEP students.

Another complication related to terminology is that the same student may be considered to have LEP for some purposes and not for others. For example, a student may not count as having LEP when the school decides whether he or she is eligible for ESL (English as a second language) or bilingual educational services. But the same student may count as having LEP when the state or district determines whether the student will participate in its assessment. In some states and districts, a test of English language proficiency may be used to determine participation in an assessment, while in other states, regardless of performance on a language proficiency test, the number of years that a student has been in the United States or in an English speaking school is the basis for determining whether the student participates in the district or state assessment. More will be covered about this later when we get into making decisions about participation in assessments and the implications for instruction, but suffice it to say that LEP is not a simple thing.

BOX 11.1

Clarification of Terminology

Term	Definition	Equivalent Terms	Nonequivalent Terms
Bilingual student	Student who speaks two languages, one of the languages may be English		LEP student
Bilingual education student	Student in the process of learning English and at the same time content in his or her first language		ESL student
English language learner (ELL)	Student in the process of learning English, either oral or written	LEP student, LM student	ESL student, bilingual ed. student
ESL student	Student learning English through English as a second language class		Bilingual ed. student
Language minority (LM) student	Student whose first language is in the minority in the educational setting where he or she is located	LEP student, ELL	ESL student, bilingual ed. student
Non-English language background (NELB)	Student whose home language is other than English, regardless of whether the student is fully English-proficient	LEP student, ELL, LM student	
Second language learner	An individual learning a second language, the first language may or may not be English		ELL, LEP student

One more complication needs to be mentioned before we move on to the LEP student who has a disability. Because students with LEP have different language backgrounds, associated differences exist in their educational histories. These students may or may not have been born in the United States. They may or may not have come from a country with an educational system. They may or may not have participated in the educational system if one existed. They may have been in their home country's educational system for 10, 5, or 1 year (and all the variations in between) before coming to the United States. Not only are the educational systems varied, but other experiential factors may vary as well, and the amount of time that the student was in them might have varied. For example, many students in the United States who arrived from war-torn countries may have spent considerable time in hiding or in refugee camps. All of these kinds of educational and experiential differences are intertwined with the language complexities that these students carry with them.

In a nutshell, IEP/LEP students are those students who have LEP (or who are ELLs) and who also have a disability. The complication, as you might guess, is in determining that a disability exists when a language difficulty impedes our ability to identify a disability. That this is a problem is obvious, because we already have difficulty identifying disabilities in those who are proficient in the English language. As you might guess, the difficulty is not so much in identifying students who have physical disabilities or severe cognitive disabilities. The difficulties arise most often related to disabilities that are not outwardly evident, such as learning disabilities, emotional disabilities, and even sensory disabilities. The challenges of conducting sound psychoeducational assessments are considerable. These challenges are complicated, as we will note later, by the difficulty of convening IEP teams that recognize the complications and that can sort them out in the decision-making process.

How Many Are There?

It is difficult to say exactly how many exist of something for which we don't have common definitions and for which we don't have a counting system. But we can get some estimates, and we certainly know a lot about trends.

First, let's get a handle on students with LEP (without the disabilities). Current estimates across the United States are that anywhere from approximately 3 to 10 million or more of all school-age children have LEP, however defined by the school, district, or state. The estimates vary greatly depending on where one lives. Several states have an estimated percentage of school-age LEP students close to 25 percent. Most of the largest states (California, Texas, New York, and Florida) and a few of the other larger states (Illinois, Ohio, and Pennsylvania) have the majority of students with LEP.

Looking at state distributions of students with LEP does not provide a completely accurate picture of the composition of school districts within the state. Some states with relatively small populations of students with LEP overall but have significant populations of these students within some of their large districts. Examples of these are in St. Paul, Minnesota. Minnesota is typically viewed as a midwestern, homogenous, Caucasian state. Yet even though the overall population of LEP students in the state is quite small, in St. Paul more than 40 percent of its students are English language learners.

When thinking about how many LEP students exist, it is also important to consider trends in numbers. It is not the case that as these students learn English, we will have diminishing numbers of such students. Current demographic estimates confirm that the number of students with LEP will continue to increase over the years, not decrease. It is expected that there will be more than 100 different languages in many of our mid- to large-size school districts.

So, given all this, how many IEP/LEP students are there? We don't know, but we can guess. Disabilities would be expected to be fairly evenly distributed across language groups. This would mean, given the current estimates of disabilities, that approximately 10 percent of all students with LEP also have a disability. The percentage may be smaller because we have a more difficult time identifying disabilities of students with LEP. Of course, you can see where this is going. Even if we are talking about only five percent of students with LEP also having a disability, then as the numbers of LEP students increase, so will the number of students who are IEP/LEP students. The numbers should skyrocket in the next 10 to 20 years.

What Is the Language of LEP Students?

Overall, Spanish is the most prevalent first language of students with LEP in the United States. This is true in the largest states as well as in many large districts, regardless of the state. It is not universally true, however. For example, in St. Paul, the most common language is Hmong, followed by Vietnamese, Cambodian, and Laotian; then comes Spanish. In many states and districts, more than 75 different languages are represented among the students in the schools. Of course, this brings lots of complications.

But the home language is only the tip of the proverbial iceberg. Students who receive instruction in U.S. schools typically receive their content instruction in English, perhaps supported by something in their first language. It is commonly accepted that students learning English first learn social English; that is, they learn to communicate with their peers and perhaps their teacher about social topics. Learning social English typically (complicated by all the other factors mentioned earlier) takes three to five years. Social English is not the same as academic English, the language of instruction. Academic English may take 7 to 10 years to master, yet it is the language in which most students receive instruction. So, the answer for assessment is not to provide a translated version of a test, because the student has not learned the content in his or her first language.

The differences between social and academic languages have been studied extensively by language learning theorists. Common terms in this field are Basic Inter-Personal Communication Skills (BICS) and Cognitive

Academic Language Proficiency (CALP). It is generally accepted that students must reach a threshold of BICS before CALP can develop. In addition, however, the development of CALP is dependent on academic reasoning skills, which are more likely to exist or develop more quickly if the student has strong language skills in his or her first language, which in turn is facilitated by coming from a literate home background. To further complicate the issues, certain content areas may require a longer time for CALP to develop than others. For example, reading, social studies, and science are generally considered to require more time for CALP to develop, and math and language arts may take less time.

These language issues, of course, complicate not only the diagnosis of disability, but they also complicate how to make good decisions about instruction, accommodations that are needed, and how to improve test scores after students are taking state and district assessments. Wow! Lots of areas to address!

Which Comes First: IEP or LEP?

This question may be unanswerable. In terms of legal rights, if a student has an IEP, all the rights that are connected to that IEP are held by the student. Yet all the issues and difficulties created by the student's LEP also apply. Instructionally, both disability and language needs must be addressed simultaneously. That is the only way in which performance on assessments (and, indeed, benefiting from instruction) can occur.

When most people ask questions about what comes first, they are really asking about who is responsible for the dollars required to meet the student's needs. This is especially true if special accommodations are needed either for instruction or for assessment. What we know is that this type of question does little to help the student. It is likely that an integration of dollars and services is needed, so that the needs of all are met equally.

We suggest that the question of "what comes first" is a nonquestion. Even if we could come up with an answer, it would be of little benefit to the student or to anyone else in the system.

Participation of IEP/LEP Students in District and State Assessments

The participation of students with LEP in district and state assessments is not something that is specifically covered by federal law, other than through the Improving America's Schools Act (IASA), which was formerly known as the Elementary and Secondary Education Act (ESEA). This act requires that Title I programs be evaluated by reporting the performance of students on state and district assessments tied to standards and that the performance of students with LEP (like the performance of students with disabilities) be disaggregated from the overall performance of all students. The intent of this requirement is to enable us to examine the performance of these traditionally low-performing groups.

Despite federal laws like the IASA, states and districts differ on their requirements for the participation of students with LEP in their assessments. This confusion, when coupled with IDEA 1997 for students with disabilities, means that we have a muddy set of guidelines for determining whether or how an LEP student with a disability should participate in state and district assessments. So, does this mean that all students with disabilities are supposed to participate in either the regular assessment or an alternate assessment, or does the complication of LEP automatically qualify that student for the alternate assessment? Does a policy in which LEP students are exempted from district or state assessments for a period of one to three years supersede the disability requirements that students participate in state and district assessments? Can primary language tests that assess students in their own language (generally Spanish) provide adequate measures of what the state or district test attempts to measure? Does the IDEA requirement that students be assessed in their native language apply to state and district assessments?

Looking at state policies gives us little guidance for how things should be for IEP/LEP students. We believe that if a student has a disability, that student should participate in the regular or alternate assessment under the same guidelines as other students with disabilities. The caveat is that the assessment must occur in the language of instruction or, even better, in the student's language of choice. We use the term "language of choice" because of the problems with social language versus academic language and all the other complications of educational and experiential background. The IEP team should take into consideration the language characteristics of the LEP/IEP student.

Of course, things are not always ideal, and "language of choice" may not always be a viable option. Certain tests, such as English tests, preclude allowing the student to use his or her language of choice. Similarly, many states insist that the student demonstrate English skills in all content areas in order to earn a high school diploma. These situations make it much more difficult to develop and implement what might be considered "best practice" in the assessment of IEP/LEP students.

It is also important to think about the goals of the students' instruction. These goals should include both academic content (or functional skills, as appropriate) and the learning of the English language. Thus, state and district assessments for IEP/LEP students perhaps should encompass more than they do for those students about whose language acquisition we are not worried. Even if your state or district is not using an assessment of English acquisition, perhaps you should be doing so to ensure that the student is making progress in this essential skill at the same time that the state/district is measuring the acquisition of content knowledge and skills.

Accommodations

IEP/LEP students often need accommodations to address their needs related to both their disabilities and their LEP. You may wonder whether the accommodations needed would be the same. It seems logical that these students may need extra time and maybe a separate setting. But are there some accommodations that might be needed for their language concerns and others for their disability concerns?

Because we are dealing with humans, whose needs don't nicely separate between those related to disabilities and those related to language, it is probably not beneficial to analyze a student's needs separately. Instructionally, this kind of division makes little sense, but lists of accommodations that are allowed for assessments may or may not be separated for students with disabilities or students with LEP. Sometimes when the listed accommodations are divided, they just say the same things but have different labels. More often now, the lists are divided and different kinds of accommodations are included in each list. If this is the case, you will need to have both lists at hand, and you will need to be able to justify the need for accommodations in one list or the other. A list of some common LEP accommodations is included in Box 11.2. These are ones taken from state-level accommodations policies for LEP students.

Making decisions about the accommodations that IEP/LEP students need should follow the same basic procedures as decisions about accommodations for any student. They should be related to what happens in

---

BOX 11.2

Common LEP Accommodations

Setting	Scheduling/Timing
Bilingual education or ESL classroom	Extended time
Individualized setting	Frequent breaks

Presentation	Response
English dictionary/glossary	First language responses acceptable
Familiar examiner	Scribe writes responses
Translated test items	

instruction, and they should meet the specific needs of the student. Setting up a questionnaire that gets at needs (like that in Chapter 5, "Accommodations: How to Make Sound Decisions for Instruction and Assessment") works for IEP/LEP students.

Reporting Scores

The reporting of scores on state and district assessments becomes even more complicated when we are talking about students with disabilities who have LEP. Should the scores of these students be included with the scores of all other IEP students? Should these scores be included instead with the scores of LEP students? Or, should a separate group of students be formed—those students with LEP who are on IEPs.

Answering the question of how scores should be reported is less difficult if we go back to some basic assumptions and some considerations about the type of data needed to make good decisions for instruction. First, our assumptions. If we assume that all students can learn and that the learning of all students is the responsibility of educators, then there is no question that the scores of IEP/LEP students must be included in the scores reported—somewhere.

When we consider what kind of information is needed to make good instructional decisions, decisions about programs for students, then it becomes clear that we need the data reported for the subgroup of students with LEP who are on IEPs. This approach, however, does not preclude the reports from also grouping students with those students with LEP and with those students on IEPs.

The reason that it is important to have data just on IEP/LEP students is that this level of information will help us to more clearly see how these students are doing relative to other students with disabilities and relative to other students with LEP. The exception for public reporting, of course, is that if the number of students in this group is too small, it should not be reported. The fact that data are not reported publicly, however, should not preclude those educators working with the students from seeing how they are performing so that instruction can be changed as needed.

With the passage of the Title I legislation (Improving America's Schools Act) in 1994, it became clear that students with disabilities and ELLs have the disadvantage of being subjected to little research. This is changing. Recent work within the Office of Bilingual Education and Minority Languages Affairs (OBEMLA) is identifying expected gains in LEP student achievement and ways to achieve and document those gains.

Recently, discussions about what to do assessment-wise for these students have also been initiated. Suggestions made by the National Research Council in *Testing, Teaching, and Learning* (see Box 11.3) are a first step in thinking about LEP students in assessments. For example, exposing stu-

BOX 11.3

Considerations for Assessing LEP Students

- Teachers should regularly and frequently administer assessments, including assessments of English-language proficiency for the purpose of monitoring the progress of English-language learners and for adapting instruction to improve performance.
- States and districts should develop clear guidelines for accommodations that permit English-language learners to participate in assessments administered for accountability purposes. Especially important are clear decision rules for determining the level of English-language proficiency at which English-language learners should be expected to participate exclusively in English-language assessments.
- Students should be assessed in the language that permits the most valid inferences about the quality of their academic performance. When numbers are sufficiently large, states and districts should develop subject-matter assessments in languages other than English.
- English-language learners should be exempted from assessments only when there is evidence that the assessment, even with accommodations, cannot measure the knowledge or skill of particular students or groups of students.
- States and districts should describe the methods they use to screen English-language learners for accommodations, exemptions, and alternate assessments, and they should report the frequency of these practices.
- Federal research units, foundations, and other funding agencies should promote research that advances knowledge about the validity and reliability of different accommodations, exemptions, and alternate assessment practices for English-language learners.

SOURCE: Reprinted, with permission, from the National Research Council (1999) report, "Testing, Teaching, and Learning" edited by Richard Elmore and Robert Rothman. Washington, DC: National Academy Press. Page 63.

dents to assessments in the classroom is one way to familiarize LEP/IEP students with the process. Another is to develop and then use specific procedures for deciding what accommodations individual students need in order to participate in assessments. These suggestions and others, of course, may need to be adapted for IEP/LEP students.

Instruction for IEP/LEP Students

Back to the bottom line! Students must be taught in order to perform well on tests. This is particularly true for students with disabilities who are limited in their English proficiency. Although our knowledge base on how best to teach LEP/IEP students is limited, we do know something. Applying even this little bit of knowledge will help students improve their test performances.

According to a comprehensive literature review conducted by Minnesota Assessment Project researchers within the National Center on Educational Outcomes (NCEO) at the University of Minnesota, a variety of factors affect their test scores. Among the factors identified by the literature were the following:

- *The degree of acculturation in the student*: the extent to which the student has acquired the customs and values of a culture.

- *The level of first and second language proficiency*: the level of social and academic language skills in both the first and second language.

- *The extent of cognitive development and literacy in the native language*: the extent to which the student has been exposed to schooling and other factors related to cognitive development.

- *Attitudinal factors*: beliefs about a variety of topics related to assessment, including attitudes about demonstrating knowledge, verbal communication, use of time, and so on.

- *Test bias*: in addition to language or cultural biases, there may be a bias in communicative style, cognitive style, or test interpretation.

Some of these factors are alterable and are affected by instruction, but others are not. It is important to identify those factors that are alterable in one's own situation and then to systematically identify ways to address the factors. These factors, of course, will also affect how students react to and profit from instruction.

When a student has both a diagnosed disability and LEP, he or she must be involved in at least three programs: general education, special education, and the ESL/bilingual program. It is critical that the three programs work with each other to form a seamless system for the student, one that does not have duplicated supports or gaps in support.

It is generally believed that effective instruction is good practice for all students (see Chapter 9, "Instruction: The Bottom Line in Improving Test Performance," for more information on instruction). Many state- and local-level materials have been developed to guide educators in ways to make sure that effective instruction really does occur for students with disabilities who are limited in their English proficiency. In general, these materials develop the following principles (taken here from Minnesota's Special Delivery Guidelines for LEP Students with Special Education Needs):

- Instructional preparation takes into account students' needs, learning styles, and available resources.

- Flexible grouping patterns based on students' needs are exhibited in the school and classroom.

BOX 11.4

Instructional Strategies for IEP/LEP Students

- Procedures and strategies that are appropriate for elementary-age students should be continued into secondary school . . . Classrooms should be "print-rich" environments.
- The classroom climate should show value for the skills and knowledge students have from the home culture.
- Teaching acculturation is part of the goal of instruction. This includes familiarizing students with the expectations of the school and other social environments within the community.
- No assumptions should be made about what a student knows. Always give sufficient background information to establish a context for new information.
- Linguistic interference may affect all areas of learning.
- It is normal for students to make certain errors as they acquire English skills. Overcorrection of linguistic errors will reduce the student's motivation to communicate.
- The student should be spoken to at a normal rate and volume, using natural intonation.

SOURCE: Reprinted with permission from the Minnesota Department of Education. *Service Delivery Guidelines for LEP Students with Special Education Needs*. St. Paul, MN: Unique Learner Needs Section, 1991.

- Effective models of teaching are employed to increase the academic learning time and student achievement.
- Parents are involved in the child's education and support the goals and expectations of the school.

In addition to these principles, Minnesota (like other states) identifies important instructional strategies (see Box 11.4).

An important part of preparing IEP/LEP students to perform their best on state and district assessments is giving them the same advantages that other students have. As noted previously, general education students generally have picked up test-preparation and test-taking strategies on their own. This is generally not the case for students with disabilities and is doubly not so for students who have LEP.

Thus, it is even more critical that sufficient energy be devoted to ensure that IEP/LEP students know what to expect in the state or district test, and that they know how to prepare and take tests to their greatest advantage. Also, as noted before, this energy should not occur in place of regular instruction, but rather should be integrated into it. Still, checks should be done to make sure that the students are learning testing procedures as well as content.

Summary

The IEP/LEP population, students with disabilities who are learning English, is perhaps one of the most challenging groups for our schools today. This is no excuse, however, for failing to give them the best education possible. Now is the time to quickly learn how to do this, because the numbers of IEP/LEP students are increasing and will continue to do so.

From what we now know, good instruction for any student is also good for IEP/LEP students. However, additional considerations must be given to these students because they have additional challenges. These challenges are related to language, the major way that we communicate information that we want students to learn. Thus, as educators, we need to rely on principles that ease the burden of language while still educating the child.

Test Your Knowledge

Once again, review what you have learned in this chapter. Feel free to review the chapter and reread parts to fill in the blanks.

1. A common mistake is to equate students from non-English language backgrounds with students who have limited English _____.

2. _____ students are those students who have LEP and who also have been determined to have a disability.

3. Current demographic estimates confirm that the number of students with LEP will continue to _____ over the years.

4. It is estimated that there will be more than _____ different languages in many mid- to large-size school districts.

5. Overall, _____ is the most prevalent first language of students with LEP in the U.S.

6. BICS refers to Basic Inter-Personal _____ Skills.

7. CALP refers to _____ Academic Language Proficiency.

8. _____ often are needed by IEP/LEP students to address their needs related to both disabilities and LEP.

9. The need for data on the subgroup of students with LEP who are on IEPs becomes evident when trying to make good _____ decisions for IEP/LEP students.

10. It is critical that sufficient energy be devoted to making sure that IEP/LEP students know how to _____ for tests and how to take tests to their greatest advantage.

Answers

1. proficiency (p. 211)
2. IEP/LEP (p. 213)
3. increase (p. 214)
4. 100 (p. 214)
5. Spanish (p. 214)
6. Communication (p. 214)
7. Cognitive (p. 214–215)
8. Accommodations (p. 217)
9. instructional (p. 218)
10. prepare (p. 221)

Resources

Liu, K., M. Thurlow, R. Erickson, and R. Spicuzza (1997). *A Review of the Literature on Students with Limited English Proficiency and Assessment* (Minnesota Report 11). Minneapolis, MN: University of Minnesota, National Center on Educational Outcomes.

Minnesota Department of Education (1991). *Service Delivery Guidelines for LEP Students with Special Education Needs*. St. Paul, MN: Unique Learner Needs Section.

National Research Council. *Educating Language-Minority Children*. Edited by D. August and K. Hakuta (1998). Washington, DC: National Academy Press.

Testing Teaching, and Learning: A Guide for States and School Districts. Edited by R. F. Elmore and R. Rothman (1999). Washington, DC: National Academy Press.

Ortiz, A. (1984) "Choosing the Language of Instruction for Exceptional Bilingual Children." *Teaching Exceptional Children, 16* (3), 202–206.

Internet Resources

National Association of Bilingual Education (NABE): http://www.nabe.org

Office of Bilingual Education and Minority Languages Affairs (OBEMLA): http://www.ed.gov/offices/OBEMLA

Teachers of English to Students of Other Languages (TESOL): http://www.tesol.edu

Chapters 8–11
Self Check:
Where Do I Stand?

See whether you agree with the following statements as a personal survey of where you stand in relation to the information presented. Base your assessment on the topics that are presented in this book and what you think you already know and are doing.

- I am familiar with the federal laws that have affected vocational and transition planning for students with disabilities. I understand transition planning and its relevance for successfully launching students into post-secondary environments (Chapter 8).

- I realize that students working on or attending vocational programs need to be learning the same standards as students in the general curriculum. I know that this is an especially difficult situation for these students because a limited number of standards specifically address nonacademic learning. I also know that no matter what assessment students take, they need to be accounted for (Chapter 8).

- A key in developing student-centered transition plans is to involve students as much as possible in the process. Developing self-advocacy and self-empowerment skills are critical to students in post-secondary school environments. I am working on developing these skills in my own students (Chapter 8).

- I recognize the dual system of educating general and special education students that has developed over the years. However, I believe that good teaching is good teaching and effective instructional strategies work for all kids in general education and special education (Chapter 9).

- Teaching is hard work; that's for sure! However, I recognize that expectations for students with disabilities are not always the same as for general education students. I am making sure that the curriculum and materials I use in the classroom or with individual students in the general setting parallel as much as possible the standards worked on by all students (Chapter 9).

- I see how the focus on assessments and high test scores has affected instruction in the classroom. Teachers are stressed out about how their students will do on the tests. I know what I need to do to improve the performance of my students: teach! (Chapter 9)

- I realize that education in general has not done a good job in evaluating the effectiveness of instruction. When students perform poorly on classroom and/or district assessments, too often the students are blamed. I know better and work every day to have instruction make a difference in students' lives rather than a predictor about their lives (Chapter 9).

- I am worried about students with disabilities who are caught in the middle. They don't qualify for the alternate assessment yet are going to do very poorly on the district assessment. However, I realize that some of the gray in gray area students comes from the lack of good instruction that provides students the opportunity to learn what is needed. I continue to focus on aligning standards, curriculum, and assessments for all students (Chapter 10).

- I understand that the bottom line for deciding what test a student should take is reflected in the curriculum and/or diploma the student is working toward. However, I also understand that the issue of assessment is more and more becoming a civil rights issue. It is not whether the student failed or performed poorly on the assessment, but rather was he or she given the opportunity to learn the content needed to pass (Chapter 10).

- I am concerned about the gray area for kids who don't have IEPs. They don't qualify for special education services, yet they are holding on for dear life in school. What can be done for these students? For me, it is all about effective instruction: how to plan, manage, deliver, and evaluate instruction. It isn't necessarily about the kids, but how we as educators take the lead in making sure all kids count in instruction (Chapter 10).

- I know the policies that my district and state have in place for making decisions about IEP/LEP students, and I know how to implement those policies so that they result in the best decisions for students (Chapter 11).

- I understand the importance of including all students in state and district assessments and know how to incorporate in my instruction ways to increase the test-taking skills of my IEP/LEP students (Chapter 11).

- I recognize the need to disaggregate the scores of students with disabilities and students with LEP. I also believe in the importance of having disaggregated information on just those students who both have a disability and are limited in their English proficiency (Chapter 11).

Resource A:
Reproducible Forms

FORM A

School Accountability Worksheet

School:_____ **District:**_____

To determine what factors contribute to school accountability in your school or district, find answers to the following questions. Complete this with your colleagues.

- Define the "stakes" associated with your accountability system(s) and specify exactly what they are:

	District Level	**State Level**

For students—

For staff—

For administrators—

- Which indicators are currently included in your accountability system(s)?

Student performance

Attendance

Dropout rate

Other

- What methods are used to gather data on each of the indicators that are used in your accountability system?

Student performance

Attendance

Dropout rate

Other

FORM B

Steps in Backmapping Standards to Instruction

1. Select a standard.

2. Identify or break down the standard according to the elements or skills that are embedded in it.

3. Locate these skills in the scope and sequence of the curriculum. Are they present or not?

4. Create an instructional blueprint of all skills that are needed to achieve the standard. Be sure to indicate those that are prerequisite skills and those that are component skills.

5. Break identified skills into units of instruction.

6. Identify instructional strategies and materials to teach the embedded skills.

7. Assess whether students have the prerequisite skills that are needed to engage in learning the standard.

8. Identify methods to assess student knowledge and understanding of the taught skills.

9. When assessment is conducted by using a norm-referenced test, review the table of specifications. This table outlines the types of skills measured, the method of assessment, and the number of items assessed. This table helps you plan for instructional areas of concentration and importance.

FORM C

A Framework for Backmapping

Standards (Domains)	Instructional Blueprint	Units of Instruction/ Materials	Instructional Strategies	Assessment

FORM D

Case Study: Kyle's Access to the General-Education Curriculum
With and Without Accommodations

Consider the following case study about Kyle. Then answer the following questions:

- How is Kyle's situation similar to that of other students you teach?
- How can this scenario be proactively managed to avoid having Kyle fall into the cracks?

Kyle was first diagnosed as having a learning disability in third grade. His reading skills were poor, but his math computation skills were excellent. He had trouble listening to the teacher and to classroom discussions and never seemed to be able to complete assignments when he was in the classroom. Sometimes when he bothered other students and kept them from doing their work, Kyle was sent into the hallway, where he was carefully watched by a hall monitor. Here, he could do his work without distraction. Despite his quick completion of tasks, particularly if they were math problems, he was made to stay in the hallway as punishment. As a result, he missed worksheet reviews and discussions between the teacher and his classmates as they reviewed how problems were solved or how word problems were comprehended.

When the IEP team met for Kyle's annual review, it became obvious that something was not working right. Despite his excellent math skills, Kyle was not enjoying the same access to the curriculum as his classmates. The IEP team identified several accommodations to restore and upgrade his access to the general curriculum.

First, being sent to the hallway to work undistracted was no longer used to help focus on his math problems (nor as punishment). Instead, Kyle was assigned to a carrel in which he could work undistracted if he needed it. Kyle was taught to figure out when he needed an accommodation to help him work undistracted. Also, to help Kyle pay attention during teacher instruction, he was given a desk at the front of the room, slightly ahead of other students so that he could not bother them. He also was given instruction in self-regulation skills, so that he monitored whether he was on task and was rewarded for bringing himself back on task (or for remaining on task without redirection).

With these instructional accommodations, Kyle rarely missed teacher instruction or review and discussion periods. Also, he resumed his excellent math performance. As he regained his skills and began again to surpass his classmates, Kyle was allowed to help other students (as long as he remained on task). His skills and behavior demonstrated that his access to the general-education curriculum was good not only for him but also for his classmates. Also, as a result of the careful consideration of what accommodations would work and which ones he would need to be taught, Kyle gained skills in knowing when he needed accommodations and asking for those that he needed when he needed them.

FORM E

Common Instructional Accommodations, A through Z

Altered assignments	Natural supports
Audio-taped directions	Note-taking aids
Bold print	On-task reminders
Bulletin board strategy reminders	Outline text
Color coding	Paper holders (magnets, tape, etc.)
Crib notes	Peer support
Darker lines	Quality monitoring
Directions clarified or simplified	Questions in margins
Enlarged materials	Reader
Extended time	Raised print
Fewer tasks per assignment	Shorter assignments
Finger spacing, counting strategies	Seat location change
Graph paper for calculations	Touch talker (communication device)
Green color as cue to continue	Tutoring (cross-age, peer)
Harder items first	Underline key points
Headphones	Use reminders
Individual work area	Visual prompts
Isolated items	Vocabulary cues on paper/board
Key words highlighted	Wider margins
Knock-on-desk cues	Word processor
Large pictures	Word list on board
Limit number of tasks	X-out text to reduce reading
Manipulatives	Yellow paper
Memory aids	Zero-wrong strategies

FORM F

Classroom Accommodations Worksheet

Follow these steps to identify accommodations that are needed for classroom instruction and for classroom tests for a specific student. Be sure to consider the specific characteristics, strengths, and weaknesses of the student for whom this worksheet is being completed. For each step, be sure to separately consider instruction and tests and use the questions to spark ideas about useful accommodations. You will find it helpful to complete this worksheet with other individuals who know the student.

	Reflections on Each Question	Possible Instructional Accommodations	Possible Classroom Test Accommodations
1. What helps the student learn better or perform better? What gets in the way of the student showing what he or she really knows and can do?			
2. What has the student's parents or guardian told you about things that they do to help the student complete household tasks or school homework?			
3. What are the student's strengths and weaknesses? What skills or behaviors often get in the way of learning or performance?			
4. What accommodations has the student been taught to use? Are there other accommodations on which the student needs training?			
5. For which accommodations have effects been observed? What accommodations is the student willing to use?			

FORM F

Classroom Accommodations Worksheet (Continued)

	Reflections on Each Question	Possible Instructional Accommo-dations	Possible Classroom Test Accommo-dations
6. Have any quantitative data (e.g., from one-minute tests) been collected on the effects of accommodations?			
7. Is there any other relevant information that might affect the provision of accommodations in the classroom, during instruction, or during tests?			

FORM G

Student Accommodations Questionnaire

Student: _____

Class/Teacher: _____

Date: _____

Directions: The following questions can be used to ask students about accommodations. Be sure first that you understand the assessment that students will be taking so that you can convey this information to the student. Adjust your vocabulary and question complexity for the age of the student.

- Do you think that the test [describe for the student] will be okay for you, or is there some way that it could be changed to help you perform your best?

- Is there anything about the content of the test or what it asks you to do [describe for the student] that could be changed to help you perform your best?

- Is there anything about the test's timing procedures [describe for the student] that could be changed to help you perform your best?

- Is there anything about when the test is given [describe for the student] that could be changed to help you perform your best?

- Is there anything about the way the test is presented [describe for the student] that could be changed to help you perform your best?

- Is there anything about how you have to answer the test [describe for the student] that could be changed to help you perform your best?

- Is there anything about the test that could be changed to help you perform your best on the test?

FORM H

Form to Track Students' Strengths and Weaknesses

Date: _____

Class/Teacher: _____

Student Name	Strengths	Weaknesses	Implications for Accommodations

FORM I

Case Study: Tracking the Effects of Accommodations

Ms. Jones decides that Mao needs to use accommodations during the state test. She already uses several accommodations for Mao during instruction, but Ms. Jones has never checked them out in any systematic way. Because she knows about the tendency to over-accommodate and recognizes the finding that over-accommodation sometimes impedes performance, she has decided to check some of the accommodations that she uses with Mao during instruction to see whether they really would have an effect during the statewide assessment.

Ms. Jones checks the three accommodations during the next three weeks. Every day except Friday, she has Mao take a short two-minute math calculation test. During the first four days (week 1), she has Mao take the test with no accommodations. Then, during week 2, she has Mao take the test under unlimited time conditions. Finally, during week 3, she has Mao take the test with no accommodations.

The following chart shows the results of Ms. Jones' tracking study. Clearly, the accommodation makes a difference in Mao's performance. The percent correct that she obtains is much higher when she is tested under unlimited time conditions. The difference is not quite as dramatic as one would initially think, however. By reinstituting testing without accommodations, Ms. Jones sees that Mao's performance is higher the second time without accommodations than the first time. This information suggests that Mao's performance is increasing simply because of the practice she is receiving taking the test (an important point: practice and instruction are as important as accommodations).

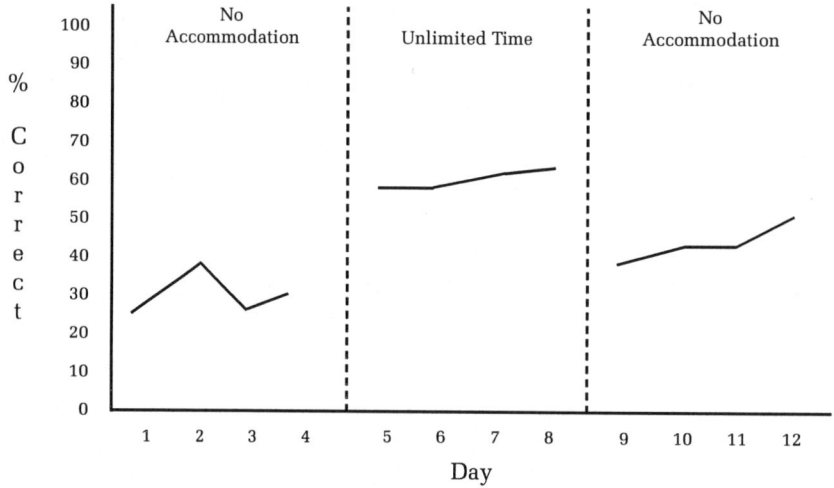

Ms. Jones could gather even more information by tracking more accommodations over a longer period of time. By extending the duration of her tracking, Ms. Jones could also get a better feel for the potential impact of simply providing Mao with practice on test formats and content.

FORM J

Determining Links between Classroom Accommodations, Classroom Testing Accommodations, and District or State Testing Accommodations

Student: _____

Class/Teacher: _____

Directions: Use this form to identify accomodations that are used during instruction. Then indicate whether they are allowed in district and state assessments. Indicate reasons for any discrepancies among the columns.

Accommo-dation	Instruction	Classroom Assessment	District Assessment	State Assessment	Reason for Discrepancy Among Columns
e.g., frequent breaks	X	X	X	X	
e.g., read text to student	X	X	X		Policy does not allow in state test

FORM K

Case Study: Accommodation Decisions for Instruction and Testing

Consider the following case study about Roberto. Use it to discuss students you currently teach who require accommodations. Answer the following questions about your students:

- How did you find out they needed accommodations?

- How have you provided the needed accommodations? Specify the logistics of providing the accommodations.

- What has been the impact of providing the accommodations?

Roberto is a third-grade student who has recently moved into the state from a state with extremely different educational supports. He now faces school daily with a certain amount of trepidation, because everyone in the school seems to be emphasizing what he cannot do, rather than what he can do. This situation is almost directly opposite of what was happening in his prior school, so he is beginning to question whether he can do what is expected of him. He is personalizing the concerns of teachers and administrators in his new school about his need for a reader (for the math test), extended time (for the reading test), and a spell-checker (for the writing test). Also, as a result, when first asked about what he needed when taking the state test, he indicated that he needed nothing. Nothing is what he got.

His performance was lower than any test score he had ever gotten before. Despite his excellent math skills, he barely finished any items, and those he did complete were mostly wrong.

Luckily, his math teacher had recently attended a seminar on instructional accommodations. There, he learned about what accommodations are, about the controversy that surrounds them, and why they are an important part of providing students who have disabilities with access to instruction. He began making sure that Roberto either worked with a peer—sharing the reading of directions and word problems—and then answering questions on their own. He also provided Roberto with tape-recorded homework assignments. With these instructional accommodations, Roberto's math performance soared. He was showing what he knew and could do without the impediment of his reading disability.

FORM L

Selected Assessment Terminology and Definitions

Alternate Assessment

A substitute approach used in gathering information about the performance and progress of students who do not participate in typical state assessments. Under the reauthorized Individuals with Disabilities Education Act (IDEA), alternate assessments are to be used to measure the performance of a relatively small population of students who are unable to participate in the regular assessment system, even with accommodations.

Alternative Assessment

A generic term that is typically applied to a variety of different assessment activities. These assessments provide an alternative to multiple-choice tests that require students to select one response. Writing samples, portfolios, and performance-based assessments might all be considered forms of alternative assessment.

Assessment

The process of collecting data for the purpose of making decisions about individuals, groups, or systems.

Authentic Assessment

Often used synonymously with performance assessment, this term can also mean an assessment that uses only real-world tasks as the basis for information about how well an individual can perform certain tasks.

Confidence Interval (CI)

A numerical range that shows the interval around a score that one would expect a person or group of persons to obtain if they were to take the same test again. A CI of 95 percent indicates that one can be 95 percent confident that if the person or group was retested, their average score would fall into the same range.

Criterion-Referenced Test (CRT)

Criterion-referenced tests are measures that are used to examine student performance relative to state and/or district criteria or standards. Instead of comparing students' scores to a national normative standard, scores are interpreted in terms of various performance standards—usually set at the district or state level (e.g., mastery versus nonmastery or low proficiency, moderate proficiency, and high proficiency within a particular subject area).

FORM L

Selected Assessment Terminology and Definitions (Continued)

Norm-Referenced Test (NRT)

Norm-referenced tests are those that provide a comparison of individual performance to that of a state or national comparison (standardization) sample. A norm-referenced test measures the performance of a student against the performance of other individuals. Use of the norm sample enables raw scores to be converted to grade-equivalent scores, percentile scores, and standard scores.

Normal Curve Equivalents (NCEs)

NCEs are standard scores that are generated from a normal distribution. You begin with a set of raw scores, convert them to percentile ranks, and then use a z-score table to convert the percentile rank to a z-score. The resulting z-scores are usually transformed by using a linear transformation to a new scale (such as the SAT, where the mean equals 500 and the standard deviation equals 100). NCE scores can be used only for students who are similar in age or grade to those in the norm sample.

Percentile Scores

These scores tell the percent of people in the normative sample that scored at or below a student's score (e.g., a percentile rank of 80 means that 80 percent of the normative group earned a score at or below that student's score).

Performance Assessment

A form of testing that requires the creation of an answer or a project, rather than the selection of an answer (as in many traditional multiple-choice tests). In many cases, such assessments are intended to represent or simulate real-life situations that require problem solving. The term is often used synonymously with authentic assessment.

Portfolio Assessment

A collection of student-generated or student-focused products that provides the basis for judging student accomplishment. In school settings, portfolios might contain extended projects, drafts of student work, teacher comments and evaluations, assessment results, and self-evaluations. The products typically depict the range of skills of the student or reveal the improvement in a student's skill level over time.

Raw Scores

These scores are simply the scores that are obtained when you sum the score on each item. If items are scored dichotomously (1 or 0), then a raw score represents the total number of items answered correctly.

FORM L

Selected Assessment Terminology and Definitions (Continued)

Standards-Based Assessment

An assessment instrument, battery, or system that has been constructed to measure the achievement of individual students or student populations in attaining certain standards, which are generally established by local districts or state educational agencies. Most state-level standards-based assessment programs that are currently in place measure student performance against articulated standards in core academic content areas, such as reading, mathematics, writing, science, and social studies.

Standard Error of Measurement (SEM)

An index of reliability that essentially converts reliability data from a test into a confidence interval around a given score. Knowing the standard deviation, the reliability, and a person's score, you can estimate a confidence band within which you would expect the individual to score (in typical cases, 95 percent of the time) if that individual repeatedly took a parallel version of the test.

Standard Scores

These scores are linear transformations of raw scores and are considered the easiest to interpret. With standard scores, the mean and standard deviation of any distribution can be placed onto a similar scale. Common examples of standard scores are the SAT, which has a mean of 500 and a standard deviation of 100, or a typical Intelligence Quotient (IQ) test with a mean of 100 and a standard deviation of 15.

Reliability

Reliability is the extent to which a test measures what it purports to measure time after time. Reliability also refers to the accuracy, precision, or stability of a measuring instrument.

Rubric

A scoring guide that facilitates the consensus of the people who are rating the students' performances on assessment tasks. A rubric provides criteria from which those students who are assessed can learn to improve their performance.

Validity

Test validity, simply stated, refers to a test that measures what is says it measures.

SOURCE: The definitions in this paper were adapted from the definitions used by Drs. Elliott and Thurlow in their work at the National Center on Educational Outcomes.

FORM M

Informing Students About State and District Assessments

Topic	Elementary (Grades 1–3)	Intermediate (Grades 4–5)	Middle (Grades 6–8)	Senior High (Grades 9–11)
School Consequences	This test is to see what you have been taught. It helps decide how our school is doing. You should do your best so that our school looks good.	This test is used to determine what you have been taught in this school. It is used to see whether this school has taught you what you need to know. You should do your best so that our school looks good.	This test is used to measure what you know so that the state department of education (or appropriate decision maker) can decide whether our school is doing what it needs to be doing to educate you. It is important to do your best so that what happens to this school is what needs to happen.	This test is used to measure what you know so that the state department of education (or appropriate decision maker) can decide whether to give the school extra money. It is important to do your best so that test results accurately reflect what our student body knows.
Student Consequences	This test is to see what you have been taught. It helps us know that you have learned what you need to in this grade to be ready for the next grade. Do your best.	This test is used to determine what you have been taught. It is used to see whether you have learned what you need to know to move to the next grade. You should do your best so that we know you are ready to move on.	This test is used to measure what you know so that we all know that you have the skills you need to move to the next grade or to graduate from high school.	This test is used to measure what you know so that the school board can verify that you have the skills that you need to move to the next grade or graduate.

FORM M

Informing Students About State and District Assessments (Continued)

Topic	Elementary (Grades 1–3)	Intermediate (Grades 4–5)	Middle (Grades 6–8)	Senior High (Grades 9–11)
School and Student Consequences	This test is to see what you have been taught. It helps decide how our school is doing. It also helps us know that you have learned what you need to in this grade to be ready for the next grade. You should do your best.	This test is used to determine what you have been taught in this school. It is used to see whether this school has taught you what you need to know. The test is also used to see whether you have learned what you need to know in order to move to the next grade. You should do your best.	This test is used to measure what you know so that the state department of education (or appropriate decision maker) can decide whether our school is doing what it needs to be doing to educate you. It is also used to see that you have the skills you need to move to the next grade or be ready to graduate from high school. It is important to do your best.	This test is used to measure what you know so that the state department of education (or the appropriate decision maker) can decide whether to give the school extra money. It is also used to measure what you know so that the school board can verify that you have the skills you need to move to the next grade or graduate from high school. It is important to do your best.

FORM N

Test Performance Chart

Directions: Use this handy chart to keep track of students' performance on state and district assessments.

Past Test Information

Class _____

Upcoming Test Content and Date _____

Student	Last Test Date	Content Area	Type of Score*	Score	Accommodations and Other Notes

*Percentile rank, raw score, and proficiency level. If there is more than one type of score noted, select and list the one that is most like the score that will be given on the state or district assessment.

FORM O

Common Test Vocabulary Terms

Directions: Take this list of vocabulary terms and expand it. Add to the list of common test vocabulary, making sure that you indicate the content area to which the terms apply, if that is appropriate.

Analyze	Estimate	List	Pattern
Best	Evaluate	Most accurate	Point of view
Categorize	Explain	Most appropriate	Predict
Classify	Fact	Not	Reasonable
Compare	Group	Not like	Sequence
Conclude	Identify	Only one	Summarize
Contrast	Justify	Opinion	Transform
Describe	Least true	Order	Verify
Discuss	Like	Outline	

FORM P

Suggestions for Answering Different Types of Questions

Item Type	Suggestions for Students
True/False	Do not be concerned with expected patterns of responses (e.g., do not try to make the number of true responses and the number of false responses equal). Attend to absolute statements—ones that contain words such as "never" or "always"—and realize that these are almost never true (but they can be true sometimes).
Multiple Choice	Treat each answer option as a true/false statement (i.e., determine whether each option is true or false); then respond to the stem demands. Mark out absurd items so that you are choosing only among the more likely options.
Multiple Choice	Proceed through items relatively quickly, going with your first guess and changing later only if you are certain of a different response.
Fill-in-the-Blank	Make a best guess based on content knowledge but look for cues in the structure of the sentence. Be sure that the word(s) you choose fits the grammatical structure of the item.
Short Answer	Recognize short answer questions as such and do not write too much. Respond directly to the point of the question; assist yourself in performing this task by underlining the key elements requested.
Essay	Write enough to be convincing. Keep your answer organized. To achieve this goal, take notes beside the item or jot notes onto a separate piece of paper. Be neat. Use strategies to help guide the writing process. (For example, use SNOW—**s**tudy the question; **n**ote the important points; **o**rganize your thoughts; **w**rite to the question (Scruggs and Mastropieri, 1992).

FORM Q

Parent Questions and Answers About State and District Assessments

Question: Why do I need to know whether my state or district assessment is a norm-referenced assessment?

Answer: Norm-referenced tests (NRTs) are developed to enable a student to be compared to other students or for a group of students (say, those in a school) to be compared to a group of students nationwide. This feature enables schools, districts, and states to know how they are performing in comparison to other schools, districts, or states. Although this seems to be important, NRTs have several limitations, one of which is that they do not directly assess standards; they assess a broad set of objectives that are not directly related to any one student's curriculum. In addition, they have many limitations for students with disabilities. One of these is that most NRTs have been developed without considering students with disabilities; items have not been checked by these students or educators who know the characteristics of students with disabilities. Furthermore, because of the importance placed on everyone taking the test in the same way, NRTs enable few accommodations to be used.

Question: Why is it important for my child to be included in assessments if their purpose is just to decide whether the school gets a reward for student performance? One student won't make a difference.

Answer: It is important that the school knows that every child counts. Although it is true that the score of one student may not make a big difference in the overall rating a school gets, it is very easy for one student to multiply into many students, and these students generally are those expected to perform less well on the assessment. When a student is not included in the assessment, there is no urgency to worry about whether they are mastering the skills that will be on the test. And if there is no urgency to worry about them, then it is easy to forget about them. Furthermore, when decisions are based on data, the missing data from students who didn't take the test will have no influence on the reforms that are generated as a result of student performance. All of these together produce a situation in which students not only are excluded from the assessment, but also from the indirect benefits of reform and often from the direct benefits of instruction.

Question: How can I tell whether the test my child is taking is based on standards, basic skills, or something else?

Answer: The best way to determine what is being measured is to ask. Often this information is provided in information about the test, but not always.

FORM Q

Parent Questions and Answers about State and District Assessments
(Continued)

Question: My student has a learning disability. What kinds of test items are going to be easiest for my child, and what kinds of test items do I need to have him work on at home?

Answer: There is no simple answer to this question. The research does not give easy answers. Most likely, the "easiness of items" is going to be related to things other than simply whether they are multiple choice, essay, or performance events. Because of this, it is important that your child's teacher knows exactly what kinds of items are included in the test, and that practice on these items is provided. The item types should not drive instruction, however. There is some research evidence that preparing the student to answer essay questions will also better prepare the student to answer multiple choice questions.

Question: How can I help the IEP team make good decisions about the accommodations that my child will need during the state or district assessment?

Answer: Making decisions about accommodations should be a collaborative effort. You should provide information that supports the information that your child's teacher and other educators bring to the IEP team meeting. It is best to keep your input to what you know. Based on your knowledge of your child's learning experiences, you have a lot to say. Think about what helps your child get things done at home. Does he or she need to be in a distraction-free environment to finish tasks? Does he or she need frequent breaks to do a good job on household chores? Think about recreational activities, household chores, and skill learning and bring information about these things to the IEP meeting.

FORM R

What Parents and Teachers Need to Know About Common Assessments

Norm-Referenced Tests: These tests are developed to measure a student's performance in comparison to the performance of other students. These tests are developed to create a spread of scores, so that some students will score poorly and others will score well. A national sample of students takes the test, and the scores of students are compared to the scores of this national sample. Because the goal is to have all students take the test under the same conditions, very few accommodations are allowed.

Criterion-Referenced Tests: These tests are developed to measure a student's knowledge and skills, which are held up to a level of acceptable performance to indicate whether the student has reached the desired criterion. These tests also measure the student against a criterion, not against other students. Because having all students take the test under exactly the same conditions is not a goal of criterion-referenced tests, many more accommodations are allowed in criterion-referenced testing.

Standards-Based Assessment: These are tests (or other measures) that are criterion-referenced in which the criterion is composed of standards identified by the state or district. Thus, the measurement is directly tied to instruction, if instruction is directly aligned to the standards. Like criterion-referenced tests, many accommodations are allowed during these assessments.

FORM S

A Guide for Translating Testing Terminology
for Parents and Teachers

Testing Term	Alternate Term	Explanation
Aggregate	Combine	The aggregation of test scores is the process of putting the scores from many students together to form a total picture. It is simply a process of combining scores, albeit sometimes in very complex ways.
Alternate assessment	Different assessment	Alternate assessments are mandated by federal law for those students unable to participate in the general assessment. The alternate assessment is simply a different assessment. It may or may not look at all like the general assessment to which it is an alternate. In many states, the alternate assessment is a portfolio, and the general assessment is a paper-and-pencil test.
Disaggregate	Separate	The disaggregation of test scores is the process of separating out the scores of a group of students. Federal law requires that the scores of students with disabilities be disaggregated from the scores of other students and be aggregated with them.
Large-scale assessment	State or district test	Large-scale assessment simply means that the test was developed to be administered to large numbers of students, usually in groups. District and state tests are large-scale assessments.
Reliability	Consistency	Reliability is a psychometric term used to indicate the extent to which a score is (in very general terms) stable over time, the same if scored by two individuals, or the same if broken into two parts.
Rubric	Rules	Rubrics are descriptions of a test performance that support scoring guides, which are used to indicate the closeness of a student to a standard. The rubrics define what kind of a performance is Below Basic and what is considered Proficient.
Validity	Accuracy	Validity is the accuracy of a measure derived from a test. It indicates that the test measures what the test developer wanted it to measure.

FORM T

Observation Checklist

Name: _____ Job Site: _____

Date/Time: _____

Outcome Objective: _____

Skills performed as follows: **M**-model, **V**-verbal, **I**-independently	Date of Observation	Date of Observation	Date of Observation
1.			
2.			
3.			
4.			
5.			
6.			
7.			
8.			
9.			
10.			
11.			
12.			
13.			
14.			
15.			

Components of the Instructional Planning Pyramid

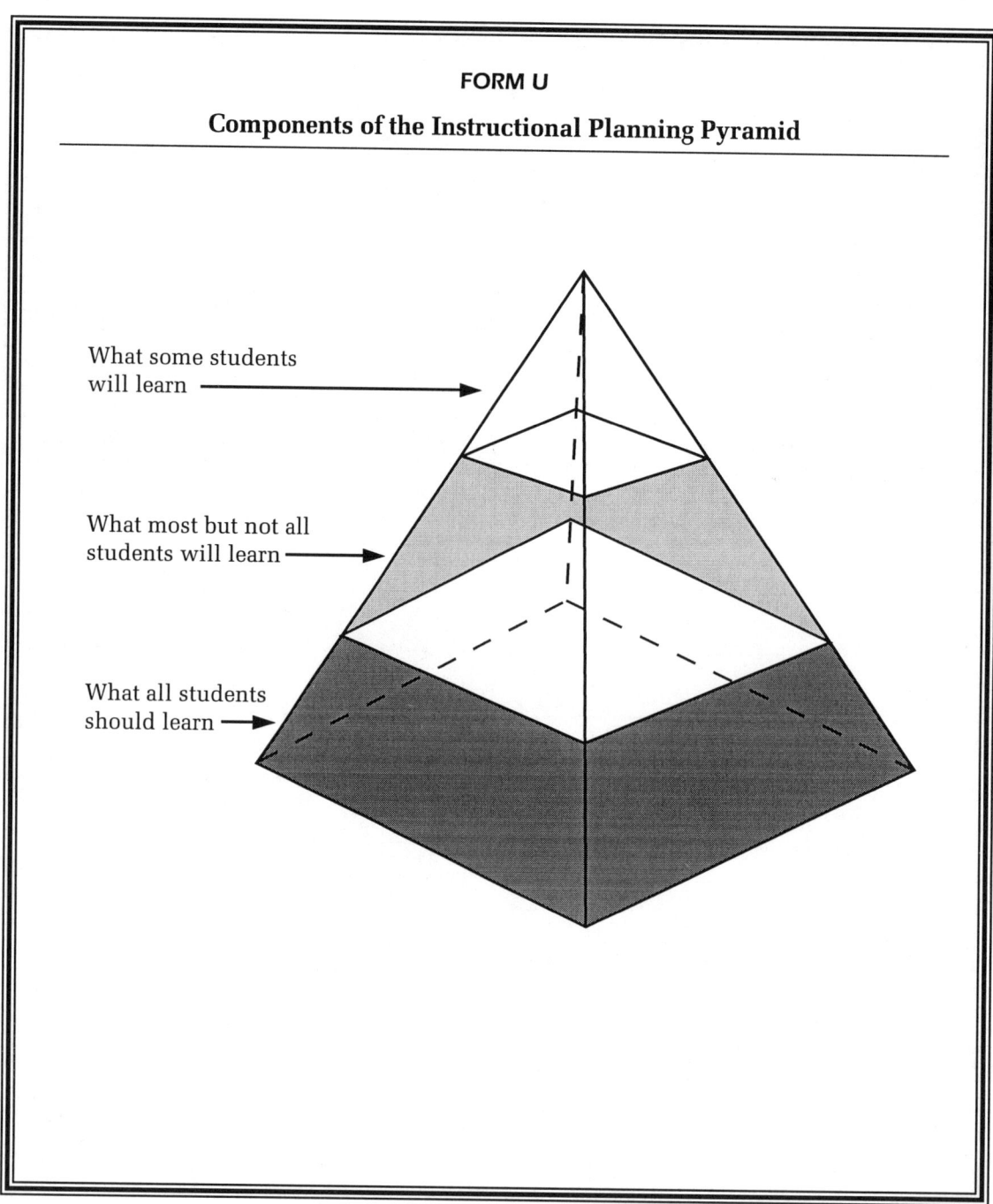

What some students
will learn

What most but not all
students will learn

What all students
should learn

FORM V

Guiding Questions for the Instructional Planning Pyramid

The following questions can be used in a self-questioning process to guide decision-making when considering topics of instruction, readiness to teach the material, and student readiness to receive the instruction.

Questions Pertaining to the Topic

- Is the material new or review?
- What prior knowledge do students have of this topic?
- How interesting is the topic to individual students? To me?
- How many new concepts are introduced?
- How complex are the new concepts?
- How clearly are concepts presented in the textbook?
- How can this material be connected to previous instruction? Can it?
- How important is this topic or parts of the topic for students to learn?

Questions Pertaining to the Teacher

- Have I taught this material before?
- How can I evaluate whether students are learning what I am teaching?
- How interesting is the topic to students? To me?
- How can students' cultural and linguistic backgrounds be connected to the topic?
- How much time do I have to plan for the unit and individual lessons?
- What resources do I have available to me for this unit?

Questions Pertaining to Students

- Will students' communication skills make comprehension of a particular topic or concept difficult?
- Will students with reading difficulties be able to work independently while learning about the concept from the text?
- Will a student with behavior or attention problems be able to concentrate on this material?
- Which students will likely have high interest in or prior knowledge of this concept or be anxious to explore this topic in greater breadth and depth?
- What experiences have the students had that will relate to this concept?
- Is there some way to relate this concept to the cultural and linguistic backgrounds of the students?

FORM W

Tracking Student Pathways

Directions: Use this form to track students' graduation expectations, opportunity to learn requirements, accommodations, and additional interventions. Keep this form handy because it serves as an on-going reminder of where students should be headed.

Student	Graduation Expectation (Regular or Alternative)	IEP/504 (Yes or No)	Needed Instructional Accommodation	Needed Assessment Accommodation	Additional Instructional, Considerations, or Areas of Intervention	Opportunity to Learn Requirements

FORM X

Common LEP Accommodations

Setting	Scheduling/Timing
Bilingual education or ESL classroom	Extended time
Individualized setting	Frequent breaks

Presentation	Response
English dictionary/glossary	First language responses acceptable
Familiar examiner	Scribe writes responses
Translated test items	

Resource B
Professional Development

An innovation is only as good as its capability to be understood. In any field, especially education, there is a critical need for training and professional development for people who work in the trenches—in other words, those who face students on a daily basis with the huge responsibility of educating them (and, of course, improving performance on assessments!). The changes in federal laws have been the impetus for creating inclusive accountability and assessment systems. This, as you know, has not been universally accepted. In fact, some of the strongest resistance comes from folks in special education, thus the need for sustained professional development.

The purpose of this section is to help you plan, manage, deliver, and evaluate needed information for improving the performances of students with disabilities on state and district assessments and including them in the accountability system. With this in mind, we present a variety of workshop outlines, activities, and reproducible handouts and overheads to use in delivering professional development. You can use this information to provide in-service training for boards of education workshops, central office and building administration, building faculty, staff, parents, and students. Feel free to adapt and adopt all or some of the information that follows to meet the needs of your potential audiences.

Overview

We have arranged the chapters of this book into four component areas: accountability, creating standards-based classrooms, standards-based instruction, and preparation and support for testing. Each component area can be addressed in individual sessions or over multiple sessions. It's up to you. Although we provide the meat of components, we strongly suggest that you tailor each with information about what is occurring in your own backyard: the issues, challenges, concerns, and realities.

Component 1: Accountability (page 261)
Component 2: Creating Standards-Based Classrooms (page 276)
Component 3: Standards-Based Instruction (page 289)
Component 4: Preparation and Support for Testing (page 316)

Professional Development Stages

The best practice for instruction is to assess the level of understanding that students have for new or revisited information. This goes for adult students as well. With any new topic, there is a continuum of knowledge that is present, ranging from awareness to synthesis and application. Using the Concerns-Based Adoption Model (CBAM) by Hall, Wallace, and Dossett (1973), you can get a heartbeat on where people are that can help drive the planning and delivery of quality professional development.

The basic premise of CBAM is that people differ in their ability and readiness to accept changes and innovations. We provide you with both an overview of the model and suggestions on ways to use it to train personnel on improving the performance of students with disabilities. The following are the CBAM stages and our adaptations for tailoring it to our topic:

- **Awareness**—This stage is characterized as having very low adult involvement. Here people either don't know or act as if they don't know much about accountability and assessments as they relate to all kids, particularly students with disabilities.

- **Informational**—This stage is characterized by general awareness and interest but still relatively little involvement. Here you may find people who acknowledge something is going on related to students with disabilities and assessments, but they still believe it will not affect them.

- **Personal**—In this stage, the "ah-ha" phenomenon begins. Folks begin to see and consider the personal impact of the innovations, polices, and/or practices. For example, site administrators may begin to be concerned about whether students with disabilities will "count" in their building test scores. Teachers may begin to count the number of students in their general education classes and those that require accommodations in instruction and on classroom assessments. The reality of the participation of students with disabilities in state and district assessment begins to set in.

- **Management**—Here informed personnel now realize that the changes in federal requirements for students with disabilities are here to stay. They begin to focus on methodologies and strategies to improve the performance of students with disabilities, both in instruction and assessments. Here there is an elevated need to find out what to do and how to do it.

- **Consequence**—In this stage, people zero in on the outcomes of instruction and assessments. They begin to raise questions about resources, including the opportunity for students to learn what is expected: the fairness of existing practices and ways that can accelerate improved results for student learning.

- **Collaboration**—This stage is viewed as learning in process. Personnel collaborate with others, especially those with knowledge and experience in working with disabled students, with the goal of learning more about these students, their needs, and their capabilities. They "get it." They see the connection between effective standards-based instruction and improved performances for all students, including students with disabilities.

- **Refocusing**—This stage is characterized by the interest and efforts surrounding the refinement of implemented strategies, plans, and methodologies. There is a fresh, focused effort in the development and improvement of results-based instruction for all students.

We have taken the CBAM and made suggestions as to how it can be tailored to proactively manage each stage you will no doubt encounter along the way. Each stage is highlighted with some general activities that can be provided to help people move through the model.

Stage	Activity
Awareness	The dissemination of articles or position papers published by recognized organizations
	Faculty meetings, workshops, or overviews
	Ongoing staff meetings
	Posting belief statements or signs reflecting the imminent future
Informational	Reading lists, video series, satellite conferences on related topics
	Presentations from district personnel who have innovative practices in place
	Testimonials of "where we've been and where we are now" from within or outside your school district
	Visits to other schools or school district programs
	Newsletters and other easy-reading professional literature on teaching strategies, accommodations, assessments, and accountability
	Full-day workshops or services developed from specific needs identified within the school or district

Personal	Tailored topical sessions that provide personnel with opportunities for discussion and reflection
	Testimonials of "where we've been and where we are now" from within or outside your school district
	Communication forums to facilitate discussions with parents, students, and others affected by current practices and the proposed changes in them
	Case studies of turn-around schools and programs and the benefits to kids
Management	Practical in-services and information on "how to's"
	Group planning and problem-solving sessions
	Networking with other districts and states working to improve the performances of students with disabilities on assessments
	Exploration of national technical assistance and dissemination networks
	Applications for grants and foundation money
Consequence	Selected current educational articles/reviews on legal consequences for noninclusive accountability and assessment systems
	Legal briefs or stances and assessment cases from the Office for Civil Rights on opportunities to learn
	Mapping out a strategy and outcomes that have set benchmark dates for efforts
	Forums to support and facilitate discussions about questions, concerns, and challenges when implementing effective instruction to improve student performance
Collaboration	Instructional/assessment swat teams to coach and monitor the integrity of program implementation
	The creation of CIA collaborative committees: curriculum, instruction, and assessment
	Providing time to collaborate on the inputs, processes, and outcomes
	Holding cross-departmental meetings
	Co-teaching across content areas
Refocusing	Attending national conferences
	Revisiting strategic plans and benchmarks
	Action research and evaluation on "how are we doing?"

Refocusing   Talking to students and parents, what insights do they offer?

Planned activities for rejuvenation and recognition of progress

Reward and reinforce efforts to move to more comprehensive instructional programs for students

These are but a few brainstorm suggestions for each stage of the model. You know your situation best. Tailor activities as appropriate to your current climate. Turn this model into a needs assessment by placing statements on a Likert scale. The needs assessment can simply depict current issues and/or key elements to the reform activities at hand. Have people rate each item from one to seven, where one is Awareness and seven is Refocusing.

Example CBAM Assessment

Item 1

1   2   3   4   5   6   7   I am aware of the recent changes in federal laws that make it necessary for us to review and revise our instructional and assessment practices for all kids, including students with disabilities.

Item 2

1   2   3   4   5   6   7   I have a complete understanding of the three ways students with disabilities participate in assessments: through standard assessments, assessments with accommodations, or alternate assessments.

Item 3

1   2   3   4   5   6   7   I know how to link student IEPs to the standards toward which all students are working.

Item 4

1   2   3   4   5   6   7   I understand the purpose and use of accommodations.

Item 5

1   2   3   4   5   6   7   I have a clear understanding of how to make decisions about instructional and assessment accommodations for students.

We provide you with a CBAM assessment for each of the four components that follow. You will find each in the Overheads and Handouts section with descriptions in the Activity boxes.

Component 1
Accountability

Purpose

- To raise the level of understanding of what accountability means in schools today.
- To raise the issue of responsibility and accountability for "all" students, including students with disabilities.

Background Information

Accountability can be defined as a systematic collection, analysis, and utilization of information to hold schools, educators, and others responsible for the performance of students and the education system (Education Commission of the States). Basically, two kinds of accountability exist: system and individual.

System accountability is where educators, schools, or districts are held responsible for the results. The consequences of nonperformance are relegated to them. Student accountability is where individual students are held responsible for their performances. The consequences of nonperformance are assigned to the students.

System and Student Accountability: A National Snapshot

National issues abound in regards to including students with disabilities in assessment and accountability systems. Here are the major issues:

- *The appropriateness of standards for students with disabilities* Because we have information that indicates most states developed their standards without all kids in mind (see Chapter 3, "Standards-Based Instruction: The Backbone of Educational Accountability"), there is now great concern that all students must demonstrate the mastery of them.

- *Participation policies or practices* Previous to IDEA 1997, most students with disabilities were excluded from state and district assessments. The changes in the law mandate that students participate, but it is unclear how well administrators and teachers understand the importance of this. Some folks are still looking for loopholes to keep kids out of the assessment and ultimately the accountability reports on how well students are doing in schools. The issue here is the integrity of federal regulation implementations.

- *Accommodation policies or practices*   Here issues surround how accommodation decisions are made. We know some tests limit the type of accommodations allowed on assessments. Moreover, a number of additional accommodations that could be used, if needed by students, are not allowed. Who makes these policies? What data are they using to make these decisions? Until very recently, little to no information existed on the impact of accommodations on test performances, yet policies were being made about standard and nonstandard accommodations.

- *Development of an alternate assessment*   July 1, 2000 is the deadline for states to have an alternate assessment in place. The big issue here is who takes the alternate assessment. The original notion behind this assessment was that it was for students with significant cognitive disabilities who could not participate in regular assessments, even with accommodations. Although it would appear that eligibility for the alternate assessment is clear, more and more concern is being raised about the kids in the middle or the gray area students (see Chapter 10, "Teaching and Assessment for Shades of Gray: The Kids In Between"). What if students don't neatly fit into either assessment? Then what?

- *The availability of data on who is excluded*   Although the requirement to include all students is encompassed in IDEA 1997, the implementation is still a concern. Although we know we must include and account for all students with disabilities in either the regular assessment or alternate assessment (starting July 1, 2000), how are we sure that students are taking the most appropriate assessment? Decisions to have students take a different assessment are not a universally defined practice. That is, some of these decisions may be based on the feeling of adults who think the regular assessment is too difficult or those students are not learning the same curriculum. We need to be sure these decisions are appropriate and in the spirit of the law.

- *The availability of data on who receives accommodations*   States and districts provide accommodations to students but often don't keep track of what kinds of accommodations are provided. Important research can be conducted with this information: cost analysis, logistics of providing them, and so on.

So many issues, so little time. It is easy to see that a lot of work remains to be done in order for us to understand the importance of inclusive accountability and assessment systems. Here is some information about what is going on nationally in system and student accountability. These policies change almost weekly; still they highlight several points.

Most states have consequences for schools and staff. The types of consequences vary from negative ones to simply publicly reporting the results of student performance. Student accountability provides a varied and interesting pattern, starting with the fact that at least 25 states have high-stakes tests for students. Most of these have graduation tests. Some of these states allow students with disabilities to earn a standard diploma by meeting IEP goals. Most states have different types of exit documents, such as a certificate of completion, an IEP diploma, and so on. Varied for sure! Where does your state stand in this mix? Do teachers know it?

Why Inclusion in the General Accountability System Is Important

Students with special needs have been excluded from assessment and accountability systems for many different reasons. Probably the main reason is the prevailing belief that these students will pull down overall test score performances. Interestingly enough, few people are looking at this issue as a symptom of a problem—lack of good instruction. For our purposes, let's focus on why it is important to include all kids:

- *For an accurate picture of education* All means each. In other words, every student is a part of all. If we truly want to determine how our education system is working for kids, then all kids need to be a part of the evaluation of the system.

- *To make fair comparisons* In order to make fair comparisons, everyone must do the same thing: include all students. Otherwise, we are comparing apples to oranges. This is in part why the 1997 IDEA amendments require the participation of students with disabilities in state and district assessments with accommodations where needed.

- *To meet legal requirements* The legal requirements for inclusion really started with the introduction of the Goals 2000 Act. It contains, among other things, the specification that all students, including students with disabilities, be a part of the overall improvement of America's schools. The passage of the Elementary and Secondary Education Act, 1994 (called the Improving America's Schools Act) also reinforced this in its Title I legislation. The group of students receiving Title I services is to include students with disabilities, if appropriate, and with provided accommodations if needed.

- *To avoid unintended effects* It is not unusual for students to be referred to special education with the intent that they be classified and provided services and accommodations that might keep them out of the assessment system. Most states and districts allow students with disabilities to use specified accommodations on tests. Some of these accommodations automatically kick out the scores of students because of the accommodations used. So, the long and short of it is that special education can provide a loophole to keep kids out of the system.

- *To promote higher expectations*   If people know that all students, including students with disabilities, will be included in assessments and reported, the impetus is there to improve the performance of students. This is most logically done through providing quality instruction and the opportunity to learn what is needed and expected of all students.

- *To benefit from reforms*   Policy makers look at test scores. Most of the nation looks at test scores. Decisions to implement new programs are based on test scores. So you tell us why it is important to include all students in tests! The bottom line: decisions made about policy and practices affect all students, including students with disabilities. It is important that these decisions be based on complete, accurate data on all students.

Activity 1

Administer the CBAM assessment for the section (Handout 1.1). Have participants indicate on a scale of one to seven (where one is awareness and seven is refocusing) where they fall on the Likert continuum.

Activity 2

Use the Myth or Truth Worksheet (Handout 1.2) as an anticipatory set for the session. This can serve as a pre- and post-test for this component on accountability. Answers for the activity are as follows: 1 through 9 are Myths; 10 is Truth.

Activity 3

In small groups, have the participants discuss what they know about beliefs, expectations, and reasons why students with special needs are left out of assessment and accountability systems. Process discussion as a large group. Be sure to address the concerns raised.

Activity 4

Use Handout 1.3 to generate small group discussion about issues surrounding accountability for "all" students (see accompanying Overhead 1.7).

Overheads and Handouts

Use the overheads/handouts on the following pages to help your presentation of material. Feel free to adapt or adopt them to suit your needs.

HANDOUT 1.1

Directions: The purpose of this Likert scale is to have you identify where you are in your ability and readiness to accept changes and innovations. Many of these are going on around you right now! Each number (1–7) has a corresponding level of awareness or concern. Read each item and rate your level of concern/awareness about each.

    1 = Awareness, I have very little involvement or interest.
    2 = Informational, I have general awareness, but relatively little involvement.
    3 = Personal, I am beginning to be affected by this. I have some concern about the impact of this on policies and current practices.
    4 = Management, I am involved and/or beginning to focus on strategies to address this.
    5 = Consequence, I have some questions and concerns about the impact of this.
    6 = Collaboration, I am working to make things happen about this through professional collaboration.
    7 = Refocusing, I am working to refine, improve, and extend strategies and practices around this.

Accountability

Item 1

1   2   3   4   5   6   7   I am aware of the recent changes in federal laws that make it necessary for us to review and revise our instructional and assessment practices for all kids, including students with disabilities.

Item 2

1   2   3   4   5   6   7   I have a complete understanding of the three ways students with disabilities participate in assessments: through standard assessments, assessments with accommodations, or alternate assessments.

Item 3

1   2   3   4   5   6   7   I know how to link student IEPs to the standards toward which all students are working.

Item 4

1   2   3   4   5   6   7   I understand the purpose and use of accommodations.

Item 5

1   2   3   4   5   6   7   I have a clear understanding of how to make decisions about instructional and assessment accommodations for students.

HANDOUT 1.2

Inclusive Accountability: Does All Really Mean All?

Read each statement below and decide whether it is a prevailing practice. If it is, write T (Truth). If the statement describes an inaccurate practice, write M (Myth).

_____ 1. A well-established accountability system is one in which all students take the same tests.

_____ 2. Educators are currently sharing responsibility in educating all students, including students with disabilities.

_____ 3. Students with disabilities are usually considered when schools adopt books, programs, and/or implement new practices.

_____ 4. Administrators are aware of the importance of an accountability system that includes all students, including students with disabilities.

_____ 5. In general, students with disabilities have access to the general curriculum.

_____ 6. Teachers are aware of what accommodations are allowed on district and state tests.

_____ 7. A direct link exists between the accommodations used in instruction and classroom tests.

_____ 8. Assessment scores of students with disabilities are a welcome addition to the scores of a school site.

_____ 9. Information on students with disabilities is included in the accountability reports that go out to the public.

_____ 10. Inclusive accountability systems impact all aspects of instruction and assessments of students.

HANDOUT 1.3

Issues Surrounding the Accountability for "All" Students

Directions: Use the following questions to guide your discussion on accounting for all students. Be sure to ground your discussion in what current practices exist in your own backyard or situation.

1. How should students with disabilities be counted for in the accountability reports or measures?

2. How can students who need accommodations that are not approved be included in assessment and accountability systems?

3. How can students who take the alternate assessment be included or count in the accountability system?

4. What can be done for school sites (or districts) that have a disproportionate number of students with disabilities?

National Issues

- The appropriateness of standards for SWD

- Participation policies or practices

- Accommodation policies or practices

- Development of an alternate assessment

- The availability of data on who is excluded

- The availability of data on who receives accommodations

Accountability

A definition:

"The systematic collection, analysis, and use of information to hold schools, educators, and others responsible for the performance of students and the education system."

Education Commission of the States, 1998

Types of Accountability

System Accountability:

Educators, schools, and/or districts are held responsible.

Consequences are assigned to them.

Student Accountability:

Students are held responsible.

Consequences are assigned to them.

System Accountability

Nearly all states have consequences for schools or staff.

Types of consequences:

- **Negative (loss of accreditation)**

- **Positive (cash awards)**

- **Performance reporting (newspaper/media)**

- **None**

Student Accountability

- **Twenty-five states have a test with high-stakes consequences for students.**

- **Twenty states had a graduation test in 1999–2000. More are on the way.**

- **Several states allow students with disabilities to earn a standard diploma by meeting IEP goals.**

- **Most states have different types of exit documents.**

Why Inclusion in Accountability Systems Is Important

- For an accurate picture of education

- To make "fair" comparisons

- To meet federal requirements

- To avoid unintended effects

- To promote higher standards

- To benefit from reforms

Issues Surrounding Accountability for "All" Students

1. How should students with disabilities be counted for in the accountability reports or measures?

2. How can students who need accommodations that are not approved be included in assessment and accountability systems?

3. How can students who take the alternate assessment be included or count in the accountability system?

4. What can be done for school sites (or districts) that have a disproportionate number of students with disabilities?

Overhead 1.7

Component 2

Creating Standards-Based Classrooms

Purpose

- To emphasize the importance of all students being held to high standards.
- To elevate the critical educational variable of the opportunity to learn (OTL).

Background Information

Standards-based instruction is a relatively recent term that has greatly affected teaching, learning, and assessment. Basically, we are talking about teaching all students, including students with disabilities, at high standards. This is very new for most folks in education. For too long, students with disabilities have been instructed in unrelated and insufficient subjects. We know, however, good things are going on in some places! But, "some places" is not enough.

A standards-based assessment is concerned with aligning the curriculum for all students with the standards that have been identified as important for students to know and be able to do. For students with IEPs, it means linking goals and objectives to those standards. The difficulty right off the bat is that many special educators have not received training in the standards; some may not even know what areas they cover or that they even exist. General educators aren't exempt from this. For them, it is a matter of being familiar enough with the standards to integrate them into the existing curriculum they teach.

What Do We Know About Standards-Setting and Students with Disabilities?

As discussed in Chapter 3, most states have developed their standards without the input or involvement of special education. Some states acknowledge that their standards are for "all" students, including students with disabilities. Others indicate that students would require accommodations. IDEA 1997 specifically indicates that students with disabilities must have access to the general curriculum, which is predominantly made up of standards that don't consider those with special needs.

Basic Tenants of a Standards-Based System

Many national activities are taking place based on standards-based reforms. However, any good structure needs a solid foundation. The following questions are based on principles that should be present in your current system:

- *Is the accountability system in your school district and state accountable to itself?* Here we mean, who monitors the integrity of the current accountability system? How do we know it is doing what it is supposed to do? How do we know it is being consistently implemented across the state, school district, and school sites?

- *Is your accountability system built on standards that reflect all students in your schools?* This requires an examination of what currently is really going on at school sites and across school districts. Even though we pointed out that standards have been developed without all students in mind, that doesn't preclude districts and schools from taking a closer look at what they have and what is needed. In doing this, school districts and states have begun to develop extended or expanded standards that better encompass all students.

- *Is the opportunity to learn a primary element in your accountability system?* That is, are all students, including students with disabilities, being provided the opportunity-to-learn identified standards? If not, why not? What needs to be done to make this happen? With the onslaught of more and more high-stakes exit exams resurfacing, it is imperative to make sure that all students are given the opportunity to learn what they need in order to improve test performances and to pass high-stakes exams.

- *Do all members of your teaching community, including parents and students, have a clear understanding of the components of the accountability system?* It is important that folks affected by the accountability system know all about it, including rewards and sanctions. Proactive communication about what is expected of students and teachers is critical to garnering support for any accountability system.

Trademarks of a Standards-Based Classroom

Now that we have reviewed some key elements of an accountability system, let's take it down into the classroom. As discussed in Chapter 3, the following are important trademarks of a standards-based classroom:

- Students know the standards and level of proficiency required.
- Students are provided multiple opportunities to learn.
- Student assignments reflect an integration of facts, concepts, and strategies.
- Each assignment is an assessment in itself.

Here the key points are that everyone understands that it all begins in the classroom. It is important for educators to analyze their classrooms for the foundational indicators of a classroom reflecting standards-driven instruction.

Making the Linkages

IDEA 1997 has prompted national attention to student IEPs and their relationship to standards. As discussed in several places, the lack of standards-based instruction for students with disabilities has done little to ready students for different learning environments, be it a mainstream class, an exit from special education, or graduation. Here are a few ways to promote the connections of IEPs to the general curriculum or standards:

- Raise the expectations of students with disabilities.
- Provide sustained professional development to administrators as well as general and special educators through "how to's" for instruction and assessment.
- Forge collaborative relations between general educators and special educators.
- Think out of the box for providing services and instruction for students with disabilities.
- Use the attitude of HANWTTAI (pronounced han-wat-ti): Here's a new way to think about it!

Positive "can-do" attitudes are contagious. We know more now than ever before about how to teach students effectively. Making standards-based instruction happen starts with making sure everyone knows that effective instruction makes a difference. It is all in the way you plan, manage, deliver, and evaluate instruction!

Backmapping for the Future

We refer to Chapter 3 for a very thorough discussion of backmapping. For our purposes here, we will simply highlight things to remember when introducing it. The goal of backmapping is to directly link IEPs to standards. It is important tht educators know what the standards are and what content areas are covered, as well as the skills. When the IEPs are linked, this activates the process of breaking down the standards into the subskills that students will need to master the overall standards. Some students with disabilities will learn only some of the subskills (for example, students taking the alternate assessment); for others, it will be important that they learn them all.

Backmapping creates a blueprint for instruction. After the skills are teased out in the standard, we refine them into instruction. Where do they appear in the scope and sequence of our curriculum? (Some people may not have a curriculum! All the more reason to use the standards as a guide for the instruction of all students.) Here it is important to plan for how these subskills and standards will appear in instruction. Lesson plans are then developed around the skills that need to be taught for the standard.

Activity 1

Administer the CBAM assessment for the section (Handout 2.1). Have participants indicate on a scale of one to seven (where one is awareness and seven is refocusing) where they fall on the Likert continuum.

Activity 2

Have a discussion about extending standards. Should standards be the exact same for all students? Should they be different for students with learning disabilities or students with developmental disabilities? Discuss the importance or opinions about having standards for all students.

Activity 3

Select a standard and extend or expand it to encompass a broader range of skills (and students!). For example, take a social studies standard and expand it to be more appropriate for students with developmental disabilities. The key here is to bridge the extended standard to the original one in some related way.

Activity 4a

Take a standard, any standard, and break it into its component parts. What are the prerequisite skills and component skills? Use Handout 2.2 as a guide for this as well as the 4b and 4c activities.

Activity 4b

Take the product of Activity 4a and identify where in the curriculum or scope and sequence the identified prerequisite and component skills are taught. Are they?

Activity 4c

Continue with this same standard and discuss how it (and the identified skills) can be integrated into a lesson for students. Although these activities sound elementary, they are not. They require knowledge of the standards, curriculum, and teaching methodologies. It is one thing to recognize or recite a standard and another to actually teach it.

Activity 4d

Use the case study in Handout 2.3 to facilitate problem-solving discussions about standards-based classrooms.

Activity 5

Use the case study in Handout 2.4 to enhance discussion about student accountability requirements, namely graduation. This case study is for states that require all students, including students with disabilities to pass an exit test to graduate. Feel free to change it to meet your specific needs or situations that you face.

Overheads and Handouts

Use the following overheads and handouts to assist you in this section. Change them to fit your needs. Be sure to enhance this section with the current issues faced in your situation.

HANDOUT 2.1

Directions: The purpose of this Likert scale is to have you identify where you are in your ability and readiness to accept changes and innovations. Many of these are going on around you right now! Each number (1–7) has a corresponding level of awareness or concern. Read each item and rate your level of concern/awareness about each:

1 = Awareness, I have very little involvement or interest.

2 = Informational, I have general awareness, but relatively little involvement.

3 = Personal, I am beginning to be affected by this. I have some concern about the impact of this on policies and current practices.

4 = Management, I am involved and/or beginning to focus on strategies to address this.

5 = Consequence, I have some questions and concerns about the impact of this.

6 = Collaboration, I am working to make things happen about this through professional collaboration.

7 = Refocusing, I am working to refine, improve, and extend strategies and practices around this.

Creating Standards-Based Classrooms

Item 1

1   2   3   4   5   6   7   I know what standards-based education is.

Item 2

1   2   3   4   5   6   7   I know what a standards-based classroom looks like.

Item 3

1   2   3   4   5   6   7   Our school/district embraces accountability for all students. That is, every student counts and is accounted for.

Item 4

1   2   3   4   5   6   7   Efforts are made to link students' IEP goals to curriculum and instruction for all students.

Item 5

1   2   3   4   5   6   7   All students are provided with equal access and opportunities to learn standards.

HANDOUT 2.2

Backmapping Standards for Standards-Based Success

Use the following worksheet to guide your backmapping process:

1. Select a standard to be backmapped for instruction.

2. Break down the standard according to the skills that are embedded in it.

3. Locate where these skills are taught in the curriculum. If they aren't present, note where they would fit.

4. Create an instructional blueprint of all skills needed to achieve the standard. Identify those skills that are prerequisites to instruction and those that are components of or the meat of instruction.

5. Break skills into units or lessons of instruction.

6. Identify instructional strategies to teach identified skills.

7. Assess whether students have the prerequisite skills needed to successfully begin instruction in the standard.

8. Identify how students' progress will be assessed.

9. Use the test matrix or table of specifications to identify instructional emphasis.

10. Begin instruction!

HANDOUT 2.3

Case Study Discusion

Directions: Use the case study here to discuss issues around creating standards-based practices. Talk about what changes could be done to increase student performance in the classroom and other requirements.

You are a member of a grade-level team. Your student Paco, a 10th grader, is currently receiving resource room services. He is bilingual and is proficient both in English and the language spoken in the home. Paco has good attendance, works hard to complete assignments, seeks extra help when needed, yet struggles tremendously in school. In particular, he has difficulty in math and science. Paco is not a candidate for the alternate assessment.

Your district/state mandates that all students must pass an end-of-course exam to get credit for courses. Paco has failed both the 9th and 10th grade end-of-course exams in math and science. In fact, he was not successful in summer school either.

What can be done for Paco? What needs to be examined or changed?

HANDOUT 2.4

Case Study Discusion

Directions: Use the case study here to enhance your discussions about student accountability requirements for all students, including students with disabilities. Be sure to link it to what exists in your current situation.

Sarah has taken the state-mandated graduation test and failed. As a 12th grader, she has failed the exam three times (at the end of 11th grade, during summer school, and at the end of 12th grade). Sarah's parents would like to request that she be allowed to graduate without passing the exam. What is the appeals process in your district (or state)? If none exists, create one.

Basic Principles of Standards-Based Reforms

The accountability system is accountable to itself.

Accountability is based on standards that reflect all students.

The opportunity to learn is a primary component.

Everyone has a clear understanding of the accountability system.

Trademarks of a Standards-Based Classroom

Students know the level of proficiency required.

Students are provided multiple opportunities to learn.

Student assignments reflect an integration of skills.

Each assignment is an assessment in itself.

Foundations to Standards-Based Change

Raised expectations for students with disabilities

Sustained professional development

Collaborations among general and special educators

Thinking out of the box

HANWTTAI

Thinking Like Assessors

How do I know my students have an in-depth understanding of instruction?

What evidence do I have?

What do my assessments look like?

How do I use assessment results to anchor my instruction?

Component 3
Standards-Based Instruction

Purpose

- To examine ways to teach all students no matter what the assessment.

- To highlight the importance of planning for accommodations.

- To elevate the importance of curricular planning for students taking the alternate assessment.

- To provide a framework in which to plan and integrate effective instruction for all students.

Background Information

Here's where the rubber meets the proverbial road: instruction. We can talk about standards and what they are, what they should look like, and how they will be assessed, but the reality comes into play in the classroom. In this component, we combine issues and considerations for accommodations, alternate assessments, gray area students, and students with limited English proficiency (LEP).

Instruction for All

There still seems to be remnants of the early days when educators seemed to be more concerned with what to call students rather than how to teach them. Although there has been some movement away from this, terms such as minority, disadvantaged, underprivileged, and special education still surface as descriptions of who is in a program, rather than the program itself. The basic foundation to any instructional program is the instruction itself. Many states are faced with teacher shortages and the challenge of employing teachers who are uncredentialed.

This makes it even more imperative to structure what we want all kids to know and be able to do, coupled with exactly how to do it. Many students exist who need special planning and instructional considerations. Let's briefly review some of the issues that surround them.

Issues in Teaching All Students

Students who require no special accommodations. We start with these students because we must never forget that they too need quality instruction. Research has shown us that students are able to survive poor instruction if they are bright, motivated, and have supportive home environments. However, we venture a guess that you know many students who otherwise fit into other situations. It begs the question, are students doing poorly because of instruction or student factors? In the end, the thing that matters most is the quality of instruction and how it is delivered to students. Although we can't control student factors, we certainly can control instructional factors.

Students who require accommodations. When planning for instruction, it is critical to know which students in your classes require or need accommodations for instruction and/or tests. For students with disabilities as well as IEP/LEP students, the first place to look is on their IEPs. Even then, you may find that a student may need additional accommodations. If this is the case, notify the IEP team leader in your school and let that person know. An addendum can be made to the IEP.

Keep in mind that a few important accommodation realities need to be documented on a student's IEP in order to ensure they are provided. Also, just because they are used in instruction and on classroom tests does not mean they will automatically roll over onto the district/state assessments. As discussed elsewhere, most of these tests have a limited number of accommodations allowed. So, even though you may hear that the best place to start providing accommodations is during instruction (and indeed it is), these same accommodations may not be allowed on the assessment.

Aother thing to keep in mind is that out-of-level testing is not an appropriate accommodation, especially for assessments used for accountability purposes (see Chapter 5, "Accommodations—How to Make Sound Decisions for Instruction and Assessment" for a complete discussion). Finally, it may be wise to look into whether an appeals process exists for students who need accommodations that are not provided to them. The appeals process is most critical when students, because they are denied the use of accommodations, are not successful on an assessment and as a result are not promoted or do not graduate.

The important piece is that students indeed receive accommodations. Here's a quick way to find out whether more students need more or different instructional accommodations:

1. Ask the student what he or she needs to be successful.

2. Ask parents what accommodations they know the student uses.

3. Consider each student's strengths and weaknesses within subject areas.

4. Teach students to use accommodations they need.

5. Watch for the effects of provided accommodations, both within the classroom and on assignments where appropriate.

6. Collect data on the actual use and impact of accommodations that are used.

7. Ask the student whether the accommodations help.

It is also important to be aware of students who have 504 plans and as a result are eligible for instruction and assessment accommodations. Often these plans specifically indicate the accommodations needed by students. Remember the following points:

1. Do not make accommodation considerations based on the student's category or type of disability.

2. Accommodations should not be based on what is easiest and available.

3. Accommodations may change over time and from subject to subject.

4. Accommodations are not provided to boost overall performance.

With information about which students need which accommodations, you are ready to plan your instruction and classroom tests for all students. This may seem like an incredible task, but after you become familiar with what is needed for students, it becomes automatic to make necessary accommodations during the instructional process.

Students who will take the alternate assessment. As discussed in Chapter 4, "Improving the Performance of Students in the Alternate Assessment," these are students for whom the general assessment is not appropriate, even with accommodations. It's not appropriate in the sense that these students are learning and working toward standards that focus on life skills, and the curriculum they are learning is no way tapped by the general assessment. The practice of educating special education students in the least restrictive environment is in full swing. (LRE is the federal term indicating students should be educated in the environment that encourages success and where they would most likely be educated if not in special education.) As a result, many more students with significant needs receive instruction in general education classrooms. It is important to know who these students are and be familiar with their instructional goals and objectives. In doing so, you can plan for how to integrate individual goals and instruction within the larger context of a lesson. For example, if a student is learning how to use a calculator, his or her math work can be completed using one while the rest of the students do the assignment without one. The key here is to know what the life skills or functional goals are for students taking the alternate assessment and plan for them.

Remember the alternate assessment is not appropriate for students who

- can take the regular assessment but need accommodations that are not allowed.

- are learning the general curriculum but need a different way to show what they know and can do.

- are struggling in general education but do not qualify for special education services.

- are performing poorly due to attendance, lack of motivation, or various socioeconomic variables.

- are expected to perform poorly on the regular assessment.

(For possible formats and examples for the alternate assessment, see Chapter 4.)

Students who fall in the middle: the gray area kids. Although we dedicated an entire chapter to these students (Chapter 10, "Teaching and Assessment for Shades of Gray: The Kids in Between"), we want to re-emphasize the importance of planning for them. These kids can be looked at in two different ways: (1) as students who do not qualify for special education but continue to struggle in school, or (2) as students with disabilities who do not qualify for the alternate assessment but are sure to do poorly in the general assessment. Either way, these are students who are in need of special instructional consideration. For kids who are truly in the middle (they don't qualify for special services), we must be sure they have the prior knowledge and prerequisite skills to successfully complete the curriculum presented to them. The use of pre-tests is one way to ascertain this. For students who are not candidates for the alternate assessment but are expected to do poorly on the general assessment, we must look into why this is. These issues begin to look the same. Are they expected to do poorly on the assessment because of poor instruction or lack of opportunity to learn? Once again, we see these as alterable variables, ones we can directly impact with good instruction.

Students with LEP. A variety of things need to be considered for these students. Among these considerations are acculturation, language proficiency, cognitive development and literacy, attitudes about assessments and other schooling variables, and any biases that may exist in assessments. Collaboration becomes a key aspect of instruction for these students because general educators, special educators, and ESL/bilingual staff all must work together to produce the instruction for students learning English at the same time they are learning other academic content. Among the key considerations for instruction are the following:

- Preparing for instruction by accounting for needs, learning styles, and available resources.

- Using flexible grouping patterns.
- Increasing academic learning time.
- Involving parents.

Instructional Considerations for Teaching All Students

In this section, we highlight some considerations to use for providing instruction that is sensitive to the diverse needs of all students. We focus on how to plan, manage, deliver, and evaluate instruction (see Chapter 9, "Instruction: The Bottom Line in Improving Test Performance," for a thorough discussion). Through the use of the instructional pyramid, we can scope out what we need to be sure of before we proceed with instruction.

The Instructional Planning Pyramid

In Chapter 9, we outlined the instructional pyramid and specific questions pertaining to the topic of instruction, the teacher, and the student. Although we do not discuss it again here, we provide you with the overheads that will be useful in your presentation of it.

A Model of Effective Instruction

The Algozzine and Ysseldyke model of effective instruction was presented in detail in Chapter 9. In addition, we provided you with specific applications or tactics you can use to address each strategy. We encourage you to use this as you desire. More importantly, we refer you to the complete resource set (*Strategies and Tactics for Effective Instruction* and *Timesavers for Educators*) for many more ideas. For the purpose of this section, we simply provide you with an overhead of the four components: plan, manage, deliver, and evaluate.

Activity 1

Administer the CBAM assessment for the section (Handout 3.1). Have participants indicate on a scale of one to seven (where one is awareness and seven is refocusing) where they fall on the Likert continuum.

Activity 2

Use Handout 3.2 to prompt discussion about accommodations. Have participants expand upon their own experiences.

Activity 3

Use the alternate assessment (Handout 3.3) case study discussion to involve participants in tough decisions about what assessment students with disabilities should take.

Activity 4a

For gray area kids: use Handout 3.4 to discuss the prevalent issues surrounding gray area students. (See the accompanying Overhead 3.11.) Simply divide participants into groups and have them talk about each point. Be ready for a lively discussion.

Activity 4b

Continuing with this group activity using Handout 3.4, have participants discuss solutions for addressing the current issues surrounding gray area kids in your school district or situation. Focus especially on question 5.

Activity 5

Use the gray area case study (see Handout 3.5) to continue discussion and problem solving around what to do for gray area students.

Overheads and Handouts

Use the following overheads and materials to assist you in preparing and presenting information on standards-based instruction. There is a lot to this section so feel free to cut, combine, or change any of the following. Good luck.

HANDOUT 3.1

Directions: The purpose of this Likert scale is to have you identify where you are in your ability and readiness to accept changes and innovations. Many of these are going on around you right now! Each number (1–7) has a corresponding level of awareness or concern. Read each item and rate your level of concern/awareness about each:

1 = Awareness, I have very little involvement or interest.

2 = Informational, I have general awareness, but relatively little involvement.

3 = Personal, I am beginning to be affected by this. I have some concern about the impact of this on policies and current practices.

4 = Management, I am involved and/or beginning to focus on strategies to address this.

5 = Consequence, I have some questions and concerns about the impact of this.

6 = Collaboration, I am working to make things happen about this through professional collaboration.

7 = Refocusing, I am working to refine, improve, and extend strategies and practices around this.

Standards-Based Instruction

Item 1

1   2   3   4   5   6   7   All students, including students with disabilities, are considered when I plan my instruction.

Item 2

1   2   3   4   5   6   7   I understand the importance of providing disabled students with accommodations during instruction and on classroom tests.

Item 3

1   2   3   4   5   6   7   I understand that the alternate assessment is for a very small number of students with disabilities.

Item 4

1   2   3   4   5   6   7   I know who the gray area kids are and how to educate them.

Item 5

1   2   3   4   5   6   7   I am familiar with an instructional model that focuses on the teaching environment rather than student behavior or failure.

HANDOUT 3.2

Case Study

Directions: Use the case study here to extend your understanding and planning for accommodations.

    Iva Haddit is an elementary teacher in Johnny B. Goode Elementary School. In her class of 35 students, she has six resource room students, one 504 plan student, two LEP students, and five Title I students. Many of these students require accommodations in order to participate in the grade curriculum and assessment program. Iva identifies the accommodation needs of each student. Her intent is to use these accommodations during instruction, on classroom tests, and then finally for the district and state assessments. Although she has 14 special needs students, not all of them need assessment accommodations.

    As the result of her student-by-student analysis, Iva summarizes her classroom accommodation needs as follows:

    Four students need oral reading of directions and questions (Jose, Rose, Jimmy, Robert).
    One student needs a written translation of tests into Khmer (Maya).
    Four students need testing in a small group (Jose, Maya, Jimmy, Paco).
    One student needs more frequent breaks during testing (Kimberly).

Focus Questions:

1. What must be done to provide the needed accommodations for the students' classroom instruction and tests as well as for district/state assessments?

2. What are your strategies for making this happen? Who will need to be involved? Be sure to consider scheduling, location, personnel, and materials.

3. How will the integrity and implementation of the provided accommodations be monitored?

Action Plan: Use the space below to plan your decisions. The logistics of providing accommodations need to be thought out well in advance.

HANDOUT 3.3

Case Study

Directions: Use the case study here to focus discussion and planning for the students who will take an alternate assessment.

Background: Howard is an intellectually challenged 10th grader. His overall cognitive ability is well below average (a full-scale score of 60). Howard's academic achievement is as follows: Math G.E. 5.3, Reading G.E. 4.0, Written Language G.E. 2.8. Howard demonstrates difficulty expressing himself but is able to understand conversation relatively well. Howard attends a special education class for most the day. He spends the morning in vocational education classes.

Instructional: Howard needs extra processing time. Directions must be given multiple times in small steps. Howard has a relatively short attention span and appears to work better in a small group. Howard's goal is to work in the local florist shop. His horticulture teacher believes that with support and supervision, Howard may be able to accomplish his goal.

Questions to Reflect upon:

1. What assessment should Howard be expected to take (district, state or both)? Why?

2. What is the basis for your decision?

HANDOUT 3.4

Issues Surrounding Gray Area Kids

Directions: Use the following questions to guide your discussion about gray area students. Be sure to ground your discussion in current situations you face right now.

1. Why are there gray area students in accountability systems?

2. Are gray area students an assessment issue or an instructional one?

3. Are there really gray area students or is it just a way to avoid responsibility for "all" kids?

4. Should we be discussing gray area assessments, rather than gray area students?

5. What can be done right now for gray area students? What needs to happen? Who needs to be involved?

HANDOUT 3.5

Case Study Discussion

Directions: Use the scenario here to further discuss the issues around educating gray area students.

Who are gray area students really? Is there such a student? Are they really gray, or is the system black and white? In your group, discuss exactly what your state/school district/school site is doing to address students who fall in the cracks of the accountability and assessment systems. Make suggestions as to what steps can be taken to address these students. Be sure to discuss what the perceived problems or issues are. Could it be the standards? Instructional practices? Unqualified teachers in the classroom?

Whose problem is it really? And what ought we to do about it?

Considerations in Making Accommodation Decisions

- **Accommodations are provided based upon a student's need, not upon his or her category of disability.**

- **Accommodations are provided based upon need, rather than ease and availability.**

- **Accommodations may change over time and by subject area.**

- **Accommodations are not provided to boost overall student performance.**

Identifying Accommodations for Classroom Use

- Ask the student.

- Ask parents.

- Consider the student's strengths and weaknesses.

- Teach the student to use an accommodation.

- Observe the effects of provided accommodations.

- Collect data on the actual use and impact of accommodations.

- Ask the student whether the accommodations helped.

Rough Realities of Accommodations

- **Accommodations must be documented on IEPs.**

- **What is allowed in instruction often is not allowed in assessments.**

- **Appeals must be processed for students not provided with needed accommodations.**

- **Out-of-level testing is not a useful accommodation for accountability.**

Alternate Assessment Participation Decisions: Who's In and Who's Out?

Who's in:

- **Students who have significant cognitive disabilities**

- **Students who are working on life skills curricula**

- **Students who are not working toward the same course requirements for graduation**

Alternate Assessment Participation Decisions: Who's In and Who's Out?

Who's out:

- Students who can take the regular assessment, but need accommodations that are not allowed.

- Students who are learning the general curriculum, but need a different way to show what they know.

- Students who are struggling in general education but do not qualify for special education.

- Students who are performing poorly due to attendance, lack of motivation, and/or socioeconomic variables.

- Students who are expected to perform poorly on the regular assessment.

Possible Formats for an Alternate Assessment

- ## Observation

- ## Interview, Checklist, and Rating Scales

- ## Record Review

- ## Testing
  - ### Norm-referenced tests
  - ### Criterion-referenced tests
  - ### Standards-based tests
  - ### Curriculum-based tests
  - ### Performance-based tests
  - ### Portfolios

- ## Various Combinations of These

Gray Area Kids
Gap Kids
Kids in the Middle
No Place Kids
Kid in Between

Two distinct definitions

1. **Students with disabilities who do not fit in the regular district/state assessments, even with extensive accommodations, but for whom the alternate assessment is equally inappropriate**

2. **Students who are not in special education but who are struggling in general education**

Why Do Gray Area Kids Exist?

- **Students have a wider range of skill levels than existing tests measure.**

- **All students are now expected to be in either the regular assessment or the alternate assessment, but neither makes sense for some students.**

Deciding What Assessment Is Appropriate for Gray Area Kids

- **What are the instructional goals of the student?**

- **Which assessment is taken by other students with the same instructional goals?**

- **Has the student received effective instructional practices?**

- **Which diploma or requirements is the student working toward?**

Considerations for Addressing Gray Area Kids

1. **If a student is expected to meet the requirements for graduation, he or she should take the regular assessment.**

2. **If passing an assessment is required for graduation, students should be learning the content/skills needed to pass the test.**

3. **If the student is to receive a regular diploma, provide the supports needed to meet the performance requirements.**

4. **If little effective instruction is going on, change it!**

Issues Surrounding Gray Area Kids

1. Why are there gray area students in accountability systems?

2. Are gray area students an assessment issue or an instructional one?

3. Are there really gray area students, or is it just a way to avoid responsibility for "all" kids?

4. Should we be discussing gray area assessments, rather than gray area students?

5. What can be done right now for gray area students? What needs to happen? Who needs to be involved?

Using the Instructional Planning Pyramid: For Topics of Instruction

- Is the material new or a review?
- What prior knowledge do students have on the topic?
- What is the interest level of the students?
- How many new concepts will be introduced?
- How complex are the new concepts?
- How clearly are they presented in the text?
- How can the new material be connected to previous instruction? Can it?
- How important is this topic for students to learn?

Using the Instructional Planning Pyramid: For the Teacher

- **Have I taught this material before?**
- **How can I make this interesting for the students?**
- **How can I make this interesting for me?**
- **How can students' cultural and linguistic backgrounds be connected to this topic?**
- **How much time do I need to plan for the unit and individual lessons?**
- **What resources do I need to make this work?**
- **How will I evaluate whether students are learning what I am teaching?**

Using the Instructional Planning Pyramid: For Students

- **Will students' skills make comprehension of the topic difficult?**

- **Will students' reading skills make textbook and independent work difficult?**

- **Will student behavior and/or concentration be an issue?**

- **Will students have prior knowledge and interest in this topic?**

- **What student experiences can be connected to this topic?**

- **What student cultural and linguistic backgrounds can be connected to this topic?**

Components of Effective Instruction

(The Algozzine and Ysseldyke Model)

Planning Instruction

- The degree to which teaching goals and teacher expectations for student performance and success are stated clearly and are understood by the student.

Managing Instruction

- The degree to which classroom management is effective and efficient.
- The degree to which there is a sense of positiveness in the school environment.

Delivering Instruction

- The degree to which there is an appropriate instructional match.
- The degree to which lessons are presented clearly and follow specific instructional procedures.
- The degree to which instructional support is provided for the individual student.
- The degree to which sufficient time is allocated to academics and instructional time is used efficiently.
- The degree to which the student's opportunity to respond is high.

Evaluating Instruction

- The degree to which the teacher actively monitors student progress and understanding.
- The degree to which student performance is evaluated appropriately and frequently.

Component 4

Preparation and Support for Testing

Purpose

- To review what good test preparation looks like.
- To examine ways parents can support instruction and assessment.

Background Information

So much to learn, so little time. Today's students are required to meet more requirements than ever to graduate from high school; close to half the states have instituted graduation exams that students must pass to get a diploma. In other places, end-of-course exams are starting to pick up momentum. These are the tests that are administered at the end of a course and assess what students must know and be able to do to receive credit for the class. Still other places allow students to pass on their average and take a teacher-made test (and pass it) to receive class credit. Things are definitely all over the place when it comes to students taking which assessment for what course.

Assessment Literacy

Too often, little is done to prepare students for the tests they must take. Consider the first time you were told to "study" for the test. How did you know what to do? Most of us found out whether our study techniques were sufficient when we got our exams back. Not an optimal way to go through coursework! Many different ways exist for getting ready to take a test, and parents and families can be major supporters. Of course, you can enroll in expensive commercial study programs and buy books, but other direct strategies can also help students prepare for tests. Among them are mnemonic strategies or memory techniques. A tremendous amount of research has proven the power of learning tricks for improving task performance, yet little instruction is devoted to study techniques, and how can there be when there is a test we have to teach for?

Probably one of the most familiar discussions around standards, curriculum, and assessment alignment is one that focuses on the lack of breadth and depth of instruction in schools today. Some argue that standards-based instruction has limited the ability of teachers to have greater breadth and depth in any one area of instruction. Rather, they must concentrate on getting students ready for what is on the test. We argue that this is not teaching to the test, but rather teaching what is on the test. With this in mind, let's talk about teaching students how to take the test.

Assessment literacy seems to be a new concept, one with which teachers and students need to be familiar. Basic assessment literacy helps teachers and students ready themselves for the assessment that lies ahead. Assessment literacy can be taught in a few simple methods (see Chapter 6, "Preparing Students for Testing," for a complete discussion):

- *Discuss the purpose of the test.* Be sure students know the stakes surrounding the test(s) they are about to take.

- *Discuss the nature of the test.* It is important that students know the format of the test (short answer, multiple choice, and so on). It may be important, depending on the age of the student, to describe the difference between NRTs and CRTs. In addition, almost every published test has a test matrix that describes the types of items and content or concepts assessed.

- *Set performance goals.* Here the aim is to work with students to have them set reasonable performance goals based on the work they have done and how they have studied (for tests other than NRTs). It could be as easy as having students pick the level of proficiency they will achieve, assuming there is a rubric of this sort. Of course, it is important for students to know what skill performance must be demonstrated at each level of the rubric (advanced, proficient, novice).

- *Set expectations.* Have students set expectations for their performances. What do they expect to achieve? What do others expect? Of course, these are to be positive, high expectations, not those that indicate "you're never going to make it" attitudes. It could be as easy as having students predict how many points of improvement will be attained or even as a class predicting what the overall average will be. Then wait and see. It's amazing how motivational this little task can be.

Test Preparation

Of course, now comes the part where students must be prepared for the test. This should be an integral part of instruction. Assessments and instruction are inextricably linked, and one feeds the other. Here are some easy ways to prepare kids for the test:

- *Get to know test directions.* Get some old tests and look at the directions. If you are preparing students for NRTs and CRTs, this is especially useful. For your own classroom tests, this task can be even easier. Being familiar with test directions can lower the level of concern and save time in the long run.

- *Get familiar with test vocabulary.* Again, pull out some old tests and scan them for the frequency of certain words. Never assume that students understand vocabulary words that you use in everyday language. Unlike conversations, taking an isolated test provides little or no context for connecting vocabulary words.

- *Review specific content area terms.* Be sure students know the terms used as a natural part of the content areas being assessed. Again, tests often give little familiar context for word usage, so be sure to provide students with lots of opportunities to read and use content-specific terms.

- *Prepare students for test administration.* When students are taking a secure test, be sure they understand the seriousness of the matter and what to expect. Friendly, familiar teachers may not appear so on test day. This alone can throw students test psyches off.

- *Provide students with practice on test item formats.* As we all know, we use certain test-taking strategies when doing matching items, multiple choice questions, and true and false. Be sure students are familiar with them and have practiced them.

- *Complete practice tests.* What better way to provide students with test preparation than by actually administering an old test? We know that this is not always possible, but you can create your own tests that reflect those that students will be required to take.

- *Provide students with specific test-taking strategies.* Certain strategies must be practiced when taking specific test formats. For example, in timed tests, it is critical to have a sense of time and pace at which you are working. Here one needs to take a look at how many problems are expected, peruse the general difficulty of them, and then make a plan for their completion. This skill can be easily learned by setting timers in the classroom and having students work until it rings, and then assess their progress.

Now we are ready to take the test! Or are we? Not all of our students look forward to being tested on anything. In fact, some of them get ill just thinking about it. To counter test anxiety, we must work at it. Teach students how to take the test mentally. Here are some suggestions on how to do so:

- *Teach personal strategies.* Provide students with practice using self-affirmations. These are statements that are positive, upbeat, and help concentrate on the "can do" attitude, rather than the "uh-oh" attitude. The visualization of treats or rewards that will follow the test is also a useful strategy. The mere visualization of a calm blue sea can also help lower anxiety.

- *Physical and mental preparedness.* Encourage students to get sleep! One of the best ways to combat stress is with a rested and well-fed body.

All in the Family: Working Together on Test Preparation

As discussed in Chapter 6, family involvement can be a very beneficial tool in preparing students for an assessment. If this is not an option, then the involvement of a person of significance and credibility is the next best thing. Some basics need to be in place, such as informing families about tests. If people are to help students prepare both mentally and physically, it is critical for them to know what they are getting students ready for. Let family members know all about the test purpose, specifications, coverage, and the like. Use of the test matrix can expedite this task. Providing family members with the opportunity to take the test is another great way to get folks on board. It is a good idea to create a parent brochure on testing and accommodations that is friendly and understandable.

Family Decisions, Participation Decisions

It is important that family members and other supporters understand all the issues surrounding participating in an assessment as well as accommodation decisions. Here are few to consider:

- What is the purpose of the assessment?
- What is the content of the test?
- What is the format of the test?
- How is the test administered?
- Who takes the assessment?
- What are accommodations?
- What accommodations are allowed on the test?
- What accommodations does my student need to be successful?
- What is the impact of testing itself?
- Understanding test results: what do they mean?

Having family members understand these areas is a precursor for helping students ready themselves both mentally and physically for the assessment. And finally, the more parents know about the assessment, the more they can help students understand their test results, something often overlooked with students. Do they really understand how they performed?

Finding out what works in preparing students for assessments is as easy as asking them. You have some straightforward ways to proceed, as outlined here and in Chapter 6, but never forget to ask the students what they need to feel prepared for any assessment. You may be surprised what you find out!

Activity 1

Administer the CBAM assessment for the section (Handout 4.1). Have participants indicate on a scale of one through seven (where one is awareness and seven is refocusing) where they fall on the Likert continuum.

Activity 2

In small groups, discuss which techniques can be used in the classroom to prepare students for assessments. Find out what kind of instruction takes place. If there isn't much, talk about what instruction can be like when teaching test preparations.

Activity 3

Talk to a student or a small group of students about how they perceive the test. Find out how prepared they feel. Ask what could help them prepare for assessments. Handout 4.2 provides an outline for discussion (feel free to make this into a written student interview form).

Overheads and Handouts

Use the following overheads to facilitate your discussions of this component. Feel free to tailor them to your specific needs.

HANDOUT 4.1

Directions: The purpose of this Likert scale is to have you identify where you are in your ability and readiness to accept changes and innovations. Many of these are going on around you right now! Each number (1–7) has a corresponding level of awareness or concern. Read each item and rate your level of concern/awareness about each:

1 = Awareness, I have very little involvement or interest.
2 = Informational, I have general awareness, but relatively little involvement.
3 = Personal, I am beginning to be affected by this. I have some concern about the impact of this on policies and current practices.
4 = Management, I am involved and/or beginning to focus on strategies to address this.
5 = Consequence, I have some questions and concerns about the impact of this.
6 = Collaboration, I am working to make things happen about this through professional collaboration.
7 = Refocusing, I am working to refine, improve, and extend strategies and practices around this.

Preparation and Support for Testing

Item 1

1   2   3   4   5   6   7   Assessment literacy is a critical component in today's world of high standards and assessments.

Item 2

1   2   3   4   5   6   7   It is critical to teach students test-taking skills.

Item 3

1   2   3   4   5   6   7   Parents and families can be key supporters in readying students for testing.

Item 4

1   2   3   4   5   6   7   Teaching students test preparation is as important as teaching the content itself.

Item 5

1   2   3   4   5   6   7   It is important to ask students what they feel they need to get ready for assessments.

HANDOUT 4.2

A Framework to Guide Student Discussions About Test Preparation

1. How do you generally feel on the day of a test? Why?

2. What would make you feel better, more confident on the day of a test?

3. How do you prepare to study for a test?

4. How long do you study?

5. How do you decide how long to study for a test?

6. What do you think would help you study better?

7. After studying hard, how do you do on the test?

8. Do you need some help from your parents or others in getting ready for a test? If so, what would this help consist of?

9. What test formats do you perform the best on?

10. If you could change anything about taking tests, what would it be?

Teaching Assessment Literacy to Students

Be sure students know:

- **The purpose of the test**

- **The nature of the test**

- **How to set performance goals**

- **How to set expectations**

Test Preparation for Students

Be sure students know and are familiar with the following:

- **Test directions**

- **Test vocabulary**

- **Content area terms**

- **Test administration**

- **Test item formats (multiple choice versus short answer)**

- **Personal test-taking strategies**

- **Physical and mental test readiness**

Preparing Families to Help Kids

Families need to be able to answer the following:

- **What is the purpose of the assessment?**

- **What is the content of the test?**

- **What is the format of the test?**

- **How is the test administered?**

- **Who takes the assessment?**

- **What are accommodations?**

- **What accommodations are allowed on the test?**

- **What accommodations does my child need to be successful?**

- **What's the impact of testing?**

- **Understanding test results: what do they mean?**

Overhead 4.3

Resource C
Technical Assistance and Dissemination Networks

For more information on research and development efforts in the areas of instruction, assessment, and accountability, contact the following organizations:

The Office of Educational Research and Improvement (OERI)
U.S. Department of Education
555 New Jersey Avenue Northwest
Washington, DC 20208
Fax: 202-219-2135

The Office of Special Education Programs
U.S. Department of Education
Office of Special Education Programs (OSERS)
600 Independence Avenue Southwest
Mary E. Switzer Building #3521
Washington, DC 20202-2641
Fax: 202-205-8105

National Center on Educational Outcomes
University of Minnesota
350 Elliott Hall
75 East River Road
Minneapolis, MN 55455
Telephone: 612-626-1530
Fax: 612-624-0879
Web: http://www.coled.umn.edu/nceo

National Center for Research on Evaluation, Standards, and Student Testing
UCLA Graduate School of Education
405 Hilgard Avenue
Los Angeles, CA 90024-1522
Telephone: 310-825-8326
Fax: 310-206-6293
Web: http://cresst96.cse.ucls.edu/index.html

For a state and local policy perspective, contact the following organizations:

> National Association of State Boards of Education
> 1012 Cameron Street
> Alexandria, VA 22314
> Telephone: 703-684-4000
> Fax: 703-836-2313
> Email: boards @nasbe.org
>
> Center for Policy Research (CPRE)
> 1012 Cameron Street
> Alexandria, VA 22314
> Telephone: 703-684-4000
> Fax: 703-836-2313
>
> National Association of State Directors of Special Education (NASDSE)
> 1800 Diagonal Road, Ste 320
> King Street Station I
> Alexandria, VA 22314
> Telephone: 703-519-3800
> Fax: 703-519-3808

For state-based regional resource centers, contact the following organizations:

> Federal Resource Center for Special Education (FRC)
> Academy for Educational Development
> 1825 Connecticut Avenue NW Ste 900
> Washington, DC 20009
> Telephone: 202 884-8215; TTY 22-884-8200
> Fax: 202 884- 8443
> Web: http://www.dssc.org/frc
> Email: frc@aed.org

Region 1: Northeast (Connecticut, Maine, Massachusetts, New Hampshire, New Jersey, New York, Rhode Island, Vermont)

> Northeast Resource Center (NERRC)
> Trinity College of Vermont, McAuley Hall
> 208 Colchester Avenue
> Burlington, VT 05401-1496
> Tel: 802-846-7009; TTY 802-846-7223
> Fax: 802-846-7002
> Web: http://www.trinityvt.edu.nerrc
> Email: nerrc@courage.trinityvt.edu

Region 2: Mid-South (Delaware, District of Columbia, Kentucky, Maryland, North Carolina, South Carolina, Tennessee, Virginia, West Virginia)

> Mid-South Regional Resource Center (MSRRC)
> Human Development Institute
> University of Kentucky
> 126 Mineral Industries Building
> Lexington, KY 40506-0051
> Telephone: 606-257-4921; TTY 606-257-2903
> FAX: 606 257- 4353
> Email: msrrc@ihdi.uky.edu
> Web: http://www.ihdi.uky.edu/msrrc/

Region 3: Southeast Resource Center (Alabama, Arkansas, Florida, Georgia, Louisiana, Mississippi, Oklahoma, Texas, Puerto Rico, U.S. Virgin Islands)

> Southeast Regional Resource Center (SERRC)
> Auburn University Montgomery
> PO Box 244023
> Montgomery, AL 36124
> Telephone: 334-244-3100
> Fax: 334-244-3101
> Web: http://edla.aum.edu/serrc.html
> Email: bbeale@edla.aum.edu

Region 4: Great Lakes (Illinois, Indiana, Iowa, Michigan, Minnesota, Missouri, Ohio, Pennsylvania, Wisconsin)

> Great Lakes Area Regional Resource Center
> (GLARRC)
> Center for Special Needs Populations
> The Ohio State University
> 700 Ackerman Road, Ste 440
> Columbus, OH 43202
> Telephone: 614-447-0844; TTY 614-447-8776
> Fax: 614- 447-9043
> Web: http://www.csnp.ohio-state-edu/glarrc.html
> Email: edaniels.121@osu.edu

Region 5: Mountain Plains (Arizona, Colorado, Kansas, Montana, Nebraska, New Mexico, North Dakota, South Dakota, Utah, Wyoming)

> Mountain Plains Regional Resource Center
> (MPRRC)
> Utah State University
> 1780 North Research Parkway Ste 112
> Logan, UT 84341
> Telephone: 435-752-0238; TTY 435-753-9750
> Fax: 435-753-9750
> Web: http://www.usu.edu/~mprrc
> Email: cope@cc.usu.edu

Region 6: Western (Alaska, California, Hawaii, Idaho, Nevada, Oregon, Washington, American Samoa, the Federated States of Micronesia, the Commonwealth of the Northern Marianna Islands, Guam, the Republic of the Marshall Islands, the Republic of Palau)

> Western Regional Resource Center (WRRC)
> 1268 University of Oregon
> Eugene, OR 97403-1268
> Telephone: 541-346-5641; TTY: 541-346-0367
> Fax: 541- 346-5639
> Web: http://interact.uoregon.edu/wrrc/wrrc.html
> Email: wrrc@oregon.uoregon.edu

Other Technical Assistance and Dissemination Networks

> National Center to Improve the Tools of Educators
> College of Education
> University of Oregon
> 805 Lincoln Street
> Eugene, OR 97401
> Telephone: 541-683-7543
> Fax: 541-683-7543
> Web: http://idea.uoregon.edu/~ncite
> Email: dcarnine@oregon.
>
> National Clearing House for Professionals in Special Education
> Council for Exceptional Children
> 1920 Association Drive
> Reston, VA 20191
> Telephone: 703-264-9476, 800-641-7824;
> TTY 703-264-9480
> Fax: 703-264-1637
> Web: http://special-ed-careers.org
> Email: ncpse@cec.sped.org
>
> National Information Center for Children and Youth with Disabilities (NICHCY)
> Academy for Educational Development
> PO Box 1492
> Washington, DC 20031-1492
> Telephone: 202-884-8200; TTY 800-695-0285
> Fax: 202-884-8441
> Web: http://www.nichcy.org
> Email: nichcy@aed.org
>
> Council for Exceptional Children
> 1920 Association Drive
> Reston, VA 22091-1589
> Telephone: 703-264-9479, 800-224-6830
> Fax: 703-264-1637
> Web: http://www.cec.sped.org/

Transition

> National Transition Alliance for Youths with Disabilities (National Transition Network, Academy for Educational Development, Transition Research Institute)
> Transition Research Institute at Illinois
> University of Illinois
> 113 Children's Research Center
> 51 Getty Drive
> Champaign, IL 61820
> Telephone: 217-333-2325
> Fax: 217-244-0851
> Web: http://www.dssc.org/ntal
> Email: leachlyn@uiuc.edu

National Transition Network (NTN)
Institute on Community Integration
University of Minnesota
150 Pillsbury Drive, SE
Minneapolis, MN 55455
Telephone: 612-624-1062
Fax: 612-624-8279
Web: http://www.ici.coled.umn.edu/ntn
Email: johns006@tc.umn.edu

Parents

Parents Engaged in Educational Reform (PEER)
Federation for Children with Special Needs
1135 Tremont Street, Ste 420
Boston, MA 02120
Telephone: 617-236-7210
Fax: 617-572-2094
Web: http://www.fcsn.org/peer
Email: cromano@fcsn.org

Technical Assistance Alliance for Parent Centers,
The Alliance
PACER Center
4826 Chicago Avenue, South
Minneapolis, MN 55417
Telephone: 612-827-2966; Toll free 888-248-0822
TTY 612-827-7770
Fax: 612-827-3065
Web: http://www.ta@alliance.org
Email: alliance@taalliance.org

Early Childhood

National Early Childhood Technical Assistance
System (NECTAS)
Frank Porter Graham Child Development Center
Bank of America Plaza
137 East Franklin Street, Ste 500
Chapel Hill NC 27514
Telephone: 919- 962-2001; TTY 919-962-8300
Fax: 919-966-7463
Web: http://www.nectas.unc.edu
Email: nectas@unc.edu

Partnerships

Associations of Service Providers Implementing
IDEA Reforms in Education (ASPIRE)
Council for Exceptional Children
1920 Association Drive
Reston, VA 20191-1589
Telephone: 877-CEC-IDEA (toll free)
TTY 703-264-9480
Fax: 703-264-1637
Web: http://www.ideapractices.org
Email: ideapractices@cec.sped.org

Families and Advocates Partnership for Education (FAPE)
PACER Center
4826 Chicago Avenue, South
Minneapolis, MN 55417
Telephone: 612-827-2966; Toll free 888-248-0822
TTY 612-827-7770
Fax: 612-827-3065
Web: http://www.fape.org
Email: pacer@pacer.org

IDEA Local Implementation by Local Administrators (ILIAD)
Council for Exceptional Children
1920 Association Drive
Reston, VA 20191-1589
Telephone: 877-CEC-IDEA (toll free);
TTY 703-264-9480
Fax: 703-264-1637
Web: http://www.ideapractices.org
Email: ideapractices@cec.sped.org

The Policy Maker Partnership (PMP) for Implementing IDEA 97
National Association of State Directors of Special Education
1800 Diagonal Road, Ste 320
Alexandria, VA 22314-2840
Telephone: 703-519-3800; TTY 703-519-7008
Fax: 703-519-3808
Web: http://www.nasdse.org
Email: nasdse@nasdse.org

Other

ERIC Clearing House on Assessment and Evaluation
O'Boyle Hall, Department of Education
The Catholic University of America
Washington, DC 20064
Telephone: 800-464-3742
Fax: 202-319-6692

Education Commission of the States
707 17th Street, Ste 2700
Denver, CO 80202-3427
Telephone: 303-299-3600
Fax: 303-296-8332
Email: ecs@ecs.org

U.S. Department of Education
400 Maryland Avenue, SW
Washington, DC 20202
Telephone: 800-USA-LEARN
Web: webmaster@inet.ed.gov

Here are some additional Web sites not listed in the chapters:

Education Newsletters:
This site connects to more than 135 education newsletters within a directory of more than 5,000:
http://www.newsletteraccess.com/subject/edu.html

Federal and State Education Organizations: Links to national and state education organizations:
http://www.ezonline.com:80/parss/edorg.html
Goals 2000 Legislation and Related Items: In this site, you will find information about Goals 2000.
http://www.ed.gov/g2k/

Improving America's Schools Act of 1994 IASA: Here you will find the law for the act:
http://www.ed.gov/legislation/ESEA/index.html/

National Clearinghouse for Bilingual Education (NCBE): The NCBE strives to address critical issues dealing with the education of linguistically and culturally diverse students in the U.S.:
http://www.ncbe.gwu.edu/index.html

Assessment Resource: Links to 14 assessment/educational resources.
http://www.firn.edu/doe/sas/othrhome.html

THOMAS: Legislative Information on the Internet: You will find Congress floor activities of the week, the status of major legislation, committee reports, and more.
http://thomas.loc.gov/

Glossary

Alternate Assessment

A substitute approach used in gathering information about the performance and progress of students who do not participate in typical state assessments. Under the reauthorized Individuals with Disabilities Education Act (IDEA), alternate assessments are to be used to measure the performance of a relatively small population of students who are unable to participate in the regular assessment system, even with accommodations.

Alternative Assessment

A generic term that is typically applied to a variety of different assessment activities. These assessments provide an alternative to multiple-choice tests that require students to select one response. Writing samples, portfolios, and performance-based assessments might all be considered forms of alternative assessment.

Assessment

The process of collecting data for the purpose of making decisions about individuals, groups, or systems.

Authentic Assessment

Often used synonymously with performance assessment, this term can also mean an assessment that uses only real-world tasks as the basis for information about how well an individual can perform certain tasks.

Confidence Interval (CI)

A numerical range that shows the interval around a score that one would expect a person or group of persons to obtain if they were to take the same test again. A CI of 95 percent indicates that one can be 95 percent confident that if the person or group was retested, their average score would fall into the same range.

Criterion-Referenced Test (CRT)

Criterion-referenced tests are measures that are used to examine student performance relative to state and/or district criteria or standards. Instead of comparing students' scores to a national normative standard, scores are interpreted in terms of various performance standards—usually set at the district or state level (e.g., mastery versus nonmastery or low proficiency, moderate proficiency, and high proficiency within a particular subject area).

Norm-Referenced Test (NRT)

Norm-referenced tests are those that provide a comparison of individual performance to that of a state or national comparison (standardization) sample. A norm-referenced test measures the performance of a student against the performance of other individuals. Use of the norm sample enables raw scores to be converted to grade-equivalent scores, percentile scores, and standard scores.

Normal Curve Equivalents (NCEs)

NCEs are standard scores that are generated from a normal distribution. You begin with a set of raw scores, convert them to percentile ranks, and then use a z-score table to convert the percentile rank to a z-score. The resulting z-scores are usually transformed by using a linear transformation to a new scale (such as the SAT, where the mean equals 500 and the standard deviation equals 100). NCE scores can be used only for students who are similar in age or grade to those in the norm sample.

Percentile Scores

These scores tell the percent of people in the normative sample that scored at or below a student's score (e.g., a percentile rank of 80 means that 80 percent of the normative group earned a score at or below that student's score).

Performance Assessment

A form of testing that requires the creation of an answer or a project, rather than the selection of an answer (as in many traditional multiple-choice tests). In many cases, such assessments are intended to represent or simulate real-life situations that require problem solving. The term is often used synonymously with authentic assessment.

Portfolio Assessment

A collection of student-generated or student-focused products that provides the basis for judging student accomplishment. In school settings, portfolios might contain extended projects, drafts of student work, teacher comments and evaluations, assessment results, and self-evaluations. The products typically depict the range of skills of the student or reveal the improvement in a student's skill level over time.

Raw Scores

These scores are simply the scores that are obtained when you sum the score on each item. If items are scored dichotomously (1 or 0), then a raw score represents the total number of items answered correctly.

Standards-Based Assessment

An assessment instrument, battery, or system that has been constructed to measure the achievement of individual students or student populations in attaining certain standards, which are generally established by local districts or state educational agencies. Most state-level standards-based assessment programs that are currently in place measure student performance against articulated standards in core academic content areas, such as reading, mathematics, writing, science, and social studies.

Standard Error of Measurement (SEM)

An index of reliability that essentially converts reliability data from a test into a confidence interval around a given score. Knowing the standard deviation, the reliability, and a person's score, you can estimate a confidence band within which you would expect the individual to score (in typical cases, 95 percent of the time) if that individual repeatedly took a parallel version of the test.

Standard Scores

These scores are linear transformations of raw scores and are considered the easiest to interpret. With standard scores, the mean and standard deviation of any distribution can be placed onto a similar scale. Common examples of standard scores are the SAT, which has a mean of 500 and a standard deviation of 100, or a typical Intelligence Quotient (IQ) test with a mean of 100 and a standard deviation of 15.

Reliability

Reliability is the extent to which a test measures what it purports to measure time after time. Reliability also refers to the accuracy, precision, or stability of a measuring instrument.

Rubric

A scoring guide that facilitates the consensus of the people who are rating the students' performances on assessment tasks. A rubric provides criteria from which those students who are assessed can learn to improve their performance.

Validity

Test validity, simply stated, refers to a test that measures what is says it measures.

SOURCE: The definitions in this paper were adapted from the definitions used by Drs. Elliott and Thurlow in their work at the National Center on Educational Outcomes.

Index

U–V–W

CORWIN
PRESS

The Corwin Press logo—a raven striding across an open book—represents the happy union of courage and learning. We are a professional-level publisher of books and journals for K–12 educators, and we are committed to creating and providing resources that embody these qualities.